RECOLLECTIONS

OF A

WESTERN RANCHMAN

BY

CAPTAIN WILLIAM FRENCH

~ ~ ~ ~ ~ ~ ~ ~

Originally published in America as
Some Recollections of a Western Ranchman, New Mexico, 1883-1899,
Frederick A. Stokes Co. New York, 1928.
Library of Congress Catalog Card Number: 61-8048
ISBN #: 0-944383-08-4

~ ~ ~ ~ ~ ~ ~ ~

Reprinted (1990 and 1997) by

High-Lonesome Books
P. O. Box 878
Silver City, New Mexico
88062

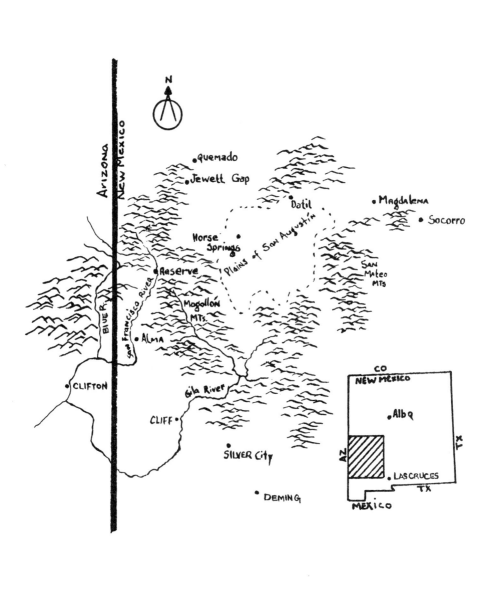

CONTENTS

CHAPTER   PAGE

I. IN SEARCH OF FORTUNE   I

Leaving Ireland—New York—The engine-bell—County Roscommon in Kansas City—San Francisco—Napa County, California—Boy's Pants in St. Helena—The coin says New Mexico

II. A TENDERFOOT ON THE ROAD   14

Silver City—Western etiquette—The W S Ranch— I buy cattle, and go to find them—Mr. Milligan—Mr. Cox —Roscommon again—A tough outfit—Socorro

III. COW-PUNCHING   26

Mr. Fowler, a border-bully—Avoiding an inquest—The dying cowboy—Branding cattle—' Qui da ho '—Merry-go-round with a steer—Rough justice in Socorro—Dutch Charlie's wages—Home without the cattle

IV. A MEXICAN WAR   39

Range-branding—Thanksgiving turkey—Politics in New Mexico—An outbreak at the plaza—Besieging Mr. Baca—The end of the warfare

V. AN INDIAN OUTBREAK   53

A French cook—A western doctor—Handling wild horses—The Meader family—An expedition for wild cattle—Traces of Indians—Geronimo's outbreak—Our cemetery·

VI. TRAILING THE HOSTILES   68

Arrival of the troops—Fort Nasty—Fool Quail and a skunk—Expedition after the Indians—A false alarm

VII. THE NAVAJO SCOUTS   80

Murder at Point of Rocks—Trailing the Indians—Navajo scouts—Deer-hunting—Incipient mutiny—The foot-race —Held for ransom

VIII. THE TROOPS IN PURSUIT   95

Failure at Dripping Spring—Mule and skunk—The stage-driver's escape—Mr. Cox in danger—A dutiful son —News of the ambush

RECOLLECTIONS OF A WESTERN RANCHMAN

CHAPTER   PAGE

IX. THE AMBUSH 112
The tragedy of Dry Creek Hill—Return to Camp
Maddox—The public funeral—Departure of the hostiles—
A Navajo bath—The young cadet—Big medicine—News
of Geronimo's surrender

X. LIFE ON THE RANCH. I 132
Drought—Mr. Cox and the deer—The pet bear—Jap's
discomfiture—A cattle convention—A marketing fiasco

XI. LIFE ON THE RANCH. II 147
Wedding-cake—Jap in trouble—Trial for murder—A
cheerful Chuck-liner—The last of Pow-a-Sheik

XII. JUSTICE IN NEW MEXICO 161
Murder of Old Charlie—How it was done—Taking the
prisoner to Socorro—The trial—Mining claims—A Federal
land inspector—Dick Deadeye and Captain M.

XIII. HUNTING BEARS AND MEN 185
A trip home—Roscommon once more to the rescue—
A shooting episode—Witty the squirrel—A bear hunt—
A cattle stampede—Trailing Black Jack

XIV. HORSE-BREAKING AND CATTLE-RUSTLING . . 210
Horse-breaking—' The Granger ' and Bullet—Laid out
by Utah—Death of Black Jack—Cattle-rustling—War
with Tuk Holoman

XV. TROUBLE AND AMUSEMENT 227
The Hall boys—Murder of Mr. Lyons—Bear cubs—An
embarrassing inscription—De Priest's religious complex—
Brother Bacon—An emergency amputation—Politics and
Pete Branson—Nearly buried alive

XVI. THE WILD BUNCH. I 251
Louie Lloyd in Mexico—The brothers Ketchum—Rustlers again—A new outfit—Train robbery—The special
agent

XVII. THE WILD BUNCH. II 266
How Mac was taken—His conviction—Complications
—Murder of Luke at Mogollon—Another miscarriage of
justice—The last of the ' Wild Bunch '

SOME RECOLLECTIONS OF A WESTERN RANCHMAN

CHAPTER I

IN SEARCH OF FORTUNE

ON 4 November 1883 I left Ireland, having taken passage in the Royal Mail Steamship *Arizona*, at that time considered to be one of the greyhounds of the North Atlantic Fleet.

I had no definite plans, only the desire to better my fortune. The immediate cause of my departure was a letter from my old friend Charles O'Conor of Mt. Druid, Belenegare, Co. Roscommon, Ireland, who at that time was living in Sonoma County, California. The letter was eloquent with the beauties of California and hinted at the desirability of settling there. I stepped aboard the *Arizona* with a blue envelope marked ' O.H.M.S.' and containing a year's leave to travel in the United States of America in my pocket.

So far my life had been that of a younger son. I was devoted to sport and had some slight military experience and a smattering of law. The last I gained through a course of lectures which I was presumed to have attended at the King's Inns in Dublin. I say ' presumed ', as I had a standing agreement with a studious friend to answer my name at roll-call.

The week before sailing had been devoted to the usual festivities accompanying departures. Two of my brothers had accompanied me to Queenstown, where we made a night of it. They toasted success to my trip while I swallowed farewells to my native land. Whether they experienced any ill effects after leaving me on board they have never related. As for me, the ship ran into boisterous weather immediately on leaving the harbour and my regrets became acute.

Up to that time I had considered myself immune from

sea-sickness, having crossed the Bay of Biscay several times. But I had evidently miscalculated my powers. It was Sunday morning when I went on board and I did not venture on deck till the Wednesday following. During that time I formed a deadly hatred for the steward, who obligingly had offered me soup, and I derived a certain consolation from the pangs of my cabin-mate, who was still slower in recovering.

Having got rid of my regrets I soon began to make acquaintances. I fell in with three men who had just graduated from Cambridge and were entered on the passenger list as E. Upcher, Alfred Hardcastle, and E. W. Lyon. They informed me that they were on their way to New Mexico, where they owned a ranch. This news interested me very much, as a few days before leaving Ireland I had met a Mr. Scott, who had told us some wonderful stories about that country, where he also had bought a ranch called 'Carizozo'. The name struck me as strange, and I asked Upcher whether the place was near his ranch. He was not sure, but thought it might be some three or four hundred miles east of them. He spoke of it in a way which suggested to me that their estimate of distances was vastly different from what I had been accustomed to.

This made me think there might be some foundation to Mr. Scott's stories, though I had a distinct recollection of my old C.O., a shrewd man, laying his hand on my shoulder as we left the dining-room and whispering to me : ' That man's friends ought to look after him ' : this after he had listened to him for fully an hour with rapt attention.

Anyway the episode served as an introduction. I threw in my lot with my new chums, and we all took up our abode at the Fifth Avenue Hotel. Our stay was limited, as my new friends had already taken their tickets over the Pennsylvania Railroad. My ticket, which I had taken in Dublin, called for transportation all the way to San Francisco, but did not specify by what route. When I produced it in the ticket office in the hotel I was besieged by innumerable touts from all the railroad systems east of Chicago. It was useless telling them that I had already made up my mind. When I mentioned the Pennsylvania, the representatives of the Nickel Plate and the Southern Pacific threw up their hands and surmised that I would be in luck if I were taken out alive on arrival in Chicago. On asking why, they said :

' The curves ! The curves are so dangerous. Why they have a curve there, near Pittsburg, they call the Horseshoe Curve, that they never pass over without killing two or three passengers. They throw them out on the road and pretend they were run over and then stop the train and pick them up, because it is as much as they can do to make the grade.' This sounded very fearful, but as my friends were travelling by that route I determined to take the risk.

We left New York on a Sunday morning, the eighth day after I had left Queenstown. My recollections of the place are made up of impressions of ill-paved streets, gargantuan bills of fare, and the haughty demeanour of the hotel clerk. This gentleman seemed borne down by the dignity of his office. I wondered if such a demeanour was confined to his particular calling, or whether it extended, in proportion, to the other high dignitaries of the country. If so, I thought, what an awe-inspiring person the President of the Great Republic must be.

I wondered about the President even more after I got on the train and met the Pullman conductor. My speculations were not satisfied until I had the honour of meeting a President in person. But that was many years later and I had changed my views on several matters. It belongs to the hereafter and has no bearing on our journey to Chicago.

Railway travelling in those days had not reached the comfort and dispatch to which it has since attained. The fastest train from New York to Chicago took thirty-six hours. I found it both slow and tedious. The Pullman car was a new institution to me. It lacked the privacy of our sleeping-cars in Great Britain, seemed to me more luxurious than comfortable, especially as the windows were kept tightly closed and the ventilators at the top let in more coal-dust than fresh air.

What struck me particularly during the journey was the great number of wooden houses. Brick or stone seemed only to be used for special buildings in the towns through which we passed and was entirely absent in the villages or farmsteads.

I thought I could trace the influence of the early Puritan settlers in the piety of the present generation, as the church bells seemed to be ringing in every settlement we passed through. True, it was Sunday, but the calls to service seemed to extend all through the day and far into the night.

I set down the Americans as ardent supporters of public worship and ascribed it to inherited piety.

We arrived in Chicago on Monday morning. I was glad to get out of the stuffy Pullman and into the fresh air. There was no doubt about the freshness of the air, for the thermometer was ten below zero and a gale was blowing from the lake.

We went to the Palmer House. Owing to the cold outside they kept the hotel at such a temperature that I spent most of the day in circumnavigating the block for fresh air. During that time I nearly froze, and during the intervals in thawing out in the hotel I nearly suffocated. My chief impression of Chicago was frozen spittle on the sidewalks. There was lots of it.

Here I parted from my new friends. They were detained in Chicago for a day by some business transaction, while my ticket called for continuous transportation. I left that evening over the Burlington route for Kansas City. The train did not leave till late, so we had dinner together and they afterwards saw me safely on board.

As soon as the berths were made up I turned in, hoping to sleep through the night, as we were due in Kansas City early the following morning. But I was restless and stayed awake long after retiring. I could not sleep on account of the bells. It was then that I began to doubt whether I had not been endowing the inhabitants with a halo, which they had not really earned.

It was now Monday night and I had no reason to believe that the residents carried on their church-going all the week. Still, every place we passed through seemed to have the bell-ringers at work and I wondered if they worked it in shifts and had relays of bell-ringers. At any rate, it seemed to be a popular occupation.

From the bell-ringers my mind wandered to the preachers, and I wondered how they managed to keep things going and if it was not necessary to divide the labours amongst the members of the congregation. In this frame of mind I dropped off to sleep, with the ringing still in my ears.

When I awoke in the morning we were crossing the Missouri River. That infernal bell was still ringing, but there was nothing in sight except water. I hustled into my clothes and made my way to the wash-room. Here

I found the coloured gentleman who made up the beds engaged in shining the passengers' shoes. He seemed to take so much pride in his occupation that I watched him in silence for several minutes.

As soon as he looked up I asked him if there was some national festival in progress. He looked at me with a puzzled expression and asked me to repeat the question. I asked what was the cause of all the church bells ringing.

I think he had serious doubts as to my sanity. He said : 'Church bells ? I ain't he'erd no church bells.' I said : 'Why, man, it's ringing now. Don't you hear it ? '

He gave a great guffaw and said : ' Lawdy, boss, that's the engineer on the locomotive. We's a-comin' to a station.' I said that I presumed so, as I had heard them whistle, but I was unable to account for the bells. He then explained to me that they rang a bell on the engine all the time while passing through a town or its environs. The mystery was solved. Shortly afterwards we steamed into Kansas City.

This was a comparatively new town built up at the meeting point of several different railroads. From the noise and confusion in the depot it looked as if the world and his wife might be passing through.

The porter was a good-natured soul and undertook to transfer my portable baggage to the Pullman on the train by which I was to leave. Pointing out the baggage-room where I was to have the heavier stuff rechecked, he advised me to hurry to the dining-room, if I wished to have breakfast before the train departed. On my asking about the re-checking, he said I would find some one around the breakfast-room who would attend to that for me.

There was no difficulty in locating the breakfast-room, for a youth with a forage cap was beating a gong outside. Reaching it, however, seemed to involve considerable risk. There were numerous tracks to be crossed, with huge locomotives moving up and down, ringing their ear-splitting bells, but otherwise disregarding the human traffic which was making its way before or behind them wherever there happened to be a clear space. Between the tracks men in overalls were wheeling barrows piled high with wobbling luggage ; they were yelling ' Gangway ' and apparently reviling everything and every one in sight.

To one fresh from a country where you were liable to

arrest for venturing on the track it looked pretty reckless. However, I followed the crowd and reached the breakfast-room without mishap.

Here, when I could make myself heard above the noise of the gong, I was directed to a gentleman just outside the door, who was inviting one and all to come to breakfast while there was time to eat it. I was loth to interrupt him, but time was pressing and I explained hurriedly my predicament about the checks. He did not appear to take any notice of me, but when I had finished he held out his hand and said : ' Give them here.' I placed the checks I had got in New York in his palm and he pocketed them while continuing his occupation. He motioned me into the breakfast-room, and I left him, without further explanation.

Having breakfasted, I came out and met him at the door. He handed me a bunch of new checks and demanded fifty-five dollars and fifty cents, in payment for excess baggage. I dived into my pocket and produced all the money I had, which amounted to three or four dollars more than the sum demanded. I paid him the money and was about to depart, when I reflected that I was still some days from San Francisco. On leaving New York I had put a hundred dollars in my pocket for my wants till I reached San Francisco, where I could use a letter of credit. In New York, though the greater part of the baggage was mine, it had been weighed with that of my friends and our joint tickets had covered it. Here I had only one ticket and I would either have to go without food for four days or contrive to avoid paying the extra charge until I arrived at San Francisco. I explained this to the gentleman who had given me the checks, but he could only offer to return the money if I gave him back the checks. I promptly did this, feeling I could do without my luggage better than without food.

When I showed him my letter of credit on a San Francisco bank he repeated that he could do nothing, but suggested I might accompany him to the baggage-room and see the superintendent. In the meantime my stuff, which was loaded on a truck ready for the outgoing train, was wheeled back and I followed it up the platform in a very dejected state of mind. I was beginning to be really home-sick.

When we reached the baggage department the superintendent was out at breakfast ; I would have to await his return. My friend with the checks handed them to a clerk in the office, and wishing me good-day left me alone with my gloomy reflections.

I sat down on the end of the barrow and tried to think out some scheme to relieve the situation. Nothing helpful occurred to me, but I suddenly remembered my things which had been transferred to the outgoing train by the Pullman porter. The man in the office told me that train had already departed ; I might wire to the conductor and have them put off at some wayside station to await my arrival.

I returned to my seat more depressed than ever. Think as I would, I could arrive at no solution of my predicament. I sat there twenty minutes or so, when my thoughts were deflected by the entrance of a youngish man chewing a wooden toothpick. I particularly remember the toothpick, because this wooden kind was new to me.

He looked at the pile of luggage on the truck, glanced casually at me, and asked the man in the office who the stuff belonged to. The clerk nodded towards me. He asked me what I wanted done with it. Here evidently was the superintendent. I explained my predicament. He listened patiently ; then, without replying, walked round the truck, counting the pieces. A considerable portion of the baggage was the field equipment I had used in Egypt, with my name and regiment painted in large letters on it.

When he had counted them he looked hard at me and said he guessed it would be all right. Why, his name was Noonan and he was the son of the stationmaster at Newtownforbes, in the County of Longford, Ireland. He would check my baggage through to San Francisco and I could pay the excess there.

From the depth of despair I was suddenly raised to joy, and I nearly embraced him. He was touched by the heartiness of my handshake, the more so when I told him that his father was quite well known to me. Indeed, he was a well-known character to every one, and his solemn and deep-sounding way of announcing the station was looked forward to as one of the events by travellers between Sligo and Dublin.

He said he guessed he had often seen me go up and down the line and that my face was quite familiar to him. When I told him about some of my things having gone off on the train, he undertook to wire for them to be transferred to an incoming train. Further, he offered to have my ticket re-routed *via* Denver and Cheyenne, over the Union Pacific, instead of over the Santa Fé and Atlantic Railroad, as originally called for. He explained that it would save me at least a day, as the A.P. at the time did not go beyond some out-of-the-way place on the desert, where it connected with the Southern Pacific and they were not particular whether they made the connexion or not.

After that we sat down on the end of the truck and yarned for a couple of hours or more. Then he arranged to take the afternoon off and show me round the town. No one could have treated me with greater kindness. He not only showed me everything that was to be seen, but lent me his overcoat until I could connect with my own things.

When I had finished seeing Kansas City we returned to the depot. Noonan was detained in his office and I put in the time watching the incoming trains discharge their passengers. I was suddenly surprised to see Upcher, ' Fairy ' Hardcastle, and Lyon, my three friends of the voyage, get off a train. They were shaking hands with another gentleman, who had stepped off a train on the opposite side of the platform. I judged him to be a fellow-countryman, and when I greeted them they introduced him as a Mr. Wilson, a neighbour of theirs, also engaged in the ranching business in New Mexico.

I thought little of it at the time, not having any idea they would come into my life after I left Kansas City. Yet when we all adjourned to a hotel to spend some hours together I was greatly interested in comparing their stories of the cattle business with those I had heard from Mr. Scott while still in Ireland. They had some similarity, but were more conservative.

My train was the first to leave, and as they bade me good-bye they gave me a general invitation to visit them at their ranches should I ever wander that way. Mr. Wilson was particularly cordial in his invitation, but I thought it very unlikely that I should ever be able to accept.

It was after midnight when I got out at Denver. I was asleep most of the time, and recollect nothing further until we arrived in Cheyenne in the forenoon of the following day. Here we had to change again, and I took advantage of the delay to stroll up town for a shave. The gentleman who operated on me was communicative, and I learned many

things about the old country about which I had previously
been in ignorance. When I told him that I came from
Ireland, he said I didn't talk like it, but he knew I couldn't
have come from England because I pronounced the letter
' h '. He claimed to be intimately acquainted with several
English lords and not one of them ever pronounced the
letter ' h '. As I had only two hours to wait I did not feel
like getting into an argument with him. I weakly let it go
at that and returned to the depot.

The trip west of Cheyenne was uninteresting. We
travelled through a country of apparently endless prairie,
sparsely covered with yellow grass and entirely without
water. Most of my time was occupied watching the prairie
dogs, amusing little creatures, who uttered feeble protests
as we came by and popped into their holes with a triumphant
flourish of their tails when we seemed on top of them. We
passed through Ogden, which, after leaving Cheyenne,
seemed to be the first place with any pretensions to be called
a city. Then there was more prairie until we reached the
Sierra Nevada Mountains. By this time everybody on the
train had become acquainted, and as the country became
more interesting we formed into groups and got out at every
opportunity, to stretch our legs and to enjoy the scenery.

It was a relief to get off those dreary plains, with their
endless expanse of yellow grass and penetrating alkali dust.
In the mountains we passed through miles of snow-sheds
built over the track, during which everything was obscured,
but the glimpses in between were magnificent. At one
point near the top we were rewarded with a view of an
extensive lake, in which was mirrored the mountain,
streaked with snow, with the railroad track and snow-sheds
meandering up the side. Even our own train with its
engine bellowing smoke was reflected miles below us.

At the summit we entered a heavily timbered country
with magnificent pines and a dark green undergrowth of
what appeared to be a species of laurel which I think they
called ' manzanita '. This continued without a break till
we descended the Pacific slope, which appeared rich and
fertile in comparison with the lands we had been through.
The country now became so interesting that the time seemed
short, until we arrived at Sacramento.

We had crossed the Sacramento River on a ferry-boat,
which took the whole train on board, first breaking it into

two and transporting it into two sections, lying alongside each other, on rails fastened to the deck of the boat. The whole arrangement was ingenious and efficient. The train was united on the other side and we steamed on. We arrived in Oakland, the terminus of the railroad, about sunset and were ferried across the bay to San Francisco.

This time we went on board the boat without our train. The trip across the bay, which was like a sheet of glass, with the rays of the setting sun burnishing it up like molten gold, well repaid us for the entire journey across the continent.

I had neglected to tell my friend O'Conor of my change of route and of the general mix-up in Kansas City, so that on my arrival I was left to my own resources. I went to the Palace Hotel, where I unloaded my checks on to the baggage porter. Having got this off my mind I retired to bed and had the first real night's sleep for more than a week.

I awoke the next morning much refreshed, but it took me several days to get the noise of the train out of my head. It stayed with me much longer than the motion of a ship after a long voyage. Some time during the forenoon O'Conor turned up, accompanied by a friend of his, a Dr. Whitwell. They were quite pleased to find me, as they had been the round of the hotels in search of me, after my failure to show up on the day appointed.

O'Conor told me that he had sold his ranch in Sonoma County and was undecided whether to return to Ireland or look out for another ranch. After some discussion we postponed the matter. We spent a week or more in San Francisco and I was shown the sights.

We took in Chinatown under the auspices of a gentleman belonging to the detective force, who seemed to have been supplied by nature with everything except a bump of reverence. The way he entered the temples with his billy-cock hat perched over one eye and prodded the sacred images with a very thick stick was a revelation to me. It must have been a lesson in Western civilization to the Heathen Chinee.

We also visited the Chinese Theatre and were treated as distinguished visitors, chairs being set for us upon the stage. The particular play had been going on for several years before our arrival, so that it was not easy to get in touch with the plot, but the costumes were unique and gorgeous. While there a distinguished Chinese family came in and were given seats beside us. They were accompanied by a little boy and a tiny girl, dressed in native costume, who were the dearest little objects I had ever seen. They might have been carved in wood, so solemn and still they sat, with faces like miniature sphinxes. After a time their parents went behind the scenes and I devoted my time to an effort to produce a smile from the children. I was successful in the end, with the aid of an old cartridge extractor, and it amused me to see the little fellow conceal it in his capacious sleeve.

What interested me most in San Francisco was the cable-cars. This was the first time I had seen vehicles in motion without any apparent motive power. They looked uncanny. I believe that at the time San Francisco was the only city in the world in which they were in use. To see these great yellow cars, with their clanging bells, moving along at some fifteen or twenty miles an hour, seemingly of their own volition and coming to a stop or starting up at what resembled a wave of the hand of the magician in charge, afforded to me endless gratification. Until the system was explained to me I was unable to figure out how the cars could maintain the same pace up hill and down.

When we had tired of the sights in the city and had enjoyed a few days snipe and duck shooting, O'Conor and I decided it was time to look out for a ranch. Dr. Whitwell had introduced us to a lady from Boston who owned a small place at Calistoga, and we accompanied her there to look it over. It was nearly a day's journey by rail from the city, which included at least one change, and both during the journey and after our arrival the lady entertained us most hospitably. But whether it was that the ranch did not suit us, or that we were fed up with the praises of Boston, I never could determine. We did not buy, and I have had a feeling ever since that Boston is too perfect for a mere mortal to visit.

But we were much pleased with the country and we decided to look it over. We wandered through Lake and Sonoma Counties, winding up at a small mountain resort called Anguin, some nine miles from St. Helena in Napa County. This was a comfortable farm-house, owned by an Englishman. There we employed our time making excursions into the neighbouring country, on the look-out for a suitable ranch.

We invariably went on foot, much to astonishment of the natives, who looked on that mode of progression as a monopoly of the professional tramp. O'Conor and I usually wore the costume common to the old country, consisting of knickerbockers and a shooting jacket, and though this appeared strange to the few people we met, they were too polite to make any demonstration. It was different, however, when I found it necessary to go to St. Helena, in order to mail an important letter.

On this occasion I went alone, and as I entered the town I happened to meet the entire youthful population coming out from school. Not appreciating that there was anything unusual about my costume I paid them no attention but went on up the street in search of the post office. I had not gone far when it was apparent, from the shouts and whistles, that something unusual was going on behind me. I turned round, but could see nothing, except that the number of small boys was increasing rapidly. Still innocent, I went on, merely wondering at the cheer that went up as soon as my back was turned. But then I had an uncomfortable feeling, and asked a man who was leaning against a doorpost, what all the commotion was about. He looked at me in a supercilious way and said : ' What you wearin' them boy's pants for ? ' I drew a deep breath and thought that I had still a good deal to learn, but I answered him mildly, saying it was the usual costume in my country. He responded by saying : ' I don't know where in hell you come from, but in this town grown folks wear long pants.'

My curiosity was satisfied. I made my way to the post office at an increased pace, and having got rid of my letter started back for Anguin at a pace far from dignified. My admirers accompanied me to the edge of the town, and I could hear their cheers long after I had turned a corner and disappeared from view.

We had remained two or three weeks at Anguin when I received a couple of letters which determined my career in the West.

The letters arrived by the same mail. They were from Wilson and Upcher, inviting me to New Mexico to spend Christmas with them. The time was short and it was necessary to come to an immediate decision. That night we held a consultation, in which all the residents at the farm took part. The question was, the respective merits of

California and New Mexico, as a prospective residence for a young man desirous of improving his fortune. The company was unanimously in favour of California. None of them had any personal knowledge of New Mexico, but they all agreed in denouncing it as an abode fit only for outlaws, greasers and cowboys. I was not convinced, however. To decide the matter I spun a coin in the air. It came down New Mexico and my future was definitely fixed.

CHAPTER II

I PROMISED O'Conor that if nothing definite turned up I would come back after the holidays. But I felt I was leaving California for good as I made my way back to San Francisco, collected my traps, and took passage over the Southern Pacific for Deming, New Mexico.

It took me about twenty-four hours to reach Los Angeles, at that time a town of no great importance. Nearly all the Pullman passengers got off at Los Angeles, and I found myself alone with a single male companion for the remainder of the journey. He was a very interesting traveller, evidently touring the continent. He introduced himself by the name of Russell, and I later discovered that he was Sir Charles Russell, who was afterwards known as Lord Russell of Killowen and was Lord Chief Justice of England.

The journey east from Los Angeles was mainly through a desert, till we arrived at Yuma on the Colorado River, where I saw my first live Indians. They bore little resemblance to the warriors I had pictured in my mind since the days of my childhood, when I had feasted on the pages of Fenimore Cooper. From Yuma to Deming the journey was without incident, except that we stopped in the middle of the desert, to see a hot mud spring. It was fully half a mile from the track, but the passengers and the entire train crew walked out to have a look at it, leaving the train standing on the track.

At Deming I was left to my own devices. I discovered that there was an hour's difference between the time on one side of the depot and the other. The north, or Santa Fé, side kept the Mountain times, while the south or Southern Pacific held on to the western or Pacific time, an hour later. The clocks in the hotel favoured the former, so I judged it to be more in use and set my watch accordingly. My next discovery was that the town consisted mainly of sand piles, with windmills interspersed between them. After that I had a more pleasing experience, for I found that the hotel was a most comfortable one, scrupulously clean, with an excellent dining-room. It was known as the ' Harvey House ' and was under the management of a gentleman named Fred Harvey, who attended to all the catering on the Santa Fé road. It was the first I had seen of those excellent institutions and it was a revelation after one's experience on the S.P.

A narrow gauge railroad had just been completed to Silver City, but trains were not yet running regularly. The six-horse stage carrying mails and passengers was still in existence I booked passage on the stage, and after a comfortable night at Deming we left the following morning about six o'clock. The coach itself was a lumbering affair, but it was well horsed and we had a delightful drive, through interesting country, in a wonderfully clear atmosphere. Mountains in Old Mexico, two hundred miles off, were clearly visible.

The driver entertained me during the trip with stories of Indians. When he heard that I was going to Alma he said that all that section had been raided in 1880 by the Apaches under Victorio and a number of people had been killed. On my asking if the Indians were still active, he said that it was hard to tell, and he pointed to some mountains west of us, saying that during the preceding year, 1882, a Judge McComas and his wife had been killed there by a party of Indians under a chief named Nana. They were out for a pleasure drive from Silver City and were only fourteen miles from the place when they were ambushed and horribly mutilated.

All this was highly entertaining and the time passed quickly. We reached Silver City early in the afternoon. It was a well-built town of brick houses, built on both sides of what appeared to be the dry bed of a stream. It had fine cotton-wood trees on both sides of its moderately wide streets; the streets themselves, which were far below the level of the wooden sidewalks, seemed to be the receptacle for all the rubbish of the city. It was carpeted with playing cards. I mentioned something about a street-cleaning department to my friend the driver, but he smiled at my ignorance. He explained that it was unnecessary. When it rained, as it usually did during the summer, the streets were converted into torrents which swept away anything that was lying around loose. If they should meet with a dry season, the wind next spring would remove the rubbish anyway.

I was put down at a substantial brick building of two

stories, which bore the legend, Southern Hotel, in large letters. Here the driver turned me over to the proprietor, a large gentleman whom he introduced as Cap Connor. I had a comfortable room at the Southern and would have enjoyed a perfect night's rest had I not been next door to the proprietor and his wife. For Cap Connor's voice was stupendous, and it was embarrassing to a stranger to hear him exchanging confidences with his better half long after every one was supposed to be asleep.

Try as I would I could not avoid overhearing him. His whisper penetrated the walls as if they were paper. After a vain effort to sleep, I resigned myself to the conversation. It began by Cap announcing that another ' Damn fool Englishman ' had come to town. Then a pause, interrupted by a chuckle from the Cap, who continued : ' He called his baggage " luggage ", or some such name. And did you hear the funny name he had for that leather trunk of his ? The damn fool called it a " portmangle," or " portmantle," or something.' This was followed by another laugh, in which both seemed to join.

After which the Cap continued : ' How in hell did he think I was to know what his portmangle was ? Those damn foreigners shouldn't be allowed to come over till they learn the English language.' All of which sounded so funny that I joined in the laughter.

I had another day in Silver City, to do the town and get acquainted. My guide was the genial Cap, who had forgiven my attempt to impose a foreign tongue. He took me to all the saloons, and I had an opportunity to see how it was they carpeted the streets with cards. Poker games were in operation everywhere, with chips or stacks of gold and silver piled high on the tables. Whenever any of the players wanted a new pack of cards they called loudly for them and the old ones were thrown out of doors.

Cap also initiated me into Western etiquette. I learned that it was a serious offence to refuse a drink when offered it. I found this embarrassing, as it was not my custom to indulge before the evening meal. It was consequently a relief when he told me that I could fulfil all requirements by accepting a cigar. My pockets were soon bulging with these substitutes. Hospitality to a stranger was one of the city ordinances, and if you succeeded in getting him drunk he was immediately adopted as ' one of the boys '. Altogether it was a most profitable day and almost repaid me for the chippy feeling experienced the following morning.

The stage for Alma consisted of two diminutive buckskin mules and a vehicle new to me, called a buckboard. It left Silver City at six o'clock in the morning. I was given to understand by the driver, a gentleman called Al, that the distance was approximately eighty miles and that it would take us two days to cover it. He added, as a rider, that this referred to fine weather and if it rained and the roads became muddy it was twice that distance and would probably take us four days.

I occupied the front seat, alongside the driver, while our only other passenger, an old Confederate soldier named Pete Branson, made himself comfortable amongst the mail-sacks and other impedimenta behind. I was anxious to start a conversation with Pete, but he was not of a communicative nature, at least to strangers; and when I asked him about his experiences in the great struggle between North and South, he merely laughed and said He didn't Want No More of It.

The day was cold, but we got out on the up-grades and had plenty of exercise. We stopped at ' The Mangus ', which had been the head-quarters of a noted Apache chief, and on the Gila (pronounced Hila), where there was a post office and a real river.

We resumed our journey next morning. The road grew worse, but by this time I had got used to the buckboard, and could hold on like the others. We stopped at noon at a Mormon settlement called Pleasanton, and were taken care of by the presiding Elder. The Mormons established little colonies in that region even before the Indians were driven out, and the Elder was intent on carrying out the precept to increase and multiply, for his families were scattered in little huts all over the valley.

Here we got our first sight of the San Francisco River, so that I knew we were getting near the end of the journey. Indeed, Alma was only some ten miles farther on, but the hills were so steep and the road so bad, that it took us several hours to get there. It was what in Western parlance was called an hour by sun when we drove into Alma, and I completed my first drive of over eighty miles on a buckboard.

I was met by Mr. Wilson and his manager, a Mr. Cook. They borrowed a horse for me from one of their cowboys, a

Mr. Erway, as it was necessary to ride the rest of the way to the ranch, which was more than a mile farther on. This was my first experience with a Western saddle, which I found at first awkward, but comfortable. At first sight they appeared clumsy, but in the light of after experience I discovered how useful they were. The only fault was an excess of ornamentation, which added to the weight.

My recollection of the first few days at the ranch is not very vivid. Upcher came down from his ranch thirty-five miles farther north, and we rode about the country, taking in the sights. The main one was the Cooney canyon, in which a mine had been located by a man named Jim Cooney, who was later killed by the Apaches, during the raid of Victorio, in 1880. Here a regular mining camp was in the process of formation. A brother of the original locator, Captain Michael Cooney, had come from Louisiana and taken over the property. He had placed the body of his murdered brother in a unique mausoleum. This was a great cone-shaped boulder, that had fallen away from the main cliff and stood forty feet high, close by the road from Alma. It was twelve to fifteen feet wide at the base and tapered up to a point. In this, about ten feet from the ground, he had excavated a place for the coffin, closing it after the ceremony with a marble slab, with the name, age, cause of death, and the date. It was a monument to stay for all time.

It would be impossible to describe the canyon itself. I still think it is the most beautiful thing I have seen in the United States. The brilliant colours, delicate tracery of the rocks, and the constantly changing prospects as side canyons open up, leave one breathless.

At the ranch Mr. Cook entertained us with an exhibition of shooting, which could only be duplicated at Wild West shows. These had not as yet come into fashion, and he was a pioneer at the game. He was a wonderful shot and the very best game hunter I have ever met. In addition, he initiated me into the mysteries of the lasso and the branding of horses and cattle.

Some ten days after Christmas, when I was thinking that it was about time to bring my visit to a close, Upcher, whom henceforward I shall call Ned, made me a proposal which changed the current of my thoughts. He and his partners had contracted for the purchase of a herd of cattle from some Mexicans named Garcia and Gallegos. It would use up all their funds and they would be willing to let me come in on the deal, should I decide to remain in New Mexico and go into the cattle business.

That evening we held a powwow over the matter The upshot of it was that Mr. Wilson agreed to let me run the cattle with his on the W S range, and I agreed to buy a hundred head of them. In return for the privilege of running the cattle along with Mr. Wilson's I agreed to stay on his ranch and make myself generally useful.

Ned had agreed to receive the cattle about the middle of January, and it was necessary for me to get into harness at once. I set about finding out what was necessary for one to blossom into a ' Cattle Baron.' The first necessity was a horse or two. Here Mr. Wilson helped me by letting me purchase from him, for a nominal sum, a compact little bay that had evidently attained to years of maturity before being haltered. I called him ' Torruno,' the Spanish equivalent of ' stag '. For a pack-horse I bought an angular-looking sorrel from one of the boys. I accepted him of necessity, but he did not seem worthy of a name, and I never gave him one.

I was able to pick up the rest of the paraphernalia, saddle—bridle, blankets, both bed and saddle, with cooking utensils and provisions—at the ranch or in Alma, so that in twenty-four hours I was ready to take the road. The only thing foreign about me was a pair of hunting spurs which I happened to have in my kit, but I found afterwards they were amply sufficient to establish my nationality.

Ned had to leave immediately after we had come to an arrangement, as he had business to transact at the county seat, Socorro ; but before leaving he gave me instructions to find the road, first to their place and from there to Socorro, a matter of two hundred miles or more. There he proposed to meet me and pilot me to where the cattle were, on a little stream called the La Jinsa, some thirty-five or forty miles north-west from Socorro.

It was not necessary for me to start for several days, and I sat down and wrote to my friend O'Conor, telling him of my determination to remain in New Mexico. Everything being finally settled, I set out on my ten days' trip alone. I had every assistance in fixing my pack on the sorrel, and considered that I had fully mastered the intricacies of the

diamond hitch. It looked a simple affair, when you had
some one who was thoroughly familiar with it helping you;
but later on, when alone, I had reason to suspect that I had
forgotten some of the details.

However, I started out full of confidence. Torruno was
on his mettle and impatient to be gone, while the sorrel, as
I was leading him with a stout rope, had no choice in the
matter. We got along swimmingly for a mile or two, but
after that it got tiresome leading the unwilling sorrel. I
took a turn or two round the horn of the saddle, but then
fearing that my little bay would get a sore shoulder, I
decided to turn the sorrel loose and drive him. This
decision met with the approval of Torruno, but the wretched
sorrel started briskly for home, as soon as I had taken the
rope off. But he had to reckon with Torruno, who quickly
headed him off and turned him in the right direction. Then
the wretched beast, by way of revenge, ran under a tree and
raked off his pack. It was here that I had my first doubts
about the diamond hitch. However, after some delay, I
got things to rights, and if I had not thrown a real diamond
hitch, I got something serviceable, and we continued our
way to Ned's ranch, generally called the S U Ranch, where
we arrived about sundown.

No one was around at the time, but I unsaddled, threw
my pack and all my belongings on to the porch, and led my
ponies round to the corral by the side of the house. Having
watered and fed them, I returned to the porch, sat down, lit
a pipe, and prepared to wait for some one to turn up.

I was beginning to think seriously of breaking in the door
when an old gentleman who might have been a near relative
cf Methuselah's hove in sight. He carried a long pole and
had a bunch of hogs running in front of him. I had never
seen a hog go where you wanted, but he seemed to have them
thoroughly broken in. They nosed along in front of him,
now stopping, now breaking into a trot to catch up with the
leaders, while he moseyed along behind them like an ancient
patriarch.

When he got close to the house he turned the hogs loose
in a clump of oak brush and left them to their own devices.
Then he came to the house and unlocked the door before
taking any notice of me, after which he turned his head and
said : ' I reckon you was waiting to get in.' I said : ' I
reckon I was ' and in this manner I was introduced to Mr.

Wallace, Master of the Hog Department of the S U Ranch.

After that he cooked supper, which we ate in silence. Afterwards our conversation was fitful, but I could see by the way he kept muttering to himself that he had something on his mind. He struggled with it for a time, but at length it burst forth and to my astonishment turned out to be a desire to know my opinion on some obscure passage in the Bible. He caught me at a disadvantage ; I asked his own opinion. Then he broke out and continued to descant on the Scriptures for the remainder of the evening. His remarks were original, if not exactly orthodox, and I could only remember them I would be in a position to found a new sect. They grew wearisome after a time, however, and I unrolled my blankets and fell asleep before thoroughly mastering his particular brand of Christianity.

When I awoke the next morning the old gentleman was already busy round the stove preparing breakfast. He told me my best way was to go through the Milligan Plaza. He said that it was not the most direct, but that it was the easiest to follow. He was also careful to explain that the Milligan was also known as the Upper Plaza and that there were two other plazas, the Middle and Lower respectively, but they were situated farther down the river, and he supposed that I had sense enough to know that my way did not lie in that direction.

He had not formed a high opinion of my intelligence, owing to my inattention to his Biblical discourse. However, it had been my intention to go by the Milligan Plaza, where I could lay in supplies, and I made no attempt to improve my status. I got on the road as quickly as possible.

I had no difficulty in finding Mr. Milligan, who ran the only store in the neighbourhood. As I stopped at his door he stepped out on the porch. His head almost touched the ceiling, and his hands were the largest I have ever seen on a human being. He was all length and breadth without any superfluous attachments except a fringe of hair some six or eight inches long on an otherwise bald head.

He supplied me with crackers (which I had previously known as biscuits) and offered me a drink, which I declined owing to the untimely hour. I took a cigar, while he punished a stiff dram, with the remark that whisky was good at any time. He told me that on the Tularosa, which was my next step, there was a friend of his, named Cox, who might put me up and treat me nicely if he was sober, but if otherwise it might be advisable to leave him alone.

The Tularosa was about thirty-five miles from the plaza, almost a full day's ride. I reached it about sundown and had no difficulty in finding Cox's cabin, which was a little way off the road. The door was open and there was a faint smoke curling up through the chimney, but the interior was black as ink, and my repeated knockings failed to bring any response. In view of the description of the gentleman's temperament I was loth to enter unannounced, so I raised my voice in a gentle ' Hallo ! ' About the fourth repetition there was a movement, followed by something between a snort and a growl, and a dark object which had been lying on the floor rose up and approached me. It was a big, unkempt, red-haired man. His bristly beard was half an inch long and he must have been sleeping in his clothes for several weeks.

As he scowled down at me I timidly told him where I was going, with whom I was associated, and expressed a desire to stay overnight. He looked me over scornfully, muttered something about a ' God damned English outfit ', and intimated that there was plenty of water in the creek. As for the rest, it was Government land and I might camp anywhere within a radius of a hundred miles, for all he cared.

Satisfied with this reception, I backed off and led my horses down to water, where, under a large pine tree, I unloaded my stuff and prepared to make camp. Grass was plentiful and as soon as I had watered and picketed my horses I prepared to make a fire and cook my first meal— that is to say, the first one for which I was wholly responsible.

The preparation consisted of frying bacon and boiling coffee, to be drunk undiluted, for such luxuries as sugar or milk would have been treated with contempt by the average cowboy. But being a novice I managed to consume a good deal of time over making the fire. I had it going fairly well when my hospitable friend came to the door of his cabin and began to saunter down in my direction. I devoutly wished that he had elected to stay where he was. I wasn't exactly afraid of him, but I had been fed on stories of the Wild West and I wasn't hunting trouble.

He came towards the fire and watched me for some time in silence. I kept a wary eye on him and wondered what would be the next move. After a time he spoke. ' You're a tenderfoot, ain't you ? ' I pleaded guilty and offered him a cup of coffee. He declined this, but continued to ask questions. ' You're not long out from England, I guess.' I told him that I had only landed in the United States the previous November. He studied over that for a while and then abruptly asked : ' What might your name be ? ' I told him and it seemed to afford him matter for grave thought.

After a short pause and considerable contortion of his features, however, he remarked, as a sort of final ultimatum : ' Well, if you came from Ireland, I'd say you came from Frenchpark.' This brought me to my feet with a jump. I said it was the very place I came from. He slapped his thigh vigorously and said : ' The hell it is ! Why, I come from Strokestown ! '

In this way I met Mr. John Cox, late sergeant in the 8th Cavalry, of the armed forces of the United States of America.

After that he insisted on gathering up my belongings and carrying them into his cabin, and also brought my horses to his corral and fed them with hay. I was grateful for the change, for we were up over eight thousand feet and the nights were cold, but in the cabin it was snug and warm, and we sat up most of the night by the fire, swapping yarns. He told me that he had not considered it necessary to get a discharge when leaving the U.S.A., and that he feared they might make a fuss about some troop horses that had been missing since he left, but he thought he was pretty secure where he was.

We slept rather late the following morning, and I expressed a fear that night would overtake me before I reached my destination, a place known as Horse Springs. Cox then told me of a camp that had been established by a man named Dan Kyle, some fifteen miles this side of Horse Springs. He wound up by remarking that they were a pretty tough outfit, but probably I would be able to put up with them for one night.

That evening about sundown I located the camp he had described. His description of the occupants was justified. They were certainly a tough crowd, and I think that every one of those who were there at the time, afterwards died in their boots. They made no objection to my staying, but they let me see that I was not particularly welcome. However, I troubled them very little. I hitched my horses to their wagon, where I fed them, and afterwards retired to a corner of the shelter, where I munched some crackers and rolled in.

When I woke up in the morning I proceeded to attend to my horses. To my surprise the little bay was gone. I had tied him securely the evening before, and I was satisfied that he could not have got loose of his own accord. Moreover, the rope with which he had been tied was neatly coiled up in the bed of the wagon. Also the old sorrel was there, looking round for his breakfast. Altogether there was need for an explanation.

I sought one from the cook and a man with him. All I could get out of them was that the bay was gone when they got up and they thought he must have got loose in the night and was probably on his way home. I wasn't so sure. There were a lot of fresh horse-tracks round and I decided to follow them. I had not gone more than a quarter of a mile, and was just coming out of the timber, when I heard a horse nicker. My old sorrel nickered back, but I could not see anything, as the sun was rising over the hill. As soon as I got out of its rays I saw a horse which looked like Torruno. He kept nickering and the sorrel kept answering him back ; as we got close to him he broke into a trot, and as soon as he was alongside I jumped off and hugged him.

He was totally indifferent to my caresses, but he had a warm spot for his companion. He and the sorrel exchanged greetings, rubbed noses, and kissed each other, with every demonstration of affection. I forgave him the slight to my own caresses, changed the saddle and bridle on to him, and rode him back to camp.

There I lost no time in gathering up my belongings and securing my pack. The rest of the outfit had gone in to breakfast, so I had the place to myself. As I was leaving one of them came to the door and shouted to know if I wanted any breakfast. I did, but I felt that it would be more enjoyable out on the prairie, where I would be free of their company.

My next objective was the Datils, where there was a road-house, kept by a man named Baldwin. He combined ranching with catering for belated travellers. Having failed to reach Horse Springs the previous day, the journey I faced was something over sixty miles, a long trip for a winter's day. It was a pretty tired traveller that dismounted at Mr. Baldwin's door, shortly after dark.

Here, however, I found most comfortable quarters. There were actually luxuries. There was milk and butter, and, for the horses, several varieties of grain. I resolved to stay over a day and recuperate. I feared it might result in missing my connexion with my friends from the S U, but I trusted to catch up with them before the real work began.

I slept most of the next day, only getting up for meals, which consisted mainly of antelope meat. After the day's rest I felt like a new man, while Torruno also showed signs of getting up on his toes. Our next stop was at a spring two miles north-west of the present town of Magdalena. Here there was a combined hotel, and general emporium, three rooms and a kitchen, presided over by a southern gentleman with a very red face, whom every one called ' Cap.' The store occupied the front room, the kitchen and dining-room combined occupied a lean-to at the back, and to the side, attached to the main adobe building, were two rooms built of undressed lumber. One of those was Cap's, and the other, entirely devoid of furniture, was for the accommodation of travellers. You were allowed to unroll your blankets on the floor. Cap collected fifty cents and every one was satisfied.

The food was what was known as ' sow-belly ' in the West, washed down with black liquid which Cap called coffee. The old gentleman himself took his nourishment principally in whisky straight. He had strong convictions against the iniquity of adulterating it. He took me severely to task for doing so and prophesied an early demise.

Another five-and-thirty miles brought me to Socorro. I took up my abode at the Grand Central Hotel, an imposing looking building, kept by a gentleman named Lockhart, assisted by an amiable wife and three charming daughters with auburn hair.

CHAPTER III

COW-PUNCHING

THE young lady in the office of the Grand Hotel, Socorro, was inclined to show me out, until I mentioned my friends from the S U. Then she assumed a more cordial demeanour and told me they had left only the day before, with instructions for me to follow them as soon as I conveniently could.

I felt a good deal like a tramp, but reflected that a new pair of overalls and a bath would restore my self-respect. I politely inquired from the young lady if there was a bathroom in the hotel. She regretted very much that as yet they had not put one in. It was so hard to get plumbers in such an out-of-the-way place, so different from their home back East. But, she said, I could get a bath at the barber's shop, just round the corner, in the plaza.

I bought the needed overalls and found the barber's shop. It was an annex to a saloon. When I stated my wants to the gentleman in charge he excused himself while he went out to light a fire, saying that the demand had not been great just lately and the water was cold. When he came back he proposed to shave me, saying the water would get hot in the meantime. During the process he proved to be a most interesting talker, and entertained me with the exploits of a gentleman named Joe Fowler, who, it appeared, was at the time taking in the town, or, in common parlance, going round from one saloon to another drinking with his friends and looking for trouble.

While the barber was speaking a crowd came into the adjoining saloon. My barber friend, who evidently held Mr. Fowler in great awe, stole to the door, and after a peep returned with his finger on his lips, saying in a hushed voice : ' That's *him.*'

When we heard them going out he took another look, to make sure, and then launched into his full history. I confess I thought he was exaggerating when he stated that Mr. Fowler's record was thirty or forty murders. He explained that Mr. Fowler was a deputy sheriff ; that the murders were committed after the victims had been arrested and disarmed, generally on trumped-up accusations ; for apparently, Mr. Fowler was in demand amongst a certain number of unscrupulous politicians as an agent for removing their opponents, and they were interested in keeping him in office. I gathered that he had grown truculent through success and was not above doing some removing on his own account. His minor crimes were too numerous to chronicle. On my inquiry whether there was no objection on the part of his fellow-citizens, my informant told me that he had them all ' Buffaloed '.

Mr. Fowler appeared to have all the qualifications of a certain Bret Harte character, except the Tender Heart. However, I was not disposed to accept all the stories as gospel. After my shave and a bath in a receptacle which appeared to have been used for a dust-bin, I returned to the hotel. But that evening after supper, while I was reading the papers and enjoying a smoke, Mr. Fowler and his gang entered the hotel, and after exchanging noisy greetings with some of the attendants made their way to the bar-room ; and as I recalled that one of his foibles was forcing innocent strangers to drink with him at the point of a gun, I gathered up my papers and retired to my room on the floor above.

I had been there perhaps an hour when I was startled by a terrific scream from below. This was followed by a hurried shuffling of feet, and then everything was still. Thoroughly alarmed, I opened the door and rushed into the corridor. From there I could hear some one groaning down below. I ran down as fast as I could to investigate.

As I entered the office several men were disappearing through the front door. In the doorway leading to the bar there was a man huddled up on the floor, groaning pitifully. Others, amongst them the bartender, were hurrying to the stricken man. He was bleeding copiously and had one hand clutching his stomach. We lifted him up and got him on to the billiard-table, on which some one had spread a blanket.

The bartender told us that he was an unfortunate stranger in the clothing line who had gone to the bar-room for a cigar. There he was invited by Mr. Fowler to drink. The invitation was backed up by a gun, but the unfortunate man had pleaded a weak stomach. This was not considered an adequate excuse by Mr. Fowler, who expressed a determination to cure him. He drew his bowie knife and actually disembowelled him.

Fowler's friends had hustled him out of the place. It

was they who were just disappearing through the door as I came on the scene.

Some one brought in a doctor, and under his direction we carried the unfortunate man upstairs and laid him on a bed. He was unconscious and died a few hours later, without regaining consciousness.

Early the next morning I heard that Mr. Fowler's friends had taken him to jail, as a matter of precaution, should any ill-advised citizens be misguided enough to resent this cowardly murder. I was advised that if I wished to get away that day I should make an early start ; otherwise there was the possibility of an inquest, and I might be called as witness. I swallowed a hasty breakfast and got under way for the La Jinsa with as little delay as possible.

I had a hard day's ride north into a new country before I found my friends in camp, when it was almost dark. I was cordially welcomed and introduced to Mr. Montague Stevens, Ned Upcher's partner, which cleared up the mystery of the brand S U. They were not to start receiving the cattle till the following morning, so I had got there just in time.

My horses were thrown into the *remoutha*, or herd which was being taken out to graze, and I soon forgot all my troubles over a hearty supper by the camp fire. Afterward the cowboys gave us songs of the prairie. One had reference to a gentleman who was *in extremis* and objected to being buried on the prairie. It was entitled ' The Dying Cowboy,' and the first verse ran as follows :

> Oh ! Bury me not on the Lone PraiRIE-E-E-e-e
> These words came Soft, but MournFULLY-Y-y-e
> From the Pallid Lips of the Youth AS he LAY-y-y-a,
> On his dying Cou-CH At the Break of DAY-a-a.

It was a mournful ditty, especially as they paid no heed to his request. I can't recall the rest of it, but it had something to do with coyotes' howls and buffaloes' paws, and finally wound up with a statement :

> They heeded not his Dying PRAY-er-r
> In a Narrow Grave they buried him THEY-er-r,
> In a Narrow Grave, just six by THREE-e-e
> They buried him There, on the Lone PraiRIE-E-e-e.

The work of receiving the cattle began the morning after my arrival, and I took my first lesson in the art of cow-punching. There was a stout picket corral, divided into three compartments, in the largest of which several stout snubbing posts had been sunk in the ground. These, I was given to understand, were a necessary adjunct to the roping and throwing of grown cattle, which in this case had to be done on foot. The cattle we were about to receive were too wild to risk horses in the enclosure with them. A number of the bulls were of a fighting breed, favoured when bull-fighting had been a popular pastime in the country.

The cattle were to be brought into the large compartment in batches of from a hundred to a hundred and fifty by the representatives of Garcia and Gallegos. There they were to be branded. Then they were to be thrown into one of the smaller partitions to make room for a fresh lot and afterwards shoved outside, to be held as a herd, by employees of the S U outfit.

This being the general outline of the day's work, we girded up our loins ready to go to it. My humble duties as a novice were to attend to the fire and to see that the brands were always hot. I was furnished with an axe and directed to a pile of wood outside the corral.

I was no stranger to the use of an axe, and managed to provide a goodly pile and get the fire started and the brands hot before the work began. While waiting, I got on the fence with the others to watch the cattle coming in. I had at first intended walking out to meet them, but was dissuaded by some men on horseback, who appeared wildly excited. I could not understand their language, but I gathered that it was advisable to keep out of sight.

From the fence I watched them come in. They were different from any cattle I had hitherto seen. Most of their growth seemed to have gone into their horns. They were coaxed inside the wings of the corral and then rushed through the gate, evidently under the impression that they were being turned loose. Their disappointment on finding no outlet was evident, and they circled round the coral for quite a time after the bars had gone up before allowing the atmosphere to get sufficiently clear for the men to go to work.

Then it was every man to his duties, and I was kept on the run carrying hot irons to the men who were branding them and then hurrying back as they cooled off to fetch fresh ones and re-heat those that had been in use.

In this way I did not have much time for observation, but I listened curiously to the cries' of the Mexican *vaqueros*, who were constantly shouting ' *Autro la haut*,' which I gathered meant to turn the animal over on the other side. Also there was a cry ' *Qui da ho*,' used when the branded animal was turned loose and got to its feet in a state of frenzy. This was followed by a general rush to the fence to escape its infuriated horns.

From my position behind the fire I began to enjoy the idea of every one else having to seek refuge on the fence while I looked on in safety. But the supply of wood began to run short and I had to replenish it. To do this I took advantage of a pause in the proceedings while they were struggling with a malicious-looking animal of indescribable colour and keen offensive horns.

I gave the brands to the executioners and climbed over the fence for more wood. I had it all neatly stacked up outside, so lost no time in securing a large armful and climbing back into the corral. I had secured as much as I could possibly carry, and the pile on my arm came up in front of my face, partly obscuring my vision. I did not therefore notice very closely the position of affairs, beyond seeing, as I got to the top of the fence, that the men were about through branding and ready to carry the irons back to the fire.

My load was so cumbersome that I threw it on the ground before jumping off the fence. Then I gathered it up again carefully and was proceeding across to the fire with it when there was much scuffling and snorting and every one rushing for safety.

I paid no particular attention till the renewed cries of ' *Qui da ho*,' followed by the good English shout of ' look out,' made me realize that I was the object of the warning. In another moment all doubt was dispelled, for the infuriated animal was within a few feet of me. Then, realizing my position, I dumped my load on his head and jumped to one side. This diversion was received with a cheer from the fence, but whether as encouragement for me or the beast I was never very clear.

So far as the latter was concerned it seemed to aggravate him. My precious load was tossed high in the air and scattered all over the place, while he kept on his way, attracted by the shouts and cheers. Seeing his persecutors out of his reach he snorted and shook his head at them while pawing up the dust and challenging them to come down and fight it out.

I, in my innocence, thought it all over and proceeded to recover my wood. I had collected a billet or two when warning cries again attracted my attention. Looking up, I perceived that the beast was coming straight at me. He was between me and the nearest fence, and so my retreat was cut off. I jumped to my feet and let fly with the billet in my hand. The aim was true and it caught him on the nose, but only produced a snort. What was worse, it increased the acceleration of his attack.

There was nothing for it but retreat. I turned and ran for the fence on the other side of the corral. I was pretty nimble of foot in those days, but the beggar had a flying start and was rapidly gaining on me. I could almost feel the hot wind of his breathing and was expecting to feel his horn when some good angel shouted to get behind a snubbing post.

It came as a heaven-sent message, and I turned sharply to one that was close by. I was only just in time. As it was, the beast's horn caught a portion of my new overalls and carried it away on the tip, like a miniature flag. His impetus carried him nearly to the fence, but when he got there he turned to take in the situation. For a moment or two he was nonplussed and shook his head in defiance at all creation.

I crouched behind my post, hoping to escape his observation, and might have done so had not his cruel rent caused my shirt to stick out and flutter in the air. This quickly drew his attention and he came at me full tilt, challenging me to come out in the open and fight it out. But I was in a strategic position behind the post and was not prepared to abandon it. My only trouble was that one hand had to be employed in holding my damaged garment in place ; also my fluttering shirt drew derisive cheers from the fence, where the assembled hands were enjoying the fun.

Not heeding their shouts, I clung to my post like a limpet. For several minutes that rampant steer and I circled it, till we were lost in a cloud of dust. I held to it, however, and having the inside berth he failed to connect with me. This might have gone on indefinitely had he not realized the position and stopped, incidentally to recover his breath but mainly to consider. He was out for blood and had no intention of being foiled.

After a few more useless challenges, he changed his tactics and took after me from the other direction. This was unexpected and almost led to disaster, for it necessitated my changing hands, relegating the one I had on the post to my falling garments and *vice versa*. I managed to elude him, however, and we took up our merry-go-round game again at increased speed.

I have no idea how long this lasted, but I was getting short of breath and beginning to think it was growing serious when my doughty assailant again called a halt, and I leaned closely against my side of the post and hitched my garments into position. All this time I was painfully aware of the ribald remarks from the audience on the fence. These gentlemen seemed to think that the performance had been specially staged for their delight, and their sympathies were entirely with my opponent.

However, it did not last much longer, for my opponent, finding his challenges of no avail, attempted to dislodge me by main force. With a final snort and a bellow he charged the post. This was firmly set and he struck it full tilt. We both rebounded from it, but in opposite directions. The result was evidently unexpected on his part. He looked at me in astonishment, as much as to say : ' Did you do that ? ' and with a twist in his neck ran off to join his companions.

I allowed him a few moments to settle down and then made a bolt for my hat, which had been lost in the early stages of the combat. I reached it in safety and stooped to pick it up, when some fiend on the fence shouted ' *Qui da ho.*' Not waiting to investigate, I grabbed it and made a wild rush for the fence. Fortunately in front of me was a picket with a large knot about half-way up, and I sprung on to it, placed my disengaged hand on the top, and vaulted over.

This exploit was received with a loud cheer from the audience and gained me their sympathy for the time being ; but I had to repeat the performance several times before we got through branding, in order to convince some of the more sceptical that it was not entirely due to the influence of that ewe-necked steer.

Then it was necessary for me to go to Socorro to have my individual brand recorded. Ned Upcher and Stevens had also business there, but we first took a hand at stringing the cattle out on their two hundred mile journey home, and accompanied them for eight or ten miles of the way before our roads parted.

While riding alongside the herd I was more than ever impressed with the disproportionate size of their heads and horns. They looked top-heavy to such an extent that if they stumbled it would raise their hind feet off the ground and they would be unable to get up again. I had visions of them all standing on their heads with their tails waving in the air. One of the last to go by was my old friend of the snubbing post, on whom I had put my individual brand, and though he still looked hostile, I bade him an affectionate farewell and followed Ned and Stevens, who had gone ahead with ' Fairy ' Hardcastle in a buckboard.

They reached Socorro some time before I did, but I joined them at the hotel about sundown. The events of the past week had almost driven Mr. Fowler out of my mind, but I was told by Stevens that there had been a meeting of prominent citizens and that every one was invited to assemble in front of the court-house that evening, between eight and nine, to decide what disposition was to be made of the gentleman.

He told me there was a rumour that his friends intended to take him away, but that other people were determined to take the matter into their own hands, as they thought it was time to put a stop to his activities. Accordingly we strolled over to the court-house after supper to see what was going to happen.

We were amongst the first to arrive, but it seemed as if the crowd had only been waiting for a lead, for it quickly grew, until there were several hundred assembled. A dozen men entered the court-house, the back end of which was the jail. We waited for ten or fifteen minutes before the committee came out again, dragging the most miserable, contemptible object I ever saw. All Mr. Fowler's bravado had gone. He was howling and begging for his life. He had so far lost control of his functions that he was loathsome to look at, and I felt glad that I was not one of those who had to drag him along.

The rest of the proceedings went without a hitch. He

was hustled into a wagon. The whole procession moved quietly to the edge of the town, where a convenient tree overhung the road. There they strung him up and drove the wagon out from under him. Somebody fired a few merciful shots into him, but I think they were unnecessary. I saw his face as they did the work, and I believe he was already dead before they swung him loose. It was a horrible sight : the face of a coward.

The crowd dispersed as quietly and mysteriously as it had assembled and we went back to the hotel, where it took something strong and ardent to mitigate the bad taste in our mouths.

The next morning Ned and Stevens left, to catch up with the herd, but Fairy and I stayed in town. He was a favourite with the Titian-haired young ladies, whom he entertained with his banjo. When they got hold of him they were loth to let him go.

During the forenoon we strolled down to the livery stable to look after our horses and while there invested in a couple of ponies. Fairy bought a very handsome sorrel pony called Dick, which was subsequently a noted animal on the cow range. I was anxious to give Torruno a rest, and, after looking round, settled on a good-looking animal of nondescript colour. The owner described him as a ' blue roan,' which was a new colour to me, but I let it go at that. He showed lots of quality, with a regular Arab head and a peculiar gait, most comfortable to ride, but rather ungainly to look at, which they called ' pacing '.

I got my brand recorded that afternoon, and the following morning, leaving Fairy to entertain the ladies, I started on my journey back to the W S. I had replaced my damaged garments with a new suit of overalls and I was feeling pretty fit. I passed over the familiar road, and looked forward to seeing my friend ex-Sergeant Cox, late of Strokestown in the County of Roscommon. When I reached his cabin about sundown of the fifth day it had every appearance of being deserted. I pulled up at the door and shouted. I was answered by a voice that sounded as if its owner was in bed.

I expressed my surprise, but before explaining he told me to attend to my stock and he would satisfy my curiosity as soon as I got back. I was somewhat delayed, because I had to give special attention to the roan, to protect him from the other two horses, who had been jealous of him all the way.

As soon as I got back, lighted the lamp, and stirred up the fire, Cox told me he had met with an accident. Sitting up in the bed, he showed me two bullet-holes, one on each side just over his loins, each one being some three to four inches from his spine. How they had got there without penetrating his stomach was more than I could tell. They did not seem to inconvenience him seriously, for he had met with the accident several days previously, yet had ridden five-and-thirty miles home and had attended to his own doctoring and cooking ever since.

All that he considered necessary in the way of medicaments consisted of a fractured bottle of vaseline and some unsanitary-looking cotton batting. With this he had plugged up the holes each side. As he showed them to me, he requested my assistance in changing the dressing, declaring that it was his custom to do so at least once in every twenty-four hours. It was evident that he came under the category of what doctors term ' good patients '.

I washed out the wounds for him, which he seemed to think unnecessary. Much to my astonishment, I found them to be healthy, with no signs of inflammation. While attending to him I asked how the accident had occurred, but as his hands were employed with the vaseline and a pocket-knife, and he had to hold the end of his shirt in his mouth to keep it out of my way, the narration was postponed until I got through.

He had gone over to the plaza to replenish his stock. There he had met an acquaintance of his, Charlie Schneider, generally known as ' Dutch Charlie '. It seemed that Charlie had been working for a Mexican named Gereen and that on his leaving Gereen had failed to pay him his wages, claiming that Charlie was indebted to him for the amount, on account of bedding or other necessaries already purchased.

The dispute had come up before the local justice and he had decided in Charlie's favour. This, however, failed to settle the matter, for Gereen still refused to come across with the money. Charlie, according to immemorial custom of the West, expressed his intention of enforcing the justice's decree. Thus the matter stood when Cox came on the scene and lent a sympathetic ear to Dutch Charlie's complaint.

To discuss the pros and cons of the case and to contrive a method of making Gereen disgorge they adjourned, with several others, to Mr. Milligan's bar. Here they were when

Gereen thought he saw his opportunity. If Charlie came to an untimely end there would be nobody to demand the money. So Gereen took advantage of the others being occupied, crept up behind Charlie, and shot him in the back. Unfortunately in his haste he had put a forty-four calibre cartridge into a forty-five calibre gun. The result was that although he had placed the muzzle almost against Charlie's back the bullet had stripped and only inflicted a slight wound. It had the effect, however, of drawing Charlie's immediate attention. As he turned he got another bullet from Gereen in his left wrist. Then Charlie got his little thirty-two and proceeded to retaliate. Gereen beat a retreat. Charlie got off one or two shots wildly, in his confusion, but, following Gereen out of the door, he sat down on the step and plugged him as he ran across the street. One bullet struck the gentleman behind the shoulder and was entirely effective. It killed him outright and settled the question, but Charlie never collected his wages.

My friend Cox played the part of innocent bystander and received one of Charlie's wild shots, for his punctures were of the thirty-two calibre brand. The only extraordinary thing about them was how they got there without interfering with his digestion.

When I rode to the S U ranch I found the cattle had got in a day or two previously. They had turned them all loose, except my little bunch, which they were still holding under herd. As they were unable to spare any help to enable me to take them along they agreed to hold them until I could get to the W S and obtain the necessary assistance. They were now so well broken in that one man could handle them and corral them every night. I went to the W S and Mr. Cook kindly let me have his brother Jack to help me home with the cattle. I had not ridden Torruno much since getting the roan, so he was fresh, and I took him along.

Jack seemed quite confident as we went over to the S U. It was a lovely morning when we started back, with thirty-five miles to go. We got along fairly well for the first few miles. This was all through a rolling country, with fine pine timber, not sufficiently close to obstruct the vision. We had not watered the cattle before starting, and as the first water we could strike was at the head of the Salise Canyon, they travelled the better as they got thirsty.

Still it took us some five or six hours to get to the Salise Canyon. When we had watered them it was well past noon. It was at this point that I began to doubt the feasibility of getting the cattle to the W S in one day. Jack was still confident, and explained that we could push them as fast as we wanted to through the canyon, which was some fifteen miles long, as they would not be able to get out on either side.

This all sounded good, and after we thought they had sufficiently rested and drunk their fill we began to round them up and push them through the canyon. It was about a hundred yards wide and thickly covered with brush, except where the road wound through it. The cattle didn't want to go out on either side ; neither did they want to go down the canyon. In fact, they didn't want to go anywhere. All they wanted was to be left alone, to lie down or graze, as seemed best to them. A few agreed to go ahead, but by the time we had got the others started we had to dig the first ones out of impenetrable brush, into which they had strayed. In this way we spent most of the day getting somewhat more than half-way through the canyon.

When the sun was getting low we thought they had at last recognized our good intentions, for they began to string out in file. They went at a reasonable gait, which after a time they actually increased to a trot. Our hopes were high, but aias ! as soon as we had brought up the backward ones we found the leaders had decided to leave the canyon and were actually climbing up the mountain at a place which would have caused a goat to hesitate.

We swore, not for the first time that day, but this was more emotional. Neither of us knew what to do next, but it was at this point that Torruno took matters in hand. While I gazed at the cattle in despair, he took in the situation at a glance. It was nothing new to him. He knew they were not going in the right direction, so without consulting me he started out to head them off.

How he was going to do it was more than I could imagine. But he carried the brains of the outfit, and I let him go ahead. The way he scrambled up the side of that mountain, over rocks and timber, while I held on to his mane and was stretched out at full length on his back, was a revelation to me. It would be impossible to describe it, for what with fending branches from my face and occasionally going over places that were not good to look at, I have only a vague idea of what really took place.

Occasionally he would throw up his head to take stock of his position in regard to the cattle and then scramble and scratch and bound in his efforts to get round them. And we eventually did get around them. We got above them on the mountain and dropped to the semblance of a trail which they were following.

When we did so poor Torruno stopped for breath, and I fell off his back and actually kissed him. I wouldn't have traded the little fellow at that moment for all New Mexico, with California thrown in. He was blowing like a grampus and the saddle had slipped back almost to his tail, but we were in front of the climbing herd, so I had time to take it off and adjust it, while allowing him to recover his breath.

We had got behind a shoulder on the side of the mountain, and we were all ready for the cattle when they came round the corner. There was an old fiddle-headed black and white cow in the lead, and as she blundered right on to us the look of surprise and dismay on her ugly face was ludicrous. She snorted and made an attempt to turn round, but the others were close behind her and crowded her off the trail. The others, seeing what was up, followed her, and that bunch of cattle literally fell off the side of that mountain. Such a crashing and smashing and rolling of rocks and clouds of dust cannot be described. It was a miniature avalanche. I couldn't see how those animals avoided breaking their necks. And I had no desire to follow them, but Torruno thought otherwise. He seemed confident, and again I let him go ahead. We got down somehow, with the saddle on Torruno's ears. As I adjusted it, Jack swung the cattle down the canyon. They travelled markedly better while the scare was on them, but it was pretty late at night before we finally got them out of the canyon and turned them loose, still some sixteen miles or more from our intended destination.

I never made any attempt to gather them afterwards. Some of them drifted back to the S U, but the majority of them stayed where they were, on the W S range, and a year or so later I sold the entire brand back to Mr. Stevens. This ended my first venture in the cattle business. But my retirement was only of short duration, for Mr. Wilson sold me a hundred head of the W S cattle on the same day that I closed the transaction with Mr. Stevens.

CHAPTER IV

A MEXICAN WAR

I HAD no definite position on the ranch, but tried to make myself generally useful. Wilson and I set out a lot of trees, both shade and fruit, and prepared the ground for a kitchen-garden, which well repaid us in late years. Our first attempts were looked upon by the old-time cow-punchers with disapproval. Fresh vegetables on a cow ranch were considered a desecration.

Our main ambition was to become expert ropers. We did not yet join the regular hands when they went range branding. We were fearful of making mistakes. A number of small bunches of cattle belonging to other owners were running on the range, and we had no wish to gain their enmity by having our brand show up on any of their calves.

When cattle shed off in the summer time it was easy enough to read brands, but it required experience to be sure you had the right animal when the hair was long. The first time we went out showed us that range branding was not easy. We sallied out fully equipped, like knights of old, only instead of lances and maces we carried running irons and *rietas*. But we were as keen as they were for adventure.

There were plenty of calves—little slick-haired things not much bigger than jack-rabbits, and capable of running, for a short distance, fast enough to make any rodent sit up and take notice. The first bunch we struck had an old cow in the lead, with a diminutive calf at her heels. She resented our efforts to approach by making for the hills.

We rode alongside to try and read the brand, but she kept swinging away from us in such a manner that it was impossible to get a good look. At length Wilson said he recognized a brand on her hip, which looked to me like a dried cow-pat, as a circle-dot, one of his own. We took after the calf. Wilson got first shot, a beautiful throw with a nice clear loop, but the little beggar saw the lasso coming and doubled, so that it missed him. It was now my turn. I got a nice throw, but failed to check up quick enough, and he went clear through the loop. By the time we had our ropes coiled up again the calf had joined his mother, and they were both disappearing over the edge of the canyon into a country thickly strewn with boulders and brush.

Our ponies tore after them. The sides of the canyon were steep and rough, and our quarry was part way up the other side when we reached the edge. The sure-footed ponies flew down the incline, jumping over fallen timber and rocks as big as themselves. At the bottom of the canyon was a dry creek bed, too big to clear and some six or seven feet deep. They never hesitated, but jumped into it and scrambled out the other side without losing their stride.

It was a most exhilarating ride. We caught up with them as they got to the top on the other side, and a successful throw from Wilson captured the calf. I got down to secure him, when the old lady, attracted by his cries, charged me. I had barely time to reach Torruno and dodge clear of her threatening horns. Having routed me, she stood by the calf and defied us to come on. But when I turned the matter over to Torruno he ran her off in short order.

While we were branding the calf the old cow stood under a tree about a hundred yards off and watched the proceeding. As soon as we turned him loose she gave a little ' moo ' and he scampered off to join her. She sniffed him all over, gave him a lick on the nose, and the pair of them disappeared into the canyon.

Wilson and I looked at each other, and our thoughts travelled in the same direction. That little squalling calf and his mother's kiss on the nose had taken a good deal of the romance out of the business. We had spent half a day getting a single tiny calf and felt that we were hardly earning our grub. We went back to our agricultural pursuits, and such sport as quail hunting, and abandoned range branding for the time being.

It was a relief when the autumn came round after the very dry summer. It was still hot in the middle of the day, but the mornings and evenings were ideal. We harvested our first potatoes, and Wilson and I were proud of them ; but the cowboys looked askance and pronounced them only fit food for a ' granger '. The average puncher's idea of luxury (excepting pie) was something put up in a tin can.

In the autumn we rode a good deal in the mountains, and had an enjoyable time hunting mavericks and branding the calves of the outlawed cattle. This was really good sport and proved our ponies to be as sure-footed as goats.

On one of those trips one of our boys, Ed Erway, generally referred to as the ' Straw Boss ', had a curious experience with a wildcat. He was following a trail along the edge of a deep canyon when the beast jumped out of a bush on to the flank of his horse. The animal plunged and reared, but the cat held on, until Erway, turning in his saddle, shot it with his pistol. The mounted head is still in my possession. The strangest thing about it is that the animal had not sneaked off before he got close to it. It was the only case in my experience of a wildcat attacking when it could easily have escaped.

In November all hands began to speculate on how Thanksgiving Day was to be celebrated. As the principle notion was wild turkey, I at once became devout. A friend of Wilson's—a Dr. Murray from New York—was staying at the ranch at the time, and for a week or more prior to Thanksgiving Day we hunted everywhere for the elusive turkey. But the eve of the festival arrived and we were still without the necessary birds.

We had been out early, and hunted all day and had got home and were attending to our horses in gloomy silence, when dear old Charlie Moore rode in to say that he had located a bunch of over twenty in the box-canyon a mile and a half above the ranch.

It was then too dark to do anything, but we made preparations to interview them at crack of dawn. At the place where Charlie located them a lot of Indian hieroglyphics were scratched on the rocks. We now recollected that these consisted mainly of rude imitations of tents, fish, and what might be considered turkey tracks. No doubt the place had been a favourite resort for turkeys from all time, but we had never expected to find such shy birds so close to the ranch.

The following morning we were out long before daylight. Dr. Murray and I went to one side of the canyon, Wilson and Cook to the other. We had a long wait and it was bitterly cold. Our first intimation that it was time to be on the alert came in the shape of two rifle-shots, fired quickly in succession. Cook was the only one who carried a rifle, and we knew the shots must be his.

Before the reports had died away some ghost-like forms, which we knew to be turkeys, appeared out of the dark with their necks stretched out, so we let them have it. It was over almost as quickly as it had begun, and we proceeded to gather the spoils. On our side we had four turkeys. Wilson had not got a shot, the distance across the canyon being beyond the range of a shot-gun. But Cook had got two with his rifle, a wonderful performance in the dim light, when it must have been hard to see and the birds were fully fifty to sixty yards from him.

The question now was how to retrieve Cook's birds, which had fallen into the bed of the river. It was a drop of a hundred and fifty feet or more, and almost sheer. I volunteered to go down, but getting back with two great birds weighing forty pounds or more was not so simple. I fastened them round my neck, and while climbing had to bring my teeth into play to avoid being choked. I finally accomplished the climb, under a fire of raillery from my companions on top. They were anxious about my safety merely as a secondary consideration. I received all kinds of advice as to the safety of the birds and how I should be careful in the handling of them.

To really appreciate our feelings one should have lived on straight beef and sow-belly for a year. How we enjoyed those turkeys can be easier imagined than described. I have eaten many good Thanksgiving dinners since, but none with the same zest.

After Thanksgiving we settled down to our usual routine. Things were going along smoothly when one afternoon we were startled by a messenger from our friends at the S U. This man brought word that there was trouble between the Mexicans and the white settlers. A cowboy from the Spur Ranch had been killed and the Mexicans were holding another in captivity at the plaza. It was feared an attack would be made on some of the outlying ranches, especially the S U, which was nearest to them. He had come for assistance and for an officer of the law. The only white deputy within reach was Dan Bechtol, over at Alma. We told the messenger to go ahead to Alma and we would wait for his return. If the deputy brought a posse along we could all go to the S U together.

To explain this interesting outbreak, locally known as ' The Mexican War ', it is necessary to enter slightly into history. During the years between 1882 and 1885 a number of cattlemen had moved their herds, and occasionally their neighbours' herds, from Texas to New Mexico. This migration was generally in the way of business, but sometimes its object was to avoid unpleasant consequences of a not too strict observance of the law. A new brand, a new name, and a new country covered a multitude of sins. Amongst those whose absence from Texas was tolerated only on the grounds of saving expense to the State were many cowboys who lost no opportunity of displaying their hatred of Mexicans. To them all Mexicans were ' Greasers ' and unfit associates for the white man.

Now, 1884 was an election year. The County of Socorro was a Mexican county with a large majority of Mexican voters. It was true that the political offices of the county were generally held by men who were not of Spanish descent, but this was largely due to their superior manipulation. The office of sheriff was the most eagerly sought-for office in the county government, because the sheriff, in addition to his executive power, was *ex officio* collector and treasurer, and for this his remuneration, in addition to his sheriff's fees, was something like four per cent of the amount he collected.

The incumbent at the time was a gentleman known as Don Pedro Simpson. Whether he had been originally Pete Simpson and acquired the ' Don Pedro ' for election purposes I never heard clearly explained, but he had held the office for a number of years and had come to look on it as his private monopoly. There had been considerable opposition to him of late years, and all new-comers who had the right of vote were eagerly canvassed by Don Pedro's party and by the opposition.

The opposition to Don Pedro was backed by the American population of the county. It was maintained, I believe not without justification, that sixty thousand dollars of the county funds were unaccounted for. Don Pedro was not openly accused, but it was intimated that a change in the Executive would be what a gentleman named Cicero termed ' *pro bono publico* '. We had not personally come in contact with the canvass of voters, because we were not citizens of the Great Republic, but our friends at the S U had declared their intention of becoming citizens and in consequence were more directly interested.

It was as an emissary of one of the rival parties that a young gentleman named Elfigo Baca had come out from Socorro to solicit the votes of settlers at the plazas on the San Francisco River. I never heard directly which side he was supporting, but from the subsequent proceedings gathered he favoured Don Pedro.

He had been staying at the plaza for some days when some of the cowboys from the neighbouring ranches, having ridden in and sampled some of Mr. Milligan's forty-rod whisky, recollected that they were citizens of the great State of Texas and that the Alamo and other historical events were closely connected with the despised Greaser. Under the influence of patriotism and whisky they proceeded to give vent to their feelings. Mr. Baca carried a deputy's commission and considered that as a peace-officer it was up to him to express his disapproval.

He did this effectually and was able to count the casualties when the fracas was over as one dead, one wounded, and one captive, with the remainder driven off in disorder. The wounded man had ridden off with the disordered party, the dead man was laid out in a shed, but the captive, whose name was Charlie McCarthy, was a real live issue.

According to the gentleman who had come to summon us, Mr. McCarthy was an inoffensive youth incapable of harming an insect. After his departure to Alma to procure legal authority, we started out on our own hook and reached the S U around one o'clock in the morning. Instead of finding the place in flames we found them all asleep. We roused them up, demanding to know where the enemy was, and they said he must be in bed. We had got in and settled down when Mr. Bechtol and the Alma contingent arrived, accompanied by the belated messenger. They were all full of zeal and whisky, and the representative of the law, Dan, was especially ferocious ; and although nobody was actually holding him, he expressed a determination that if he was only allowed to get at them not one would be left alive on the following day.

It was almost daylight when they got through telling us their programme, so that we got no further rest that night. We prepared breakfast, then waited around for several hours, till nine or ten o'clock, for Dan, who was sleeping it off. We all moved some time before noon and rode twenty miles to pick up a justice of the peace so that McCarthy could get a fair trial without being carried off to Socorro.

We presented quite a formidable appearance as we rode into the plaza. There were some twenty or thirty men, the majority of whom had slept in their clothes for several nights and none of whom had shaved for probably a still longer period. Consequently it was not surprising that when we drew up opposite Mr. Milligan's hospitable portals we found the place almost deserted. But the genial proprietor was in evidence and prepared to attend to the wants of the crowd, which seemed afflicted with a perennial thirst. Most of the boys tumbled into the place, while we, who had as yet taken no active part, made ourselves comfortable on the outside.

After a short interval the justice, Dan, and Mr. Milligan came out, accompanied by a Mexican, and we learned that the entire population had migrated to the middle plaza and taken their prisoner, Mr. McCarthy, with them. The Mexican was dispatched with a note addressed to Mr. Baca and signed by Dan and the justice. This note was a request to bring Mr. McCarthy and they would hold court and deal with him according to the laws of the territory.

About an hour later the messenger returned, accompanied by four or five men, amongst whom was the prisoner McCarthy and I think a Mexican justice of the peace. Mr. Baca, a young man scarce out of his teens, rode at the head of the party, and as they drew up at Mr. Milligan's the latter, accompanied by our justice and the deputy Dan, came out and met them. They all dismounted and went down the street to a house fifty or sixty yards south from Mr. Milligan's emporium. They were followed by the crowd which had streamed out of the saloon.

Some two or three of us belonging to the foreign contingent, who were not sufficiently interested, remained outside. We sat on the ground, and indulged in the exciting game known as ' mumble-de-peg '. This consisted in throwing an open-bladed knife so as to stick in the ground and remain upright. The pastime drew an audience of a few stragglers who had been left in the saloon, amongst them being two or three boys belonging to the Spur outfit.

These gentlemen took a supercilious interest in our game, and after watching us for a few moments one of them, whose name was Hern, discharged a Winchester which he held in his hand into the ground within two or three inches of my feet. The bullet tore a great gash in the ground, but, presuming it had been done in order to test the nerves of the tenderfoot from abroad, I took no notice of it. This indifference not seeming to be to their taste the crowd dispersed, and when my attention was again directed to the street they had disappeared into Mr. Milligan's Hall of Entertainment.

The proceedings in the court-room must have been conducted with due formality, for they were in there fully half an hour. The first to come out was Mr. Baca, who strode hastily through the door, pulling his hat down over his eyes. None of our party took any notice of him, but I happened to be faced in that direction and saw that he went into a cabin farther down the street and on the same side as the court-room. Then came the crowd, who told us that the prisoner had been fined five dollars, which he had paid, and was now at liberty. He came out almost immediately, surrounded by his friends, who were congratulating him, and we were all formally introduced.

This apparently ended the matter. Our party proceeded to get their horses and return to the S U ranch, where we proposed to spend the night. I went along with the rest, but was waylaid by Mr. Milligan and my friend Cox, who proposed that I accompany them to the saloon and have a parting drink. I told the rest of our party that I would catch them up. The drink took only a very short time, and as I came out of the door I noticed that ' Old Charlie ' (Charlie Moore), who was the last of our party to leave, was just mounting his horse and getting under way.

I shouted to him that I would be right along and crossed the street to my horse. I was getting him loose when I was approached by the gentleman who had shot his gun off so close to my feet, accompanied by three others. They asked me if I had seen where Mr. Baca went when he came out of the court-room. I pointed out the cabin and was preparing to mount when they told me they had authority from the presiding justice to arrest Mr. Baca. The ostensible reason was the shooting of the man at the time of McCarthy's arrest. They said it was only just that he should be made to answer according to law.

This sounded all right, so I said : ' Let's go ahead and arrest him.' The four of us walked down to the cabin. Hern, who had taken the lead, walked up to the door, and I followed close behind him. He knocked, asking if there was anyone there. Receiving no reply, he kicked the door violently, demanding admittance. The reply this time was decisive. It came in the form of a bullet through the door, which took him in the abdomen.

He swore a marvellous oath and fell back into my arms. I dragged him as quickly as I could round the corner of the cabin. The others scattered in all directions, but joined me almost immediately, and we laid him out on the ground.

In the meantime Old Charlie, who had heard the shot, came tearing back down the street at full gallop and pulled up short, immediately opposite the door. He was greeted by a regular *feu de joie* from inside the cabin, one bullet passing through his tall, peaked hat. Assuming that something was amiss when he heard the shot he had picked up my horse, which I had left standing by the rack, and had led him along with him. Not appreciating his pretty close call, he was endeavouring to get out of the way as quickly as he could, but the led horse was hampering his movements. Seeing this, I left the wounded man and ran to Old Charlie's assistance. In doing so I also came under fire, but the shooting was wild. I took the led horse from him and got back with the loss of my own hat, which lay in the street in front of the house.

The wounded man was now propped up against the wall. He had regained consciousness and was able to speak. While discussing ways of getting him up to the store, he said that he thought he could ride up if we would assist him on to one of the horses and keep him from falling off. So we hoisted him on to Charlie's horse and while two held him on either side led him along to Milligan's.

There we examined the wound and washed and dressed it as best we knew how. There was little or no blood from it, but it was in a dangerous place and must have penetrated the bowels. His main anxiety was a desire to get even with the man who had shot him, so we promised that we would do all in our power to capture him and deliver him to the authorities.

After this Charlie and I went to look for our deputy, who, with the Alma crowd, had not yet left. We discovered him in a wareroom at the back of the store, where he said he had gone to get a little rest after his strenuous exertions the night before.

Dan agreed with us that Mr. Baca should be arrested and that it should be done at once, but personally he seemed more interested in catching up with lost sleep. After an unsatisfactory interview we left him and I went down to recover my hat. I made a dash for it, but no sooner had I stooped than our friend inside turned loose. I did not waste any time, and when I got back with it to shelter there were bullet holes through the leaf in three places.

Then Old Charlie and I made up our minds that it was up to us to fog him up a little and not to let Mr. Baca think he was the only man in the plaza who possessed ammunition.

We accordingly made our way to the opposite side of the street, where there was an adobe church with buttresses. From behind one of them we amused ourselves by exchanging compliments with him. One of us would stick out his head to draw his fire and the other would fog up the little window or the door, whichever we thought he was using. He returned our fire and kept knocking gobs of mud off our sheltering bastion with tedious regularity, while we in our turn made the splinters fly from his window and door.

We had been at this interesting game for probably fifteen or twenty minutes when the rest of our party, headed by Wilson and Cook, came flying into the plaza. They had gone a mile or so when the echo of the first shots caused them to pause. When these were followed by the fusillade they made up their minds that the ball had opened and came hurrying back. Charlie and I explained the circumstances, and at Cook's suggestion some attempt was made to parley with our intended prisoner, and Mr. Baca was addressed eloquently in Spanish from the shelter of an adobe wall. This, however, did not prove very effective. All we got was more shots.

The chances of taking the place by assault were discussed and rejected. No definite decision was come to, but by way of intimation the crowd moved out and, taking up safe positions on all sides of the unfortunate cabin, fogged it up for about twenty minutes with an incessant fusillade.

When over we thought that surely Mr. Baca must have been reduced to a sieve, but were much disappointed when one of our boys, Ed Erway, ventured into the street to reconnoitre. He had hardly shown himself when he met with such a bombardment that he was forced to retreat hastily, while by way of diversion we resumed our onslaught on the cabin, searching every nook and cranny where a bullet could possibly penetrate. This had the effect of quietening him, for his demonstrations ceased ; but where he sought shelter from our fire, and how he escaped the numerous bullets that must have passed through the building, was a mystery to us.

It was getting late by this time and it became necessary to take precautions in order to prevent his escape during the night, so we posted regular sentries. I then paid a visit to the wounded man, but found him very low, and it was evident that he had only a short time to live. I was unable to visit him again until nearly daylight, when I found that he had petered out.

I took up my sentry-post by the buttress of the church, whence I had a good view of the front and side of the cabin. I stayed there for the rest of the night, with occasional visits to the other sentries, who did not seem to think that sleeping on their posts was in any way detrimental to their duty, and I suppose Mr. Baca must have been asleep too, for otherwise there was nothing to prevent his walking out of the door and going where he pleased.

I made several attempts to see our deputy, Dan, but he was either asleep or too busy to attend. As he expressed it, Milligan's bar was good enough for him, and when he was tired of it he could retire to the back room and take a rest. Things were at this stage about five a.m. when I woke up my friend Cox. He expressed surprise when I told him I had been up all night, and advised me to find a shakedown.

The advice struck me as being sound, as I had been without sleep for forty-eight hours. I found the door of the Milligan residence ajar, and pushing it gently open thought I might find a resting-place without disturbing the occupants. In this I was disappointed. I had hardly crossed the threshold when I struck my foot against something soft. This was Mr. Milligan himself, lying across the entrance, no doubt surmising that his presence was more effective than a lock.

He sat up and demanded who was there. I explained the reason I had sought his hospitality. He was not in the least disconcerted, but raising his great hand waved towards a back room, saying if I went in there I would find several mattresses on the floor and could lie down with the children.

Greater hospitality could no man show, for the rest of the family, of all sizes, ages, and sexes, were sprawling in the back room. The ladies seemed to be laid out on one side with their heads towards the wall; the gentlemen occupied a similar position towards the opposite wall. By the light of a match it was not very easy to distinguish them, but seeing a vacant spot several inches in width on what appeared to be the gentlemen's side I took a chance, blew out the match, and throwing myself down on the mattress with my hat as an impromptu pillow was soon fast asleep.

I was awakened by the rising sun shining through a little window directly on my face. I found I was now the sole occupant of the mattress, probably because I had lain down in my spurs. The men had rolled away on the floor and were still fast asleep ; so were the ladies.

I gathered up my hat and slipped quietly from the house without further disturbing the occupants. I found my friend Cox already up and preparing breakfast I discussed with him the possibility of Mr. Baca having got away during the night, but Cox seemed quite confident he was still there. To decide the matter I agreed to run across the street at an acute angle, which would give him a glimpse of me if he was still on the watch. The experiment satisfied me that our friend was still at home.

His shots roused the whole camp, and we returned his morning salute with interest. After that we made several more attempts to get in communication with him, but without effect. It only resulted in the expenditure of ammunition.

During the early hours of the day a report came that the Mexicans were approaching in force. A reconnaissance disclosed the fact that a number of them were riding over the hills on both sides of the village, and amongst some of the belligerents there was almost a stampede to get away, but a few shots at long range caused them to diverge. It turned out afterwards that they had no direct hostile intentions, but were on their way to Socorro to seek the intervention of the authorities.

When the excitement quieted down we again tried to induce Mr. Baca to come out and give himself up, assuring from secure shelter that he would incur no personal harm ; but the only response we could get from him was by exposing some one or something for him to shoot at. We tried all kinds of devices, even tried to set the house on fire by hurling blazing logs on to the roof ; but the darn thing was made of dirt about a foot or more thick and refused to ignite. We could only sit out and wait, hoping eventually to starve him out, while we fogged him up occasionally, fearing that he might be inclined to rest.

This was not a very exciting game, and the sun was getting low and we were all getting grumpy and drowsy when there was an unexpected diversion. This was a buggy containing three men, which drove in rapidly from the direction of Socorro. From it stepped a tall American, who said that he was a deputy sheriff, and he actually possessed a badge to prove it. He had come in response to a report furnished by a Mexican, who was along with him in the buggy. It was evident that Mr. Baca's friends had lost no time in sending an account of the situation to the proper authorities, for Socorro was fully a hundred and sixty miles away by the most direct route.

Our own deputy, Dan, who did not sport a badge, and if he owned one must have left it at home, had up to this time taken no active part in the proceedings. But now he was very much in evidence, reciting what he had not done to enforce respect for the law. Mr. Rose did not pay much heed to him, but turned to others of our party for information in regard to the whole affair. Dan, I think, was a little peeved, but returned to Mr. Milligan's for consolation. Mr. Rose now took charge, and another attempt was made to communicate with Mr. Baca, through the medium of the Mexican who had come in the buggy.

This time everything was successful. Mr. Baca stipulated that every one else should stand away from the building and Mr. Rose and those who were with him remain in full view, after which he would come out and surrender to them When this had been complied with he made his appearance, not through the door, from which every one had been expecting him, but through a little window in the gable end of the house.

I had gone to the back of the adjoining house while he was making his exit and thus unexpectedly happened to be close to him as he came out. He was like a wild animal, stripped to his shirt, with a revolver in each hand, looking suspiciously on every side of him, as if fearing treachery. I withdrew behind my shelter as he came in sight, and after satisfying himself that no one was lying in wait for him he went up to Mr. Rose, who disarmed him.

Our Dan and his party concluded it was time to go home, but before doing so he rode up and formally turned over the prisoner that he had not captured ; after which satisfaction to his dignity he and his party rode off and we saw no more of them. Our party had intended going to the S U, but stayed on at the request of Mr. Rose, who was uneasy lest the men belonging to the other outfits, who had gone off to pay the last rites to Hern's body, should return and attempt to take away the prisoner.

Anyway, Mr. Rose turned Mr. Baca over to our custody shortly after his surrender, and we took him over to Milligan's for a wash and some refreshment. How he had escaped death was a miracle, for the cabin was riddled with bullets. He explained to us it was only by lying on the floor, which was a foot or more below the level of the ground, that he escaped being hit. Everything else in the cabin was reduced to splinters.

We turned him over to Mr. Rose the following morning and the two left for Socorro. Thus ended what was known in that section for several years to come as ' The Mexican War '. It might seem the honours were with Baca, unless one heard our own deputy, Dan, swell up and relate what he and his posse had done.

CHAPTER V

AN INDIAN OUTBREAK

AFTER our little flutter at the plaza things on the ranch returned to the normal. All went along smoothly and nicely, and the only thing I can recollect which disturbed the peace was a slight disagreement between our cook and myself.

This was a Frenchman named George Hudon. He had served in the U.S. cavalry and taken up the profession of *chef* as a means of livelihood after his discharge. George was a nice fellow when he was sober, but those intervals only occurred when he was unable to procure stimulant. If a ban was put on whisky, he fell back on pure alcohol or methylated spirit, which he got by claiming it was necessary for the restoration of his hair, he being extremely bald.

His particular grievance against me was that I was British. When, in a weak moment, fired by ancestral pride, I told him that my father served under Wellington and was even present at Waterloo, it put the final touch on his resentment, and only the fact of my being armed at the time prevented his having my blood. He made all sorts of attempts to force an open outbreak, of none of which I took any notice.

But matters eventually came to a head. While in camp one day I came in from the herd along with one or two others to get a cup of coffee. Having helped myself I sat down on the end of the wagon tongue to enjoy it. I had no thoughts of anything unusual, when George, who had been doing something around the fire, suddenly made a rush at me with a huge butcher's knife in his hand. The darn thing looked as big as a scythe-blade, and I jumped to my feet to beat a hasty retreat. The wagon tongue impeded my movements somewhat, and he was too close to me before I could get away. The prospect of cold steel in my back not appealing to me, I seized the first thing that came to my hand, which happened to be the neck yoke, and smote him over the head with it. It was shod with iron and took him fairly on the bald spot, and he went down like a pole-axed ox.

I thought for a moment or two that I had killed him, and

must confess that the blow had been delivered with that intent ; but on examination we discovered that his skull was thick, and beyond a bad scalp wound and the loss of a considerable amount of blood he would probably come round all right. We put him in the wagon and drove him to the ranch, where we enlisted the services of the local postmaster, a gentleman named Doc Lee.

Whether Doc Lee had other claims to the practice of medicine beyond his title I never really knew, but he was sympathetic and useful, and had been known to attend some of the ladies in the community on certain auspicious occasions. Between us we put some stitches in Frenchy's scalp, bandaged him up, and put him to bed.

George came out of it all right after a couple of weeks in bed, the only result being a rather prominent scar on his bald pate. While he was sick Doc visited him every day. It was a real treat for Doc, the only professional call with a fee attached that I ever knew him to get. His services on the other occasions mentioned were generally voluntary or paid for in kind. He visited George every day and always carried a little book in his pocket, which he made a pretence of consulting, before venturing an opinion as to the condition of his patient. From its general appearance we were inclined to think that it was an abridged edition of the Bible, but he was careful not to let it out of his possession.

George himself had really only a vague idea of what had occurred, as he was pretty well loaded when it happened, and was glad ever afterwards to allude to it as an accident. The boys as a rule thought he only got what was coming to him, and personally I had a sort of feeling that it raised me in their estimation.

Doc himself was an interesting character. In addition to his duties as postmaster, which only occupied a portion of his time on two days of the week, and for which he received as a salary the amount of the value of the stamps which he cancelled, he also was the local schoolmaster, and was paid a salary from the local taxation. There were some ten or a dozen pupils from the different ranches round, and they were supposed to attend five days during the week, but the school term only lasted for about three months during the year.

Doc himself was conscientious and would have carried out his duties to the letter, but he was sadly hampered by the possession of three sons, all of whom had ambitions to imitate Jesse James and other border bullies. These boys were named Thurston, Theodore, and Theophilus. Their ages ran from about nineteen to fifteen years, and they spent most of their time tearing around on horseback with a couple of six-shooters, practising to be quick on the draw. They sadly interfered with Doc's duties as a schoolmaster, and eventually broke up his ' Academy of Learning ', as he himself called it.

The matter came to my knowledge through our having to construct a new diversion dam in the creek. We had to employ extra hands for the purpose. Amongst the applicants for work was Theodore, then about sixteen. We really didn't want him, but not wishing to tell him so in too abrupt a manner advised him gently to go to school, saying that when he had finished school he would have plenty of time to work. ' Aw ! ' he said, ' Theophilus busted the school up.'

Questioning elicited that Theophilus had pulled a gun on the old man and run him out of the Academy in the presence of all his pupils. They at once took advantage of the situation to declare a general holiday, and there was no more school in Alma for several years to come. The old gentleman did not long survive the humiliation and died in Alma about a year later. After his demise Alma was without a physician for a considerable time.

As for George, he and I were good friends after his recovery and he stayed on for a year or more, but his weakness for alcohol became so persistent that we were compelled to get rid of him. When he took to what we called a hairwash spell he was entirely useless for several days. His final offence was a disappearance for forty-eight hours. He was only discovered then by some visitors of the gentler sex who happened to have stopped at the ranch and were desirous of seeing the place. The ladies were left to their own devices after partaking of some refreshment, and one of them, inspired no doubt by curiosity, had seen the key of an outbuilding which was kept for the exclusive use of distinguished guests. On opening the door she received a terrible shock.

Attracted by the screams we all rushed up and discovered George in a state of nudity, with a bottle which had been emptied of its contents in one hand and a rosary in the other. The situation was embarrassing. While the ladies retreated to the house, we dragged him out and carried him off to the bunk-house. The rough handling woke him up, and he smiled angelically on all of us, but he was deemed to have imperilled the good name of the place. He got other jobs on ranches, but his thirst for hair tonic proved fatal and he died a year or two later in the hospital at Silver City.

It was this spring of 1885 that I had my first experience in handling wild or semi-wild horses. There were several hundred mares on the ranch, none of which had ever been handled or interfered with, other than to be driven into a corral for the purpose of having their colts branded or the necessary separation of those intended to be broken for use.

These mares ran in various-sized bunches on the range, each bunch under the control of a stallion, who jealously guarded his harem. The boss stallion appropriated the largest and most select bunch, and had no hesitation in raiding a rival's bunch if any of its inmates attracted his fancy. This led to fierce conflicts, until one of the combatants established his superiority. .

The master stallion on our range was a little sorrel called Dandy Ball. He had originally come from Missouri and was gentle both to ride and drive, but had been given his liberty after coming to New Mexico. He quickly established his supremacy on the range. His bunch was by far the largest and most select, and it was interesting to see how he lorded it over his rivals. He trotted round with his crest erect, inspecting them, and appropriating any fair lady who took his fancy.

We had a large round corral constructed of two-inch planks set on end and leaning outward from the base, in which to handle the wild horses. They could run around it to their heart's content, but as the walls leaned outward, there was nothing for them to come in contact with and injure themselves. Also, they were always within range of the lasso from the centre, and the faster they ran the easier it was to forefoot them and throw them.

In this forefooting of an animal it was always necessary to get both forefeet in the noose, otherwise you were liable to break the animal's leg. True, it often threw them hard enough to break their front teeth, but seldom caused any permanent injury. The shock of the fall generally stupefied the animal for a sufficient length of time to allow one or two to rush in and secure its head, either by sitting on it or turning its nose upwards in the air, while the man on the rope carefully watched any attempt by the horse to gather its forefeet under it. When such an attempt was made the man had to use his entire strength to frustrate it, otherwise the animal would regain its feet and have to be roped and thrown all over again.

It was nice delicate work and resembled playing a monster fish. While one man's strength was seldom sufficient to keep a horse's forefeet extended, the extra pressure of his weight was generally sufficient to prevent its getting its feet under it, and thus he would work his way close enough to the animal to raise the feet completely off the ground, when all the help he could get was gratefully received and both forefeet and one hindfoot would be secured. Thus the animal was anchored.

This work with the horses was always very attractive to me, and was certainly the most interesting work in connexion with cattle-ranching. The breaking of the horses to the saddle was rough work and has been described many times. It was cruel but effective, and its interest mainly depended on the disposition of the horse that was being broken. Outside of the actual riding the main thing was to establish friendly relations with the animal and teach it to lead.

Our nearest neighbours on the east bank of the river were a family named Meader. They had homesteaded eighty acres of land immediately south of the ranch and between us and Almo. They consisted of the old gentleman, always known as ' Pa '; Mrs. Meader, generally disrespectfully alluded to as the ' Old Lady '; and two young ladies. All sorts of excuses were invented by our boys to gain an opportunity of having a chat with them. But they were well guarded by the Old Lady, who had no use for ineligible parties.

My own introduction came about unexpectedly. The mails were late one Saturday evening. They were usually due in Alma a little before sundown and some one used to ride down to return with the letters and express. This evening I happened to be the messenger from the ranch. While waiting I met Pa on a similar errand, and we sat on the ground outside the post office and swapped lies. I was thinking of giving it up as a bad job when some one came over to Pa from the saloon, which was opposite, and invited him to join in a game of cards.

This appeal to the old gentleman was irresistible. He immediately expressed his willingness. At the same time he asked if I would kindly get his mail and leave it at his house as I rode home. In common courtesy I could not refuse. Then he came close and whispered mysteriously to me that should the Old Lady make any inquiries as to his whereabouts I was on no account to mention that he was in Alma. If she was persistent he suggested that I might say he had gone to Cooney to see his boy Ed. He gave a colossal wink and left me.

It was quite dark when the stage got in and about nine o'clock before I had collected everything. I had Pa's mail neatly tied up in a separate bundle and I trotted gaily along in anticipation of a pleasant chat with the young ladies.

As I approached the house it was very dark, but the light from a little window enabled me to find my way, so I stepped boldly to the door and knocked at it. There was no response, but I could hear some one moving inside. After some delay I summoned up courage to repeat the knocking. This time my summons was answered almost immediately. The door was opened about three or four inches and a double barrelled shot-gun thrust in my face. It almost struck me in the mouth, and if it had not been for the light shining on the barrels I would have been unable to avoid it.

Startled by the reception I jumped to one side, struck my heels against something, and sat down ignominiously in some kind of receptacle that had been thrown out on the ground. While endeavouring to extricate myself I heard the Old Lady's voice exhorting me to make myself scarce or she'd blow the daylights out of me. I endeavoured to explain from my humiliating position and the sound of my voice had a soothing effect on her, for she immediately opened the door wider and called to one of her daughters to bring a light.

A light being brought, I explained that I had merely brought her the mail at the request of her husband. She said : ' Well, well ! However did that come to be so ? ' She then called to the young ladies, telling them that it was only Cap Frenchy, and inviting them to come out to be introduced. She asked after the old gentleman, and I, according to instructions, told her that he had gone to

Cooney to see her son. She shook her head, and said she'd bet he was in the saloon drinking and playing ' keerds '.

They invited me in and asked me to stay for supper, but somehow my little romance had got nipped in the bud and I didn't feel like reviving it, so I bade them goodnight and resumed my way. The boys had a good laugh at my adventure when I related it, and it was a standing joke amongst them for some time that I always made a circuit on my way to and from Alma to avoid getting too close to the cabin.

In May 1885 we prepared an expedition to capture some wild cattle reported to be in the hills between the ranch and the Blue Creek in Arizona. There were rumours of an unbranded bull amongst them, about four or five years old, which had been seen occasionally by some of the boys, but there was nothing really definite about him, except that the watering-place of the bunch with which he was supposed to run was more or less a mystery.

The expedition consisted of five men with Ed Erway, ' The Straw Boss ', in command. Two of the others were Henry Sellick and John Bertrand. The latter was a debonair individual, much given to recounting his own exploits. He never travelled without his gun, and on this occasion bore the only arms and ammunition that accompanied the outfit.

Henry was the reverse of John, reticent, but true as steel and fearless of anything that moved on the surface of the earth. Another member of the party was a full-blooded Indian, known as Indian Jack. He was a Ute or Piute who had been captured by the Mormons when an infant and brought up by Elder Maxwell. Jack had always lived amongst whites, but he preserved many of his Indian characteristics. He could disappear from sight on a level *mesa* or table-land where there was apparently no cover or other object to conceal him from view. Also he could reappear in the same mysterious manner, apparently from nowhere. He also had the faculty of being able to see what was going on behind him without moving anything but his eyeballs.

The party left early on the morning of the 15th May, following the usual route up the Pueblo to the mouth of Bear Creek, which was a main canyon coming in from the west with little permanent water beyond a few seep springs.

Here the party separated. Ed and John continued up the main canyon to Pueblo Park. Henry and his partner followed the Bear Creek canyon, with instructions to proceed to its head and if possible explore the extinct crater under which it headed and bring definite information as to a lake reported to be the watering-place of the cattle. Jack took control of the pack-train and extra horses, with instructions to follow the west fork of the Pueblo and to proceed to its head, where on the divide between it and the Blue Creek there had been constructed a temporary corral. Here he was to make camp and have supper ready for the rest of the outfit when they got in that evening.

Everything went off as expected. Ed and his party rounded up a considerable bunch of wild cattle, while Henry and his companion made a successful exploration of the lake in the extinct crater, from which they got a magnificent view of the surrounding country, as well as discovering a sizable bunch of unbranded cattle, evidently the ones that had been reported as belonging to the maverick bull.

The lake itself was a fair-sized pool with a diameter of from one hundred to one hundred and fifty yards or so, and evidently sustained by the rains and melting snow, as it was entirely stagnant and without outflow. The cattle, on being disturbed, scattered like a bunch of quail, but they had to come together again to get off the steep peak, and they went down the steep trail like a whirlwind, scattering rocks and boulders in all directions. Henry described it as being ' Like the clatter wheels of hell ', which was expressive and seemed to fill the bill.

The tumult evidently disturbed their lord and master, wherever he had been hiding, for he unexpectedly joined the bunch as they reached the bottom of the canyon. From there it was only a matter of keeping them in sight until they were turned up the main canyon of the Pueblo, and shortly afterwards fell in with Ed and John, who were coming down it with their bunch.

They were guided safely to the head of the west fork, where all were branded except the bull, it being considered safer to take him on to the ranch, where there was plenty of help and he could be dealt with more easily.

Thus passed the first day, and that night every one slept peacefully and unsuspectingly in camp at the head of the Pu.cblo. The next morning the cattle were thrown on the trail and the whole party dropped over into the Blue. Jack and another took charge of the herd and the spare horses, while the others rode both sides of the creek and threw what cattle they found into the creek, where they were picked up by Jack and his companion.

In this way the herd gradually increased, until towards evening, when they arrived at the point where the trail leading to Alma crossed the creek, it had attained the dimensions of some seventy or eighty head. This was rather more than twenty miles from where they had dropped in that morning, so that every one was anxious to get over to the Little Blue, where there was a corral and the cattle could be penned for the night.

The horses which were in the lead and the cattle which were following them showed a decided repugnance to climbing the trail which led out of the creek and on to the table-land dividing the two creeks, and this unusual conduct caused all to notice that there were a number of fresh or fairly fresh horse tracks across the creek.

They were barefooted tracks of small size and caused some surprise, owing to the fact that none of the range horses were in the habit of using that section of the country. However, the conclusion was that a bunch of loose horses, probably driven by some one, had recently crossed there. No more was thought about it, and the cattle and horses were forced up the trail.

The only sceptical one was Indian Jack, who declared : ' It look to me like Indian.' He called their attention to what he called a moccasin traced in the bed of the creek ; but it was in soft sand, and the running water had so distorted its shape that it had lost all semblance of a human foot and might have been a depression made by a round stone or any other object. He stuck to his guns, however, and as they climbed the hill asserted that the cattle would never scare at a bunch of loose horses or the aroma left in their wake.

But no one paid attention to him and Jack relapsed into silence. The herd was pushed up the trail as quickly as possible, but it was a long, steep climb and took almost an hour to accomplish, so that when they arrived at the top it was less than an hour by sun.

At the top the tracks had entirely disappeared, and all devoted their attention to pushing the cattle along, so as

to reach the pen before it got dark. To expedite matters
Ed took the lead and the others dropped back to keep the
cattle up with him. In this way they pushed along till
approaching the descent to the Little Blue. Here Ed, who
was in front, probably some eighty to a hundred yards,
pulled up opposite some cedars, on which several turkey
buzzards were perched.

He was not watching the buzzards. His attention seemed
to be attracted by the same object that the buzzards were
watching. Seeing him hold up his hand, the others ceased
from pressing the cattle, and Henry rode out and joined
him. Then they both rode a little way off the trail to a
clump of bushes, where they dismounted. After a moment
or two all joined them except Jack, who remained to hold
the herd. There were a number of dead horses, all lying
close together behind the clump of bushes. They had been
killed. Some had their throats cut and all had knife-marks
on them in vital places. The whole thing was most mysterious, and some one rode back to relieve Jack and see what he
thought about it.

When Jack came he laconically pronounced it Indian,
adding: ' They catch fresh horses on the range and kill tired
ones.' There were only some three or four in the first
bunch, but some two or three hundred yards farther on there
was another pile of eight. That they had been killed, and
that recently, was evident, for *rigor mortis* had not set in
and the blood was still clammy.

Evidently Jack was right. What to do was an open
question. It was decided to keep on with the cattle, but to
proceed cautiously, and if possible keep on to the ranch
during the night. It was generally known that the Apache
Indians seldom molested people after dark, so it was considered feasible, if the cattle could only hold out.

As a precautionary measure the cow-bell was removed
from the neck of the pack-horse and tied to the pack, the
tongue being tied to prevent its sounding. Assuming the
dead horses to be the work of hostile Indians the party
were in a defenceless condition should they happen to come
in contact. The only weapon was John's pistol, a remark-
ably ornamental affair, but his supply of ammunition was
discovered to be two cartridges in the chamber.

Still, at the time no one except Jack gave much consideration to the defenceless state they were in. Jack was uneasy

however, and kept his eyeball constantly on the move. As they went down the trail to the Little Blue he thought that the bell was still making too much noise, and to soothe him it was taken off the pack and thrown into a bush.

The others were still rather sceptical, but thought it advisable to push on to where the Luther boys lived, a short distance up the Little Blue from where the trail crossed it. With this intent the cattle were driven down to the water, and one of the boys rode a short way up the canyon towards the cabin. He returned in a moment or two and invited the others to come and look at what he had discovered.

This was the body of one of the Luther boys lying close to the trail. He was quite dead, having been shot in two places and his skull also caved in, apparently from a blow administered while he was on the ground. There was now no doubt that it was the work of Indians, and it was decided to abandon the cattle. Where they went to we never found out, as we never saw the unbranded bull again, though some of his companions which had been branded may have been recovered.

As for the dead man, he was hastily covered up with bushes. Having secured him against the depredations of wild animals, they pushed on to the cabin, where they found his brother lying huddled up by the doorway—dead. He had also been shot and clubbed and everything inside the house turned upside down and ransacked.

The work was recent as both bodies were still flexible. The body of the second Luther boy was hastily covered with old boards, and then there was a consultation as to the best course to pursue. The party scattered out and took refuge under the brow of a hill until it should be sufficiently dark to make an attempt to reach the ranch. Jack was of opinion that there was little danger after nightfall, as he said the Apaches were superstitious and seldom acted after sundown.

After an hour or more of anxious waiting John and Indian Jack started for the ranch, taking separate paths. After a further half-hour Ed took a chance, leaving Henry and his partner to bring in the horses. This they did, after waiting for a considerably longer time, as it was considered advisable to give the Indians, wherever they were, a chance to get sound asleep. It was a delicate matter moving a bunch of horses on a dark night, as they were bound to make a considerable amount of noise, and to those in charge

of them every little rock they kicked seemed to light up
the whole country with sparks and the noise re-echoed
through the surrounding hills.

However, every one reached the ranch without mishap,
much to the relief of its occupants ; for Old Charlie, who
had got up to assist when the horses got in, related that in
the afternoon he noticed a large bunch of horses being
rounded up in the neighbourhood of a round hill some ten
miles west of the ranch.   They were a long way off, probably
five or six miles, but they felt sure it was not being done by
white men.   From what they say they felt sure there were
a bunch of hostiles in the country.

Of course the story related by the party returned from
the Blue confirmed the worst fears of every one at the
ranch.   Matters were put beyond all doubt the following
morning, for not only were moccasin tracks found in the
garden, but the Indians themselves put in an appearance
close to the house.   Some of the horses were grazing in the
alfalfa field, which was fenced in, and some of the Indians,
having seen them from a distance, made an attempt to
drive them off and capture them.

They must have seen only the horses and not the barbed
wire fence, for they came riding out of a side canyon at full
gallop.   They did not notice the fence till they were close
to it.   Then they pulled up with a jerk, and as by that
time we had begun to bombard them with long distance fire
they quickly rode off up the canyon.   My three ponies had
wandered up that canyon when they were turned out the
previous day and I never saw them again.

This was the Indian outbreak under Geronimo, and the
W S ranch happened to be their first camping-ground after
leaving the Reservation.   It took the entire armed force of
the United States a year and a half to round them up and
return them to their Reservation.

At this time we were all busily engaged polishing up our
guns and collecting ammunition, but it was a party from
Alma who got pot valiant and went out with the benevolent
intention of exterminating the whole band.   They came by
the ranch and endeavoured to get some of us to accompany
them.   We did everything possible to dissuade them from
going on such a foolhardy expedition, but they were full of
stimulants and insisted on going.   So confident were they
that they had brought a pack-horse along, intending to

stay out till they had accomplished their object. Th result was that they had scarcely got five miles from the ranch when they were ambushed, the two leaders, Luce and Orwig, being killed.

This put an end to any unofficial attempts to run Mr. Geronimo out of the country. It might be mentioned that Geronimo was the Medicine Man of the band, but not its fighting captain. The latter position was filled by Nana. It might also be mentioned that the outbreak was principally due to the bad faith of whatever branch of the Legislature was responsible for refusing to ratify the treaties made with the Apaches when they surrendered under Mangus Colorado and Cochise. These were Warm Spring Apaches, who had always been in conflict with their brethren at San Carlos. When they surrendered they stipulated that they should not be placed on the same Reservation, and the U.S. commander in the field had agreed to this ; but when the matter went back to Washington the authorities refused to ratify it and broke up the band, placing half of them on the San Carlos Reservation and the other half at Fort Stanton Reservation in Lincoln County, along with the Chriqua Apaches, with whom the Warm Spring Indians also had a feud. Hence their constant attempts to break out and return to their old hunting-grounds, which had been thrown open to settlement.

This condition was only put an end to eventually by the practical annihilation of the whole Warm Spring tribe, who after the surrender of Geronimo were eventually taken to Florida, where they died like flies from disease. The miserable remnant that was brought back and placed at Fort Sill only survived a very few years. The whole transaction was a discredit to a great country, which might very well have supported the pledges of its representatives. Though the Apache had many unlikeable qualities he was the greatest natural warrior that the white man had ever come in contact with in the West.

It was pretty well on in the afternoon when the war-party which had met with mishap returned to the ranch. Nothing could be done at the time in regard to recovering the dead bodies, but it was arranged that an attempt should be made to do so the following day. This was not carried out, for the troops from San Carlos arrived at the ranch the following day. To the best of my recollection they were a troop of the 6th Cavalry under the command of a Captain Hammond. We did not see much of them at the time, as they continued their pursuit, despite the tired condition of their stock. They were little more than twenty-four hours behind the Indians.

On their approach the Indians departed, taking with them seventy head of horses belonging to the W S Ranch. They had rounded up everything and picked out those that could be made use of, either for food or transportation. If it had not been for the fortunate circumstance that a number had been brought into the ranch immediately before their arrival, and that those in use had got back safely, the outfit would have been afoot.

As it was, we had great hopes of the troops catching up with them. It was not to be, however, for the Indians, in addition to being unexcelled mountaineers, were now freshly mounted and their stock had had the advantage of an entire day's rest. Furthermore, they divided when they struck the San Francisco, the main body taking the most direct route to the Mogollon Mountains and keeping up Deep Creek, while a portion of them had taken a more northerly route and followed Devil's Creek to the same destination.

The troops followed the former and caught up with their rear-guard about sunset. A few shots were exchanged and one of the troopers was wounded, while the others pressed so hard that the Indians were forced to abandon their squaws and a few of their more tired ponies. With these the troops returned to the ranch, arriving there about ten o'clock at night. Amongst the captives was Mrs. Geronimo, a repulsive-looking lady, but built on generous lines and no doubt valuable as a beast of burden. The boys took charge of the prisoners, in order to give the tired soldiers a chance to rest, and held them in the bunk-house that night. They christened Mrs. Geronimo as ' Biddy '. As far as one could judge the ladies seemed indifferent to their fate, and certainly exhibited no signs of regret at having been made prisoners.

The next morning the soldiers left with their prisoners, and I think returned to San Carlos. Before leaving they told off a party to assist in bringing in the bodies of Luce and Orwig and also to make a search for young Lyon, who had gone down for mail from the S U and was missing.

Luce and Orwig were found on the trail leading up from the river, where they had fallen. There was quite a search before they discovered Lyon. His body was found some five miles farther on, behind a clump of brush, twenty or thirty yards off the trail. It had been exposed to the sun for several days and was badly decomposed. The poor fellow had evidently been reading his mail and was utterly oblivious to such a thing as an Indian when shot, for an open letter of his was picked up on the trail, evidently where he had fallen off his horse and a short distance from where his body was found. He had evidently crawled into shelter to die and the Indians took no further notice of him. He was the first occupant of our little cemetery at the ranch.

CHAPTER VI

THE total strength of the U.S. Army at that time was only twenty-five thousand men, and those were scattered over a vast country in small detachments at outlying posts. To get a sufficient body together to cope with Geronimo's outlaws was a task which called for a very capable staff. I think the immediate credit for the rapid organization which took place is due to General Crook, who was then in command of the Western District. He was later succeeded by General Miles, who carried the work to a successful end. With the limited means at their command it was little wonder the search should last for a matter of nearly two years.

The country was unsurveyed and unmapped, containing ninety thousand square miles, sparsely watered, and consisting of one mountain range after another, intersected with almost impassable canyons and running up to an elevation of nearly twelve thousand feet. The amateur critics, principally in the local Press, were wont to be captious at the slowness of the military operations, but their comments for the most part displayed their own ignorance. The soldiers themselves treated them with good-natured contempt.

Immediately after the first outbreak the country around us was badly demoralized. We at the ranch were feeling sad over the fate of young Lyon, but it was necessary to find out just what our losses in horseflesh and other property was.

Our first round-up was conducted with great caution and with a disposition to discover lurking redskins in all sorts of unlikely places. It took several days to round up all the horses in the country, and they were all thrown together on the Thomson Flat, a few miles north of the ranch. Here we found that practically all our loose horses and all our stud, including Dandy Ball, were gone.

We were advised by our lawyer in Silver City that we had a claim against the Federal Government for damages, which was consequently filed and forwarded to Washington, but that was all it amounted to. Some seven or eight years later a curt note informed us that as we were not citizens of the United States we had no legal standing, which was tantamount to saying that the property could be appropriated by the Indians or any one else that chose to take it, as far as the Federal Government was concerned. We let it go at that and said no more about it.

Though things quieted down after the first few days, there were still all sorts of rumours in regard to the Indians. Every one who came in had a different report, and consequently it was a great relief when one day, in an incredibly short space of time, considering they had come from San Antonio, Texas, a troop of cavalry showed up, inquiring for a convenient place to camp.

They introduced themselves as Troop C, of the 8th U.S. Cavalry under the command of Major Sam Sumner. They were dusty and travel-stained, but had a smart, business-like appearance and made an impressive show, all mounted on grey horses. The major was all business, and when we had escorted him up the creek he selected a place some four or five miles above the ranch, on what was known to us as ' The Old Man Thomason Place '. This was afterwards officially named Camp Maddox, in remembrance of the doctor who accompanied the troop.

Accompanying the major were Dr. Maddox and Lieutenants Williams, Fountain, and Cabell. Dr. Maddox was a splendid-looking man, the most imposing figure among them. Every one was pleased with the camp site. It had a substantial cabin, with two rooms, plenty of big shady trees, and, above all, a nice cool spring of clear water, which welled up beside the creek. The major's only grievance was caused by an old tumble-down wagon which had been following him for several days and camping close to him every night.

This contained a regular scarecrow of a man and a lady of masculine proportions with only one eye. Their equipage was loaded down with a disreputable tent and several barrels of what was presumably whisky, which they proposed to sell to the men. When the major saw them looming up in his wake before he got fairly settled in his new quarters he nearly had a fit. They came snooping along in their little old waggon, drawn by a remnant of a horse and a mangy-looking burro, with a long pole sticking out behind on which was a blue flag. We wanted to know what the pennant was for, but the major was called away and we felt disappointed, for his language was picturesque and educational. Also, it was getting late, so we waved a hasty farewell and promised to return early next morning.

When we got to their camp the following morning we found them pretty well settled down, but the major was still agitated. Just below him and within about a hundred yards of the camp his Nemesis had set up shop. The measly old tent had its torn canvas flapping in the breeze ; the whole front of it was open, and inside was an improvised counter of planks set on barrels. The long pole was sticking up from the centre, with the blue pennant on top, and just below it a larger flag bearing the legend ' Fort Nasty ' in yellow letters on a pale blue ground.

The whole thing was very funny, but the major was inconsolable and said they would poison his men if we didn't get rid of them. He suggested that as they were on our ground we could warn them off. We essayed the task with some misgiving and going over to the tent politely informed the man that he was on private ground and would have to move off it. He wanted to know how in hell he was to know whether it was private ground or not, and asked where the public domain began as he didn't want to move unless he was obliged to. We politely informed him that he could move out on the *mesa* at either side of the river, but not nearer than within half a mile of it ; or he might move down the river, below Alma, which, it was true, was some six miles or more from there ; or they could move up the river, some three or four miles into the box canyon, and at any of those places they would be on Government land, and it would require an emissary of the Land Office to remove them.

At this point the gorgon who had been listening from the inside took a hand, and coming out with a gun said that she'd be damned if she was going to move for anybody. We judged it wise to return to the camp and inform the major of the result of our conversation.

We told him of the defiant attitude assumed by the lady. He swore volubly and said that if we would delegate the authority to him he would quickly make them move. Needless to say we gladly did so and accompanied him back to Fort Nasty along with an orderly sergeant and a file of men. Here the major informed them that he had taken over the land on behalf of the United States Government and that if they didn't move within a hour he would send a fatigue party to burn up the tent and all its contents. This had the desired effect, for they immediately packed up and pulled out. So perished Fort Nasty.

The arrival of the troops speedily restored confidence, more especially when we knew there was another camp at Dry Creek, fifteen or sixteen miles below us. There was also a camp on the Gila and another on Mogollon Creek. The infantry was used to form small posts at all the known waters that the Indians were likely to visit, while the cavalry did extensive scouting from those points.

The troops at Camp Maddox stayed with us until Geronimo and his band finally surrendered and were taken captive to Florida. All the time our relations with them were of the most friendly description. Though almost constantly away on scouting trips, they always made it a point to call in at the ranch and have a friendly powwow with us, and we frequently accompanied them on their expeditions. These expeditions generally lasted four or five days, and they were glad of our company and appreciated the assistance given them in making them acquainted with all the outlying waters as far as they were then known in that section of country.

Altogether they were pleasant days, and I have always looked back to them as some of the most enjoyable in my ranch experience. We always went prepared for a little hunt and generally managed to keep the camp supplied with game, either quail or deer. The latter were merely a chance, if you should happen to run on to them, but the country was well stocked with quail, and one was almost certain to find some within a limited radius of the permanent waters.

Of these, the little fellow with the black topknot was by far the most numerous, but on the higher *mesas* and close to the mountains you were almost sure to find a flock or two of the mysterious type we called the ' fool quail.' He was by far the most delicate for the table, but once you took your eye off him he vanished into thin air and was no more to be found, no matter how close you hunted for him. He had no fear of death, either from a gun or a stick, but he objected to being sighted.

We had rather an amusing experience on one of our early

trips. The major delegated a party under the command
of Lieutenant Williams and assisted by Lieutenant Cabell
to find out just where a little-known spring—the Webster
Spring—lay. It was about nineteen miles from the ranch,
and Cook and I accompanied them as guide.

On the way we spread out with a view to getting some
game, and at'our end of the line, where the only shot-guns
were, we had considerable success amongst the quail. At
the other end they had an exciting chase after some deer
and a small bunch of antelope, but were not successful. As
we approached our destination we drew together again, and
I happened to be on the outside, near the edge of the canyon
when I spotted a bunch of fool quail thirty feet below me on
the side of the canyon.

They evidently had not seen me and were in the full light
of the setting sun, which was getting low on the mountains.
I pulled up and slid off my horse as quietly as I could. Our
friends the soldiers had never seen any, and I was anxious
to show them, so standing as still as possible and keeping
my eye on them I waved to Cabell, who was a little distance
from me. He, sensing that something was up, rode over and
also slid off his horse as he came close, and was followed by
Williams, who did the same.

They had come as quietly as possible, but the slight noise
made by their movements had evidently reached the quail,
for they immediately evaporated. They didn't run into
the bush, which, was quite close to them, but apparently
sank into the earth. I, however, had never taken my eye
off one particular bird and felt positive that I could still
distinguish the particular spot of earth into which he had
seemingly turned. I tried to point it out to both of them,
for some time without success, but at length by sighting
along my gun I succeeded in getting Cabell to distinguish
the particular spot of earth I alluded to. He didn't believe
it was a bird, but failing to find a stick with which to rout it,
he picked up a large clod of earth and going down quite close
to it plumped in right on the spot.

It immediately began to flutter and another flew up from
close beside it, which I shot and ran down the hill to retrieve.
It had fallen within twenty yards of us and was quite dead,
so that I picked it up without the least delay and immediately
returned to where Cabell was still examining the one he had
smothered with the clod. There were certainly a dozen or

more when I first saw them, but although the three of us beat about that spot close enough to find a pin on the ground, we could never flush another.

However, we had two good specimens, which Cabell put in his pocket, to have them stuffed. We pushed on to the bottom of the canyon, where we made camp by the spring and enjoyed a hearty meal.

When it was time to turn in we took our bedding out from the main camp and rolled it out on an inviting bed of sand which was a little farther down the canyon. We had two beds—Cook and I in one, the officers in the other. A slight movement about the place woke me during the night. It was a beautiful night, with the moon shining and lighting up the place as if it was day. As I awoke I pushed back the tarpaulin, which we had drawn over our heads. I could hear the pattering of feet and a light movement amongst the fallen leaves on the ground, so I peeped cautiously out and immediately covered up my head again, for there was a full-grown skunk pottering about close to the other bed.

He was unpleasantly close and I was loth to disturb him for fear of the consequences. However, his movements fascinated me and I could not help peeping out again. After watching him for a short time I woke Cook. In a whisper I asked if we should do anything to scare him away, but he said : ' Lord, no. We'd have to burn our bedding if we did.' We both watched him for some time, and it was evident that there was something in the other bed that he was desirous of investigating.

He'd sniff around the foot of it and scratch a little, and this not getting him anywhere, he'd go away a little. But whatever it was he wanted, the attraction was too strong, for whenever we thought he was about to depart he would always come back again and resume his investigations. At length he got on to the bed and began to scratch on top of the tarpaulin. Here his feet made quite a noise and woke the occupants, or one of them ; for a muffled voice came from under the covers, saying : ' Hello, what is it ? '

This caused the scratching to cease and the skunk to raise his tail, but everything becoming quiet again, he resumed operations. We were both getting interested now and wondered what would happen next. The skunk sniffed around a bit on top of the bed, and evidently having located the spot he wanted, began to scratch again. This time the sleeper woke up with an oath and demanded angrily who was there. Getting no reply he swore audibly. Thinking it was the sergeant with something to report, he wanted to know what in hell was up that he couldn't speak up and tell him about it.

The dear little animal vouchsafed no reply beyond assuming a defensive attitude, raising his tail and turning his back towards the speaker, who now provoked beyond endurance, threw the tarpaulin from over his head. For one brief moment he gazed at that spreading fan and exposed offensive glands within some two or three feet from his face, and then with a wild shriek dived back under the clothes and protecting tarp.

He was too late. The outraged animal was not to be treated in this cavalier manner, and he loosed his batteries, polluting everything in the neighbourhood ; after which he presumably took his departure, though none of us were in a position to testify to it. As soon as Williams had shrieked we also had sought refuge under our tarpaulin, suppressing our laughter until we nearly smothered.

We got no more sleep that night. How offensive everything was can only be appreciated by those who have come in close contact with a skunk on the warpath. Had we had anything else to put on we should have burned everything we had with us. As we related to the soldiers the manœuvres of the animal preceding the climax, we all wondered what he had been in search of. After some thought Cabell reached down to the foot of his bed under the tarpaulin where he had put his discarded clothes and pulled his jacket towards him. Turning it round once or twice, he put his hand in the pocket and produced the fool quail : evidently the skunk's Thanksgiving dish.

A bigger excursion after the Indians occurred in our neighbourhood and as it promised a little excitement we accompanied it. The man who ran the greatest risk at the time was the stage driver, Al Lauderbaugh, who had to make the trip each way every week. True, he confined his driving as far as possible to the night, but even then it was impossible to avoid being on the road frequently at sunrise and sunset, which were really the most dangerous hours to be abroad, and I don't think he missed a single trip during the entire Indian raid.

Al left Alma one evening a little before sundown, and

having gone some three or four miles on the road to Silver City met with a horseman, whose name I forget, who was in a very excited condition. This man told him that he had been out in the hills hunting for a horse and that he had seen a bunch of Indians crossing the Robert's Park in the direction of the Frisco River. They were some way off and he had not been able to observe them closely, but had made all possible haste to get to Alma and give warning of their approach.

He strongly advised Al to turn round and go back to Alma or they would certainly get him. To emphasize his report he called his attention to a number of moving objects which had just come over the skyline at the top of the hills several thousand feet up and some two or three miles from the river on the opposite side. The light was not very good at the time and, as Al reported, the objects not very clear, but as sound carries a long distance in that country, they both declared they could distinctly hear the noise of rolling rocks, which would necessarily accompany a body of horsemen coming down the side of the mountain.

The upshot of it was that Al agreed to accompany him back to Alma, saying that he would postpone his trip for an hour or two. They both made all possible speed. From Alma the news was conveyed to us and by us to Camp Maddox as quickly as horsemen could saddle up and get there. The troops had only got in from a long scout earlier in the day, and both men and horses were badly in need of a rest, but they turned out without the slightest hesitation.

Men were dispatched at once to take up post on the hills and on the east bank of the river, so as to command the only three places at which it was feasible to get across, while the others prepared to follow as quickly as possible. We accompanied the vanguard, as being familiar with the country, to show the way.

In explanation I might relate that the Frisco River entered a box canyon a short distance below Alma, and ran a zigzag course through it for about five miles to a point where a creek known as Whitewater emptied into it. Here there was an opening of about a quarter of a mile in extent, with easy access to the river ; but between that point and the mouth of the canyon below Alma there was only one possible place by which a horseman, or for the matter of that a man on foot, could get from the river bed to the top of the bank on the east side.

As this particular place was only accessible to animals with the climbing qualities of a goat, possessed by the native ponies and cattle, it was not much used, and consequently was only familiar to those who were in the habit of riding the range. Thus all that was necessary was to post guards at the mouth of the canyon, leave some one to watch the lone trail, and take a small body down to Whitewater and watch the opening at that end.

This we proceeded to do as quickly as possible, dropping three men at the mouth of the canyon, leaving three more to guard the trail, and the rest of us, four in number, going on to Whitewater, where we took up post till joined by the main body. This took time, and we had no idea whether the Indians had passed on before we got there ; but we were inclined to think not. The night was pitch dark, and those who were best acquainted with their habits declared that they would be sure to camp on the other side some little way from the river and wait for the first crack of dawn to cross over.

We were all worked up and as keen as mustard and consequently in a mood to accept any theory that was favourable to success. All agreed the Indians could not possibly have got across before we got into position. We had not been long in position before we were joined by the main body of the troops. It was black as ink, and though we could hear their horses' feet for a considerable time before their arrival, they almost rode on top of us before we felt sure they were really there.

The plan of campaign was then outlined to us. The main body had dropped some twenty men at the mouth of the canyon, who, along with the original scouts, were left under the command of a non-commissioned officer with instructions to guard the place, and after an hour's delay, if no attempt was made to force an outlet, they were to proceed slowly down the canyon till they met the party coming up from Whitewater. They were informed that the latter would follow up the canyon until they came to the point where the trail on which the Indians were presumed to be travelling entered the river bottom, and there they would wait for them.

I was delegated to go back along the road and guide the

party who were watching the goat trail into the river bed, and also instructed that, as probably we would be the first to arrive there, we were to locate the trail going out to the west and wait there until the others arrived.

I was familiar enough with the trails both leading into and out of the river bottom, but on a night like that I didn't feel very confident of finding them of my own volition. I had, however, great confidence in my horse, and as the trail going to the west was the only one leaving the canyon in that direction I felt sure that he would want to follow it when we got there.

I hurried to my appointed place, and having got there left the matter entirely to his discretion. It was like going up against a black wall, going down that breakneck trail, but he shook his head for a loose rein, and having got it made his way down without a blunder. It wound in and out and dropped off precipitous places, but he never put a foot wrong, and when he got to the bottom, I felt myself blushing in the dark on being congratulated on an achievement with which I had little or nothing to do.

Things were a little better when we arrived at the bottom, as we had a little more elbow-room, but it was still as black as ink, and again I had to trust to my horse for guidance. I knew he would try to turn out when we came to the trail leading to the west, and the moment he did I pulled up and announced that we were there. In this way I acquired a reputation for having an abnormal bump of locality.

We were the first to arrive there, so we all dismounted and sat around to wait for the others. They did not keep us very long—perhaps half an hour or so—till we heard the noise of their horses, and as they came nearer we thought we discerned some muttered oaths at the darkness and the roughness of the road, but the latter were repressed, as every one was keen not to betray our presence.

When all got together it was arranged that all were to dismount, and while a strong party was to be left in the river bed to take care of the horses the others were to go up the trail for a short distance, and if they failed to locate anything were to scatter out on each side and lie concealed till the moon, which was due shortly, should show up. They were then to advance in a skirmish line until the Indians were located, and the party in charge of the horses were to bring them up as soon as the first shot was fired.

This, roughly, was the programme laid out, and we proceeded to carry it out to the best of our ability in the inky blackness. We scrambled up the rough trail for a couple of hundred yards or more until the ground was rather more feasible, when we began to spread out, still retaining our forward movement. This continued for a quarter of a mile or so, when, the ground still improving, we were able to maintain some kind of touch with each other, and arriving shortly afterwards at a kind of sag behind a steep rise, the order was passed to halt and make ourselves comfortable until the moon came up.

I found myself squatting behind a large boulder in company with Dr. Maddox. The doctor was a keen soldier and never missed an opportunity of taking the field. All his senses were on the alert, and we had been there only a short time when he called my attention to some faint noises which came from some distance up the side of the hill.

On listening intently to them for some time we came to the conclusion that it must be the horses belonging to the renegades who were moving uneasily at the end of the tether ropes. We were all worked up and felt confident that even if we did not succeed in capturing the entire party we would certainly capture their horses and set them afoot. When the moon came up the word was passed to advance quietly and extend the line as much as the nature of the ground would permit. At the same time a messenger was sent back to the party in the river bed to allow a quarter of an hour after the receipt of the message and then bring the horses forward quietly. They were, however, instructed that if they heard shooting they were to come forward at once and as quickly as possible.

Things looked much brighter, but the moon was not at its full and the shadows were deep and objects took on all sorts of queer shapes. Moreover, the ground was rough and covered with loose rocks, so that there was many a slip and a muttered ejaculation owing to a barked shin as we scrambled up the hill-side. Every now and again there would be a halt to ascertain if we had given an alarm. But we could still hear the slight movement and everything seemed all right.

The number of times we kept pointing out to each other what we supposed was the Indian camp or a horse or something, could not be kept track of ; but on closer inspection those objects invariably turned out to be rocks, or soap-weeds, or some other inanimate object. In this way we scrambled along for about half a mile or so, and just when we could hear the noise of the horses coming out of the canyon something did actually jump up in front of us, while every one dropped down with guns at the ready, prepared to shoot.

Whatever it was had turned end on and was evidently taking stock of us, and we were just about to turn loose when a damned calf bleated and was followed immediately by a low ' Moo ' from the ground. We were right in amongst ' the Indians '—a measly bunch of cattle that the frightened horsemen had spotted coming over the mountain.

Nobody said anything, but we looked carefully around to see if the bearer of the intelligence was amongst us ; but he was far away, and Al too more than half-way to Silver City by that time. There was no need to prolong the search for Indians any further. If there had been any Indians in the vicinity the cattle would never have been there.

As soon as the horses came out we all mounted and started for home in silence ; but after a time the ridiculous side of the situation began to dawn on us and we had a good laugh over it. Still, I think that if we had got hold of the man who had seen the Indians it would have gone pretty rough with him.

I have dwelt rather long on this particular incident because it was the only one of the kind that came under my personal observation, but it was by no means the only one with which the troops had to put up. They were frequently called away on false alarms, and many times had to go long distances on expeditions which occupied many days, only to find that the reported Indians had not been within a hundred miles of the place. They were expected to guard a scattered population over hundreds of square miles of territory and hunt down a band of Indians who could give points to the finest body of guerilla troops that were ever raised. Hostile criticism from critics who had never been in the field, and whose only conception of an Indian was derived from the pages of dime novels, made some of us, out of uniform, feel pretty rotten.

CHAPTER VII

THE NAVAJO SCOUTS

THINGS settled down to normal through the summer and a feeling of confidence that the worst was over began to prevail. Still, the troops were kept pretty busy and all kinds of rumours were rife. We heard that Geronimo had gone far into Old Mexico and was about to join forces with the Yaquis, who were giving that Government a certain amount of trouble. Then we heard that he had held a powwow with General Crook and had surrendered to him. This again was shortly denied, and it was said that he had broken into the United States, and he was reported to be in half a dozen places at the same time. A most ubiquitous gentleman.

Naturally we began to grow careless and resume our usual mode of life. We ceased herding the horses and rode about the range unarmed, except on special occasions. The stage had been running in daylight for some time and we made several trips to Silver City on our own account, sometimes in company and frequently alone.

Sometime in the early part of October I had occasion to go to Silver City. So confident were we at the time that I did not even take a gun along. My business was of no great importance, and when I got through I went across to the Post to pay my respects to Colonel Morrow, a fine soldier, who was in command there. In the course of our conversation he asked when I was returning to the ranch. I told him the following morning. He asked if I had brought a gun along; on my saying no, he strongly advised taking one, and said they could let me have one from the Post and I could turn it in to the officer commanding the troops at our place.

I was pretty heavily loaded and not very keen about packing a gun, so I suggested that if I was waylaid I would probably get no opportunity to use it, and that my best chance was to rely on the speed of the team, while if I were unlucky enough to fall a victim I would only be supplying them with another weapon.

Morrow, however, said that we were in a state of war and it was up to them to protect the lives of the citizens, so I had better take one. I made no further demur and they loaned me a cavalry carbine and a belt full of ammunition, for which I signed a receipt.

I got out of town bright and early the following morning, loaded to the gunwale, and got through to the White House, or L C Ranch, without any serious mishap. I had some trouble with the Government carbine, which was considerably in my way, until at last I tied it firmly to the back of the buggy and forgot all about it.

The next day I was on the road before daylight. Two miles or a little more after leaving the White House the road approaches close to the edge of Duck Creek, and at this point a more or less dry creek they call Buckhorn runs into it. There is a little water to be had in both creeks, and it was a favourite camping place for freighters going to and fro between Silver City and the mining camps in the Mogollons. As I approached it I saw a wagon pulling into the road and a man on foot walking beside it. When I overtook them I found it to be a Frenchman named Saburin, who had a general merchandise store at Cooney.

He and I were well acquainted, so I pulled down to a walk and drove along beside him for some distance. I advised him to be cautious, but he said he was tired of Indian reports, and after a time, as my team was getting restless, I drove on.

About half a mile or so farther on the high *mesas* jutted out towrads the road in a sharp, rocky point. The *mesas* themselves towered above the road for possibly some seven or eight hundred feet, but the point of the hill was the culmination of a steep rocky canyon which divided them, and the floor of which was some fifty or sixty feet above the level of the road. This point was known throughout the country as the ' Point of Rocks ' and was distant from the L C Ranch between five and six miles in a north-westerly direction.

When I had last looked back Saburin was still walking beside his team, and as he disappeared from view after I got round the point I thought no more about him. I got to the ranch all right a little after sundown and found Mr. Cook was away, so I had my hands full attending to the disposal of the supplies I had brought.

The next day was Sunday. In the afternoon a messenger passed, saying that a man had been killed by the Indians at the Point of Rocks. It was Saburin. I can only conclude that the Indians let me go by in order to secure the prize of his larger and heavily loaded wagon. No doubt they could have easily potted me, but in that case they might have warned Saburin.

The following morning all available soldiers were sent from Camp Maddox to investigate, and I accompanied them. Word had also gone up to Cooney that Saburin was killed and a party was coming from there to reclaim the body. It appeared that Saburin had no kin of any kind at Cooney, but the inhabitants of that mining camp determined to do the proper thing by him, and sent three of its leading citizens in a light wagon to bring the body home, where they proposed to give it burial with all due ceremony.

We all drew up at the Point of Rocks, where the newly-dug grave was, within a few feet of the road, and we all dismounted and stood solemnly around while they unrolled a great rock that had been rolled on top of it.

The actual disinterment was a matter of only a few moments. Death had evidently come quickly. They had not molested him beyond removing his six-shooter and cartridge belt, taking no notice of the contents of his pockets.

It was now determined to follow the Indians. There was no difficulty in picking up the trail, for the wagon tracks were quite distinct where they had crossed the *arroyo* and led up an open draw on the east side of Duck Creek Canyon, towards the mountains. Before we had gone three-quarters of a mile we found the empty wagon most adroitly concealed in a little clump of cedars, behind a knoll, where it was invisible from all sides until you actually rode on top of it.

The contents were scattered all around, covering a radius of twenty or thirty yards from the wagon. Everything they could not carry away with them was destroyed. The flour sacks were cut open and the contents strewn on the ground where their ponies had fed on it and afterwards wallowed in it and trampled it into the dirt. There were several cases of canned goods which they had opened and sampled, and then scattered all they could not use.

Their weakness, after the gun and ammunition, appeared to be leather goods and chewing tobacco. There were two cases of the latter bearing Mr. Lorilard's familiar brand, and these they had completely emptied. They had cut up the harness and carried off all that was capable of being converted into strings, throwing the heavier portion away.

They had carried off most of the buckles, presumably for ornament.

At first we were disposed to give the red man credit for cleanliness, as there were two cases of soap, the contents of which had been heavily dipped into, especially a coloured kind with stripes through it, which was known as ' Hard-water Soap '. This compliment had to be abandoned later on when we discovered that they had mistaken the soap for an article of food. No doubt the nice pink marbly stuff looked tempting. I would have given a good deal to have heard the red man's grunt of disgust when he bit into it.

We had no difficulty in following his course from the wagon for ten miles or more, for beside the soap he had carried off a quantity of large flat lozenges with mottoes on them. These also had not appealed to his appetite and he had scattered them promiscuously over the country. It struck us as funny, as we were following up these savages, with poor Saburin's blood still fresh on their hands, to discover a large flat lozenge with ' I love you ' or ' Kiss me, Mama,' or some other homely motto stamped on it in red letters.

The Indian also was not without his sense of humour. The first gentleman who had sampled the soap had evidently not proclaimed it from the house-tops, but had dropped it surreptitiously and waited to see what the effect would be on his neighbour. We came across pieces scattered here and there for a distance of many miles, each piece bitten into and displaying the marks of sound teeth. Each one must have had good fun recommending it to his neighbour after he had got rid of his own supply.

The trail led directly towards Mogollon Creek, and we hoped that the soldiers who were in camp there would have the opportunity of heading them off and keeping them out of the mountains.

After they got on the high *mesa* and their supplies of candy and soap were played out they were not so easily followed. But we had further confirmation when we came across a big fat stallion belonging to the L C Ranch which had been recently killed and a great hunk cut out of both flanks. Their plunder from the wagon had evidently not interfered with their taste for fresh meat. As we approached the edge of the *mesa* going down to Mogollon Creek the sun was getting low, and we wondered how the Indians had got across. There was no known trail leading directly into the mountains.

However, we presumed the Indians knew of some way and concluded that if they could find it we could.

But it took us some time. The course taken by the Indians had evidently led to the edge of the *mesa*, but when we got there it was apparently a sheer bluff, as far as the eye could reach on either side, and the bottom of the creek was several thousand feet below the level of the *mesa*. It was only after considerable search that we found a possible trail, and then only through the accident of somebody's hat having blown over the bluff.

When found it was not very inviting and all the horses had to be carefully led down it ; but once on it it was apparent that the Indians had used it. It certainly had not been used before for many years. The only possible guide mark to it was an old dead cedar tree a few feet from the edge of the bluff, which must have served as a guide to the Indians for many generations. They had evidently taken great precautions to prevent anything like a path being worn towards it.

It now seemed almost certain that they would run into the soldier camp ; but they evidently knew their country, for after following the stream down for about a quarter of a mile they found an exit on the other side which, if anything, was less inviting than the way they had come in. By this time the sun had disappeared, so after exploring the exit for a little way it was decided to return to the creek and make camp for the night.

While they were unpacking and getting ready for supper one of the officers and myself rode down the creek to find the infantry camp that was permanently located there. We stumbled right on to it within about half a mile, but found everybody gone except a sergeant and a few men, who were left to take care of the place. They had received the message of a man being killed within five miles of the White House and had left to investigate, while the actual perpetrators had crossed the creek within half a mile of them higher up. Such are the fortunes of war with a defective intelligence department.

We gave them all the information in our possession and sorrowfully returned to our camp. We followed the Indians all next day into most difficult country ; but at length we got tied up in a labyrinth of fallen timber where all signs of the Indians disappeared, and the chase had to be given up.

The next morning the soldiers decided to stay in the field until they could learn something definite in regard to the latest movements of the Indians, while we returned to the ranch, needless to say carefully avoiding the road or any likely looking places that might conceal an ambush.

The soldiers did not get back to Camp Maddox for nearly a week, and when they did they brought tidings that the main body of Indians was no longer in Old Mexico but back in our immediate neighbourhood, comfortably ensconced in our own Mogollon Range.

This news threw us back into the condition we had assumed at the outset of the raid. All regular work was brought to a standstill, the outlying cattle had to be left to their own devices, and all the saddle-horses again held under herd ; in fact, our work for several months was confined to caring for the horses and rounding up the necessary beef to supply the soldiers and ourselves.

More troops were sent into the country, and several companies of Navajo Indian scouts having been raised, were scattered here and there to assist the regulars. Two of them were sent into our neighbourhood. One, under a Lieutenant Scott, as well as I can recollect the name, only stayed for a couple of days, after which it was moved up the creek some five-and-thirty miles, to the neighbourhood of the S U. The other, under Captain Rogers, took up its quarters at Camp Maddox, along with the regular troops already there.

It was about this time also that Major Sumner was called away, and the command of the camp taken over by Lieutenant Fountain. Also a little later we were joined by Wilson, who had come out from England, and Mr. Cook went east to Nebraska to pay a visit to some of his friends.

The hostiles soon began to make their presence felt, for they managed to waylay and kill several settlers on the upper Gila and the Sapello. This kept the soldiers constantly on the move, and we did not see a great deal of them for quite a time. But we saw plenty of the Navajo scouts. Captain Rogers had his hands full keeping these employed and drilling them into the semblance of soldiers.

The Navajos were as keen as mustard, but they did not take much stock in the white man's methods. Such exercise as marching or doing the manual they looked on as mere waste of time ; but when it came to shooting at a mark or having a foot-race or a pony-race, on, in fact, anything they could gamble at, they were all there and as enthusiastic as a lot of schoolboys.

Scarcely a day passed that they did not have a meeting of some sort, and there was great rivalry amongst them as to the respective merits of their ponies. On those occasions the rate at which Navajo blankets and Government ammunition changed hands would have done credit to a large department store. The race was by no means always to the swift, for all kinds of jugglery and interference were considered legitimate, and although this led frequently to disputes which looked as if they might develop into bloodshed they hardly ever materialized. They were like a lot of children and easily diverted from the point at issue. They were supplied with an unlimited amount of ammunition, free, and this constituted their ready cash. When it came to a matter of blankets, which were of their own or their squaws' manufacture, it was a different affair and was like drawing on their bank account. Each blanket had a relative value, which was entirely regulated by its texture and had nothing to do with its size. One constantly saw several large blankets, big enough to use as bedding, given in exchange for a little one that was not big enough to go under a saddle.

They were pretty good sports, however, and were ready to engage in any kind of contest for the smallest possible consideration. It had, however, to be in sterling coin ; such things as bills they had no use for. I think any one of them would have gladly exchanged a ten-dollar bill for a dime or a nickel.

We constantly had foot-races for their benefit, and they would gladly run a mile or two for twenty-five cents, or even less. It was always necessary, however, to have a second prize, owing to the fact that one amongst them who was known to us by the sobriquet of Slim Jim had established such a superiority as to defy competition. In consequence, while it was always understood that Jim would take first prize, we generally had keen competition for the second.

We tried making the second prize more valuable than the first, but Jim was foxy and refused to extend himself as soon as he caught on to it. With the ponies it was different, for they were constantly changing hands, and what with jockeying and foul riding of all descriptions it was not easy for any of them to establish a permanent superiority.

After they had settled down a bit their commander, Captain Rogers, was anxious to make himself acquainted with the topography of the country, and as we at the ranch were the most available guides it brought us into close contact with him. One day he proposed a trip to the Blue and the intervening waters and I gladly accompanied him. He took the Navajos along with him. He said they were strangers to the country and might as well learn all about it. This had been the choice hunting-ground of the Apaches, and they had jealously excluded all other Indians. As he wanted to do the whole business in one day, which meant a ride of sixty miles or more, it was necessary to start early, and we were well on the way before sunup. He and I practically rode alone, for he had turned his dusky warriors over to a non-commissioned officer of their own colour and they had scattered out all over the country.

The N.C.O. turned up from time to time, just to see where we went to and possibly to make a report, but otherwise we saw very little of them all the way on our outward trip. We had a fine ride together and got to the Blue some time after midday. There the orderly paid us one of his periodical visits, and Rogers notified him to gather up his charges and have them all together before we got back to the Frisco. The latter explained to him in Spanish that they were off hunting deer, after which he rode away and we saw no more of him until we were more than half-way home. The first to arrive there was the orderly, accompanied by another Navajo. They bore between them the carcase of a magnificent black-tailed buck.

After a little the others began to drop in. They came in twos and threes and sometimes half a dozen or more, but without exception they all carried on their saddles, deer of all ages, sizes, and sexes. Where a carcase was extra large they had divided it, but as a rule each man had at least one whole deer on his saddle. When they all got together we looked like a butcher's convoy.

In addition to the carcases they had taken great pains to salvage both the hides and the intestines, and each man carried a bundle of the latter immediately in front of him, which juggled and gurgled in a most unpleasant manner as they jogged along. These things were tied up in all sorts of receptacles, from gunny-sacks to Navajo blankets, and wriggled about in such a way as to seem endowed with life. They resembled large-sized plum-puddings, and I christened them ' haggis ', just why, I don't know, for I have never seen a haggis. But I read a description of one in the *Sporting Times* in my early youth, and this had its influence.

When they all got together I said to Rogers that they must have slain all the deer in the country. He agreed with me, saying that at best they were a destructive lot of savages, but he thought that on this occasion they had really gone too far. As nearly as we could estimate they had eighty-four deer between them. It meant venison and to spare for every one, but it took fully twenty years for the deer supply in that section of country to become normal. Rogers and I were both disgusted at the wanton destruction.

When we struck an open piece of ground he remonstrated sharply with them through his orderly. They had evidently been in high feather over their success and were bitterly disappointed, not to say mutinous, when they came to understand that El *Capitano*, or the White Chief, as some called him, did not approve of it. Several of them harangued him through the interpreter to the effect that they considered they had done a praiseworthy action.

It took a good while for the interpreter to make himself understood, but we gathered that they considered the captain's rebuke to be entirely unwarranted. They said in effect that they had taken the field as allies of Uncle Sam, to put an end to the depredations of the detested Apache and that they knew of no better way of bringing him to time than by destroying the game in his favourite hunting-ground, which would deprive him of sustenance and bring famine and disease into his wigwam.

They didn't see what right the White Chief had to censure them for their praiseworthy action, and they intimated several things in their resentment, none of which we understood. The White Chief shrugged his shoulders, muttered something about their drawing rations and Uncle Sam's good pay, and he'd be damned if he thought they were worth it.

The thing wasn't over. They soon began to whoop apparently to encourage each other, and then two or three of them would race their ponies and dash out in front of us, with their infernal haggises juggling and sputtering. When they got about a hundred yards in front of us they'd pull up and wait till we passed them, all the time endeavouring to look defiant, while we entirely ignored them.

I asked the White Chief what he was going to do if they all quit him, and he said : ' Hell ! I'd have a nice time explaining matters at head-quarters.' When this sort of thing had gone on for a little time and was beginning to grow monotonous the White Chief scratched his head and said that he thought he'd have to create a diversion to get their minds off the deer question. I suggested a horse-race, but he said they were too heavily loaded, and if they delayed long enough to unpack and repack again it would be long after nightfall before they got to camp.

The idea then sprung up to hold a foot-race. We immediately searched our clothes for the necessary prizes. After a diligent search I dug up a quarter and the O.C., after turning out all his pockets, shook a dime out of an old note-book. With those princely sums in our possession our confidence returned and we began to feel masters of the situation.

The question arose as to what distance the race was to be, and as we happened to be at that time in a valley, known as Weedy Flat and within eight or nine miles of the river, I suggested that they race all the way to camp, which would keep them employed until they got to where they could consume some of their ill-gotten gains.

As soon as the question was propounded to them through the orderly it was received eagerly, and they at once began to dismount and consult noisily amongst each other as to who were to be the contestants. The clouds disappeared from the White Chief's brow and he smiled all over as amicable relations were again resumed.

Great is the power of wealth. Mr. Kipling had not as yet come on the scene to delight the world with his inimitable tales, but the little incident might, not inaptly, be termed ' The Incipient Mutiny of the Mavericks ' ; nipped in the bud through the expenditure of five-and-thirty copper cents.

The next thing was to arrange the details. There were over a dozen competitors, selected apparently by mutual consent, all ready to grunt and sweat over eight or nine miles at an elevation of over five thousand feet, presumably for the honour and glory as well as the very modest remuneration. They had already forgotten all about their grievance.

Conspicuous amongst them was, of course, Slim Jim, who looked all over a winner, but many of them had placed their hopes on a heavy-set Indian of unusual shape, from the fact that he had conspicuous bow-legs. Such malformation is very unusual amongst Indians, and his were sufficiently bowed to attract attention in any company. He had a name, but it was unpronounceable ; as Bow-legs I have carried him in my memory for over forty years. The hopes of his supporters seemed to rest on his staying powers. They thought he would be able to wear down Slim Jim. But I was unable to hear details of the argument, as to me it was delegated to ride swiftly to camp, where, on the edge of the *mesa* overlooking the river, I was to assume the combined duties of guide-post and judge.

The sun was getting low and all the competitors in place, so that it was necessary to ride fast in order to be of any use to them when they emerged into the open country adjacent to the river. I lost no time in getting there, and probably did the distance in thirty-five or forty minutes.

I had not long to wait, however, for I had only just filled a pipe and lit it when I could discern something moving in the cedar brakes nearly a mile off. It was undoubtedly a man on foot, and he was coming along at a great pace. The sun by this time was just sinking behind the mountains immediately behind me, and it threw long shadows in the timber ; so much so that the runner disappeared from my view for several seconds.

Presently he emerged into the sunlight and there was no mistaking who it was. It was Jim in all his glory. He was now half a mile or more from me, but as he came into the glare of the setting sun he made a most picturesque figure. I would have given a great deal to be able to reproduce the impression. Distant as he was one could distinguish the band around his forehead, while, with his head thrown back, he was running with a smooth, even stride that looked as if it might stay for ever.

I had taken up my post a little out of the direct line of the Indian camp, and as soon as he saw me he altered his course and came directly towards me, which threw him out of profile and rather spoiled the pretty picture, but he was running as if he was greased and was soon alongside of me. I was evidently only a guide-post to him, for he passed me by without notice, continued down the steep hill to the river bottom and across a narrow strip of sand that divided the *mesa* from the river.

As soon as he arrived at the latter he stopped, put one foot in the water, and then lay down and took a drink. After which he scrambled up on the bank, sat down, and waved a hand to me, some two hundred yards off against the skyline, as much as to say : ' We have arrived.' I waved back an assent and then turned to see if any of the others were in sight. Sure enough Bow-legs was just emerging from the timber, fully half a mile behind, but none of the others were in sight.

This did not seem to discourage Bow-legs, however, and he was bursting himself to maintain his position as second best in this great contest. His running was in strong contrast to Jim's smooth gait, and he was striving as if it took brute force to get him over the ground. As soon as he came up I accompanied, or rather followed him, for he negotiated the steep descent off the *mesa* much faster than I did, down to where Jim was sitting.

He also insisted on putting one foot in the water, after which he took a drink, as Jim had done, except that it required more muscular exertion and he took longer over it. He then joined Jim on the bank and they both looked up inquiringly at me. I congratulated them on being the winners of the rich prizes but doubt if they understood, and that did not seem to be exactly what they wanted.

They began to make signs, from which I gathered they were anxious to get hold of the prize money. I had turned it over to Rogers. I made a halting effort to explain my position, but it seemed to convey no meaning to the victors and they evidently expected that I was the stake-holder as well as the judge and guide-post.

The position growing embarrassing, I led them over to the soldier camp, in hopes of finding an interpreter. Everybody there was away, however, except a sergeant and a few men. The cook of the officers' mess could speak Spanish, but it evidently was a different dialogue from what the Navajos used, and I only succeeded in arousing their suspicions that I was withholding the money.

By this time the other Indians that had taken part in the race were dropping in, and with a guilty feeling I felt they were imparting my misdeeds to them as they came. Had I not promised the White Chief to wait for him I would have got on my horse and made a bolt for it ; but as it was there was nothing to be done except wait, so I gave my horse a drink, hitched him to a tree, and sat down on the bank.

That I was in custody was evident, for Jim and Bow-legs sat down, one on each side of me. It was getting dark, and hoping to get rid of them I got up after a time and started to walk back to the soldier camp. For a few brief moments I thought I had got rid of them, but happening to stumble over a tent-peg I was soon made aware of their presence, for one of them caught hold of my arm, while the other picked up my hat, which had fallen off. Till they did so I hadn't the faintest idea they were alongside.

After that I gave up the idea of making my escape and sat resignedly down to await the White Chief. When he came along after an interminable age I at once appealed to him for the stakes, explaining that I was being held in custody till they were produced. At this he laughed, and slapping his breast pocket said : ' What in hell did I do with them ? ' By way of consolation he told me to wait till he had unloaded his kit, when he would produce them.

I begged of him at least to explain to Jim and Bow-legs that I was not trying to appropriate that five-and-thirty cents to my own private use, and after a conversation with the orderly this explanation seemed to be forthcoming, but I doubt if it entirely cleared me of suspicion. It relieved me, however, from being in close arrest, and though I was kept under surveillance I was allowed thereafter to wander round the camp unmolested.

The White Chief said that he would be busy for a little while, but when I mentioned something about getting back to the ranch he demurred, saying that I should stay and help him sample some of the venison. I was really nothing loth, but to make assurance doubly sure he said that he would hold on to the prize money until supper was ready.

This practically sealed my fate, for I felt that Jim and Bow-legs would never let me out of their sight until I forked out that thirty-five cents. Had I started for the ranch I felt positive they would have gone along with me, and if I failed to dig it up when I got there I would probably have had to sleep with them. The prospect of fried venison was more enticing and I accepted my fate without further protest.

The Indians had been busy since their arrival in building

fires and had one large one in a corner of the camp, alongside which they were digging a trench, so I strolled over to see what they were at. I found them busy round a trench about ten feet long, a foot or more deep, and about the same width. They were on both sides of it and busy distributing red-hot coals along the bottom of it, as fast as they could be procured from the fire.

It seemed to be a serious operation and I watched them with interest, soon forgetting all about Jim and Bow-legs. They distributed the coals evenly with much shouting and laughter and were evidently preparing for a feast of some sort. I wondered what it was and whether they were going to bury the venison in the hot trench and leave it there all night, as I had seen a cow's head cooked in camp, with hide and everything intact—and very good it was.

When they had got to a nice glow with the red coals along the bottom some of them ran back a little way into the darkness, from which they quickly reappeared again, bearing something in a blanket. That they meant to feast on a gargantuan scale was evident, for there were two loads, and it took several men on each side of the blankets to handle them.

Their advent was received with vociferous expressions of satisfaction, and I pressed forward along with the crowd to see what was forthcoming. The pressure behind me brought me to the very edge of the trench, and I was immediately over it when they unloaded the contents. Faugh! they were the accumulated haggises that had so disgusted me when attached to their saddles. When they were unloaded on to the hot coals a thick vapour and smoke arose that obscured everything.

No words can describe the flavour of that smoke. My head was immediately over it and I got the full benefit. It was a mixture of dungpits and blood and offal and a slaughter house and a tannery and everything that was vile. I was smothering, and I fought like a tiger to escape and get some fresh air, much to the disgust of those who had crowded in behind me. They evidently thought I had gone crazy, and as a crazy man is treated with great respect by the Indians they made room for me and allowed me to escape.

When I had coughed and spat enough to get my lungs partially free from the vile concoction I made my way feebly to the tent of the White Chief. He was busy over the fire on the outside, but he saw that I was in distress and told me to go inside and help myself. By the flickering light of the fire I was enabled to discover a monstrous flask on his bed, and when I had filled and drained the cup, which held about half a pint, I felt able to speak.

I was about to explain my predicament, but he cut me short and said that the aroma had reached him. He then wanted to know what I meant by bringing a couple of ill-smelling Indians over to his quarters, which was my first intimation that I was still being stalked by Jim and Bow-legs. I hurriedly explained that he still held the stakes and that I was impecunious, whereupon he stuck the handle of the spoon or fork, or whatever he was using, in his mouth, and with the frying-pan in one hand fumbled in his clothes with the other until he found them.

With a light heart I turned the stakes over to the victors in their respective portions and watched them retire hastily to their prospective feast. Each one had said '*Bueno!*' as he received his dole, and I muttered a silent prayer that I might never set eyes on them again.

Things looked brighter after that. The White Chief was no mean performer in front of a camp-fire, and the feast of venison we had that night would have made Lucullus envious. How long we sat by that camp-fire I have no conception, but imagine it must have been near midnight when I rose to go. My poor horse had grown impatient and had pawed a great hole in the ground, but as I tightened the cinches before mounting him I had no idea there was any one near me except the White Chief.

He was carrying on a lively conversation, to which I was endeavouring to listen, but I had hardly got into the saddle when I was prodded in the leg on each side by somebody's forefinger, and damned if there weren't Jim and Bow-legs, each grunting ' *Bueno!*' ' *Bueno!*' They evidently wished to assure me and make amends for their unworthy suspicions, but they nearly scared me out of the saddle. I wished them ' *Bueno!*' back, told them not to mention it, shook hands with the White Chief, and rode hurriedly home.

That night I dreamt of a bow-legged Indian trying frantically to race through the air, but making no progress. I made a solemn resolution never to act as judge in a race unless I could control the stakes.

CHAPTER VIII

TWO days later Fountain, Dr. Maddox, and Cabell dropped in to see us. They were on their way back from a lengthy scout in the Mogollon Mountains, and their object in calling on us was to secure a supply of fresh beef. They said they had sent most of the troops on to camp, but there were a few outside holding a bunch of horses, and that if we had any beef on hand they could pack it and take it along.

Now, it so happened that I had brought a supply of the Navajo venison from the White Chief's head-quarters the day before, and no demand for beef coming from that direction we had not slaughtered our regular weekly allowance. Result, no fresh meat for the poor soldiers returning after being saturated with sow-belly and Government hard tack, not to mention fatigue and hard knocks while they were drumming up Mr. Geronimo and his pals.

However, I told them I would consult Old Charlie, who at the moment was the only one within hail. Old Charlie's opinion was not encouraging. It was that time of year when animals with sufficient flesh on them even to be palmed off on Uncle Sam ranged far and wide. Charlie's opinion was that should we be fortunate enough to catch anything handy to the river it would be after dark before we got it to the ranch and got it butchered.

Armed with this authoritative statement, I returned to the house and told them the outlook for beef was apocryphal. I recollect I had only discovered the word a short time previously and thought I would spring it on them. They ignored it. They simply said that they supposed they could exist another day on salt junk.

Then I bethought me of the Slaughter of the Innocents and brought comfort to their souls by telling them there was plenty of fresh meat in camp. And so long as their favourite portions were unmolested the Navajos were not averse to dividing it liberally.

On the way to the corral and back, when I went to consult Old Charlie, I had noticed, standing by the fence, the bunch of horses on which they proposed to pack the meat. They struck me as an unusual bunch to be in the custody of Uncle Sam's troopers. There were pintos and yellow and gruyères, which is a slaty kind of roan, and altogether they looked unsuitable for cavalry purposes.

On inquiring as to their origin, Fountain told us they had belonged to Geronimo and his gang, and that they had just captured them, and if it had not been for an unfortunate incident they would in all probability have captured the gang too.

This was real news. He related how they had got tidings of mysterious fires in the mountains which were undoubtedly Indian signals. Word had been brought from Dry Creek by a Mr. Elliott, who was foreman, entire cow outfit, and general factotum at the Siggins Ranch there. He was always alluded to as ' Old Man Elliott ', not necessarily on account of his age, for he was a much younger man than Mr. Siggins, his employer, but rather on account of his long experience on the frontier.

I believe his entire life had been spent up there, and he was familiar with all sections of it. He was slow of speech, but when he spoke pearls of wisdom dropped from his mouth. When he reported Indians in the vicinity it was pretty certain that they were adjacent.

Fountain then related how Old Man Elliott had guided them over the most impossible trail it had ever been his lot to follow. It was near the head of Dry Creek, and shortly after reaching the top they struck unmistakable Indian signs. There were all kinds of barefooted pony tracks, which indicated that the place had evidently been used as a horse pasture at no very distant date.

They followed the tracks over the roughest kind of country, crossing deep canyons and climbing steep bluffs, until near nightfall, when they found themselves under a great cliff close to the summit of one of the principal peaks, called Baldy, because its summit was above timber-line and devoid of vegetation.

There was water here, dripping from the cliff into a natural basin, which was evidently made use of by the Indians. They christened it ' Dripping Spring ' and resolved to make camp there for the night. The only drawback was there was no room and no grass for their horses, so they were obliged to take them back a considerable way to form a camp and leave a strong guard over them.

At the same time, not wishing to leave the spring unguarded lest it should be visited by the Indians in the early hours of the morning, half the force were told off to lie in ambush there until relieved by a party from the horse-camp. The party at the horse-camp did not have the most enviable quarters, but their lot was Paradise compared to that of those who were watching the spring.

The latter, Fountain and Dr. Maddox among them, nearly froze to death before being relieved, as the temperature at that time of year and at that elevation, almost ten thousand feet, must have been many degrees below zero. However, it was all in the game, and the next day, as soon as it was daylight, the trail was taken up with alacrity. Everybody had to get along as best they could on cold rations, for they dared not light a fire for fear of betraying their presence.

They had not gone many miles the next morning before they discovered the Indian ponies grazing in a valley and apparently unguarded. Every precaution was taken, and after exploring around on foot for a little time they located the Indian camp in a deep canyon, where they were busy preparing their food, for they had a small fire going.

Great pains were now taken to surround them and if possible to capture the entire bunch. The troopers were all dismounted, the main body worked in between the Indian camp and their horses, while others were detached to guard the sides of the canyon. Everything was going beautifully until they were just dropping into the canyon and preparing to rush them, when one unfortunate trooper lost his footing and in his efforts to save himself unluckily discharged his carbine.

The report acted on the Indians as if they were a flock of quail, and they all disappeared mysteriously in every direction. A glimpse of one or two was had for a second, and then they simply weren't there. But the troopers had effectually got between them and their horses, and the result was the bunch of cayuses standing outside the fence.

When Fountain got through we went out to inspect the ponies. They were in wretched condition, but no doubt a useful lot. They were all covered with brands and strange devices, until they looked like the Babylonian inscriptions that used to appear in *Punch* over the title ' As it Tickleth-My-Fancy The Scribe '.

After this the ponies were sent on to camp and we adjourned to the ranch and sampled some of the venison, while I related to them the devastation committed by the Navajos among the deer. It was an ill wind, etc., for at any rate it supplied them with fresh meat until we could round up some beef. On this latter point we assured them they could rely on our having a supply the following evening. It also occurred to us, after witnessing the taste of those Indians for the portions of animals that are usually thrown away, that in future we could dispose of the beef offal, and we asked them to notify the White Chief to send some of his myrmidons over the following evening when they sent after the beef.

The next day everything that we possessed in the horse line that could be ridden or driven was rounded up and placed under herd, and while the bulk of the outfit were thus engaged Charlie and I rode wide and rounded up the necessary beef. This in due course was butchered about sundown, or a little before it, as it was our custom to let it hang overnight before delivering it. This time, however, they were in a hurry and had sent a detail after it, with several pack mules, their big wagon being engaged elsewhere.

They were also accompanied by a band of the Navajos, who brought me a letter from the White Chief asking me to send him a quarter. He said there was plenty of deer meat still in camp, but, like last week's wash, it was strung out on a line and his digestion was beginning to rebel against ' jerky '. These Indians made most efficient scavengers and while in our neighbourhood saved us much labour, as before their arrival the offal had had to be disposed of quickly and buried ; otherwise in that powerful sun it would have been impossible to exist in its vicinity.

They now seized on all the interior portion as quickly as it was produced, and dragging it off to one side, reduced it to portable conditions and stowed it away in their clothes or on their saddles, till they were festooned with the ghastly stuff.

As fast as the beeves were killed they were cut into quarters, which the soldiers packed on the mules, as each one was led up close to the pen for the purpose. Each mule carried three quarters, one slung on each side of the *aperejo*, or pack-saddle, and one placed on top, while over all was spread a canvas sheet, which was tightly roped down.

As each pack was completed the animal was turned loose and grazed off a little to one side of the slaughter-pen. They were splendid animals, nearly sixteen hands high, and I recollect admiring their glossy coats as each one was packed and wandered off to join its companions. All would have gone well had it not been for the intrusion of some other pretty little animals.

Skunks were plentiful around the ranch. In those days their skins were of no great value, and experience had taught us that they were least offensive when entirely unmolested, so that even the dogs were not encouraged to disturb them. The slaughter-pen was a favourite resort of theirs. Prior to the advent of the Navajos they had been of some assistance in getting rid of the offal. True, they were not so thorough as the latter, but they were an undoubted help and consequently had not been discouraged.

From long habit they had got to know the regular days of slaughter, and as the hour, about sundown, coincided with their hours of recreation, they used to reconnoitre until every one had cleared off and left them in undisputed possession of the feast. Several of them appeared on the scene now and toddled around on a tour of inspection. They didn't quite come into the pen, but they were undismayed by the presence of human beings and came sufficiently close to note everything that was taking place.

As for the mules, the skunks simply ignored them. Were there not plenty of four-footed animals just like them on the range, and did not they all respect the skunk? They prowled gently around with their noses close to the ground and their graceful tails drooping, till their wanderings brought them to the vicinity of Uncle Sam's animals.

Now these mules had been recently shipped out from the East. They did not know the skunk in all his pristine beauty. The attention of one of them was immediately attracted. But a few moments before he had been downcast; no doubt regretting his warm stable and flesh-pots of Egypt. Now, here was evidently the prettiest thing he had ever seen in his life. He raised his head and with cocked ears gazed at it in silent admiration.

All would still have been well had he been content only to gaze. But he was fascinated and determined to make closer acquaintance with this lovely object. With outstretched neck and extended head he approached it cautiously.   The skunk ignored his presence until he came quite close, when it raised its beautiful tail, spread out like a fan in silent protest.   This was more than any lovesick mule could stand, and he raised a front foot carefully, with the evident intention of stroking it   Then the skunk turned loose and that mule must have thought that he had struck a cyclone.

For a moment or two he was completely paralysed.   Then he twisted his neck to one side and with his nose up in the air gave expression to his feelings in the choking tones between a bray and a whinny peculiar to the mule tribe. This failing to relieve him, he became perfectly demented and tried to get rid of his skin by a succession of buck-jumps and plunges which were simply amazing.   He didn't get rid of his hide, but he quickly got rid of the beef and everything that was on his back except the rope, the loose end of which been fastened round his neck.

All proving futile, he again raised his voice in protest and started for the hills like an express train. With lowered head and plunging knees, as if endeavouring to rub the foul aroma from his nostrils, he disappeared over the nearest rise and was lost to view.

Now the other mules who were packed had at first looked on his antics with surprise, but as the effluvia reached them they began to take an interest, and when he started for the hills they evidently thought it was time for all to move, so they followed him kicking and plunging, until the ground for the best part of a mile was strewn with quarters of beef, canvas sheets, and other impedimenta.

For a brief period every one was helpless with laughter, and then there was a rush for saddles and such mounting in hot haste as put one in mind of the feats of the Netherby clan and the elopement of young Lochinvar.   We pursued them until away into the night, when the leader got snarled up with the rope amongst some cedars and was led back ignominiously to the ranch to have his pack replaced.   He was a different animal from the debonair dandy that had been first packed.   He looked depressed and had evidently been cruelly deceived by the glamour of the West.

The first definite move made by Geronimo's band after they had lost their horses was an attempt to hold up the stage.   Al, the driver, had a pretty narrow escape.   Had it not been for the half-broken condition of the little mules that he drove, which caused them to run at the slightest opportunity, he would hardly have got off with a whole skin.

Like the rest of us, Al had gained confidence while the Apaches were down in Old Mexico and had returned to his day-time trips. But the killing of Saburin again made him scary. The attempt took place about five miles nearer Alma than where Saburin had been killed, and at the point where Duck Creek Draw merged into the more open country adjoining Cactus Flat.

Fortunately the approach to the place was down a long incline affording a good view on all sides, and Al, having his eyes peeled, noticed that the cattle were running as he came over the top from the aforementioned Cactus Flat. Failing to see any one on horseback or any cause for the disturbance of the cattle, he became more suspicious and kept a keen look-out as he approached the place There was nothing whatever in sight, but there was a shallow *arroya* some eighty or ninety yards from the road which might possibly conceal a hidden foe.

Watching this intently he noticed that there were some ten or a dozen ordinary-sized stones or rocks, the largest probably not exceeding thirty or forty pounds in weight, scattered here and there on the ground, about half-way between the *arroya* and the road. He wasn't sure whether those had always been there, as they were separated by considerable intervals, but they were more or less in line, and somehow they seemed strange to him and he never recollected having seen them before. They were inconspicuous objects and did not seem large enough to conceal a jack-rabbit, much less a human being, but as he came closer to them he thought he detected a slight movement behind one of them.

Whether he actually did or not he was never sure, but filled as he was with Indian scare and his nerves all unstrung, he gave vent to a regular scream, and dropping into the bottom of the buckboard, behind the mail-sacks, loosed off the gun, which he had carried across his knees, at the supposed object. He never knew whether his shot had gone in the air or into the ground, but its result was instantaneous. The little mules, who had been turned loose, tore down the road like a tornado, and so quickly did they pass the spot that the Indians who were actually concealed behind those rocks failed to return the fire until Al had put some sixty or seventy yards between them.

The report of the gun had taken them by surprise, but as soon as they opened fire they filled the mail-sacks and other packages which were tied on behind with lead. The more they fired, however, the faster the mules ran, and they soon put such a distance between them that they were out of all danger. Fortunately they kept the road, and Al let them run for a mile or two before making any attempt to recover the reins and check them.

As soon as he got them under control he made the L C Ranch as quickly as he could, and there he remained till after nightfall before resuming the other half of his journey. That was the last daylight trip he made for some time. When he returned to Alma on his return trip, he was wearing one of the Indian bullets, which he and the postmaster had recovered out of the mail-sack, as a charm on his watch-chain, where we all duly inspected and admired it.

The most extraordinary thing about the whole performance was how the Indians managed to conceal themselves behind those rocks. I visited the place in company with the soldiers shortly after the event, and we tried it from all angles, but our curves showed up at some point and we failed to make ourselves invisible. It was the Indian faculty. The stones lay there for years undisturbed and were pointed out to strangers when the subject of Indians happened to come up ; and I recollect one trip in company with Indian Jack. I got him to try it and he concealed himself without difficulty. But then Jack could flatten himself out on the ground like a badger trying to maintain his hold—a gift not given to the white man.

Our poor soldiers had to turn out and make another effort to connect with the Indians after this escapade before their horses were nearly rested, and needless to say they were unable to get any satisfactory results.

Shortly after this we celebrated the Christmas of 1885. The festivities had no special feature, beyond the fact that we introduced our friends the soldiers to genuine English plum-pudding. At least we called it genuine, and if they were in a position to contradict us they were too polite to say so. They said they enjoyed it, and there were no fatal results ; which was all in our favour.

Immediately after the New Year of 1886 our friends again

took the field and were out for a week or more. When they came back I thought that Fountain, who always accompanied them, looked rather ill, and my mind reverted to the plum-pudding, with vague misgivings. Poor Maddox, however, whom I took into my confidence, assured me that he was run down and suffering intermittently from a mild attack of dysentery. He said that he was badly in need of a rest, and that he had urged him frequently to take one, but he was such a conscientious beggar that he had to work day and night.

I was relieved in regard to the plum-pudding, but I added my voice to the doctor's in urging him to take a rest. Our combined efforts proved fruitless and drew nothing from him beyond a good-natured smile, so we left him, and the doctor accompanied me to the ranch with the expressed determination of beating me at putting the weight.

Maddox was a splendid specimen of manhood, but I could never persuade him that throwing the weight was not altogether a matter of strength. We had an old 16-lb. shot at the ranch, and whenever he had any spare time he liked to come over and try his luck. He could handle that weight as if it weighed only an ounce, and would shake and endeavour to throw it as one would a cricket ball, but he never acquired the knack of getting his weight behind it, and both Wilson and myself could output him, especially Wilson, who was really good at it.

The doctor would scratch his head, and in order to get even would take the weight in both hands, swing it between his legs, and throw it back over his head to a distance that we made no pretence of competing with ; but at the legitimate game we were always a little ahead of him. I have dwelt on this weight-putting because we engaged in it the last time the poor fellow came to the ranch.

When he returned to camp I accompanied him and found Fountain and Cabell deep in discussion with Old Man Elliott from the Siggins Ranch. It seemed the Old Man had come up to report that the Indians were in the neighbourhood of Dry Creek and that they were busy signalling to each other in the nearby mountains.

When he had left us Fountain said that there was some information he was desirous of obtaining from me. This brought our old friend Sergeant Cox, late of the U.S. cavalry, again on the scene. I had not seen nor heard much of him since our little escapade at the *plaza*, and was much surprised when Fountain asked me if I knew him. I said that I did, and then he asked if I knew that he was a deserter from the U.S. Army. I owned up that I did. He then told me that it had been reported to him that he was at present residing in the mining camp at Cooney and that it would be his painful duty to arrest him if he could find him. I asked what that meant, and he said probably a long term of imprisonment at Fort Leavenworth, Kansas.

I then told him about our first meeting and how the old fellow had befriended me for the sake of the old sod, at which he was much amused, but declared that the old rascal was a hardened offender and had appropriated a lot of Government property, and that it was his duty to hunt him up as soon as he had time to get around to it.

After that I rode home lost in thought about the coming fate of my friend Cox. I consulted Old Charlie, and he said that it was liable to go hard with him if he was arrested, and suggested my going up there and giving him a hint to make himself scarce.

Resolving to act on this advice, I made an early start the following morning and went to Cooney. All the way to Cooney I carried on a fierce mental struggle between my loyalty to Fountain, combined with a natural detestation for the crime of desertion, and a sense of gratitude to Cox for his kindness to me on my first trip through the country, when I felt very much like an orphan. Sometimes I was inclined to turn back, but tribal instincts were too strong. After all, wasn't he an offshoot of the town of Strokestown, in the barony of Elphin, and the County of Roscommon, Ireland? Away with the idea of consigning him to Leavenworth!

When I got to Cooney I hunted up the abode of the Shelhorns, where Cox was supposed to be, but found all the menfolks away. There was no one at home but the old lady, and she had no disposition to discuss Mr. Cox or his ways with a stranger. After an extremely brief interview I hunted up one Uncle Billy, and he told me he had seen Cox the evening before while on his way to a new camp they had started on Silver Creek. Somebody had discovered promising ore there, and this was the foundation of the town of Mogollon. Uncle Billy hinted vaguely at a lady who he said kept a boarding-house there. He winked and looked knowing, but I did not enter into particulars.

It took me nearly two hours to ride across the mountains dividing Cooney from Silver Creek, where the new mining camp had started, but I was fortunate enough to discover the boarding-house and its fair proprietress before actually striking the main creek. It was situated in the draw I was following, almost hidden in the shadow of a great bluff.

It was really a dilapidated tent, festooned with gunny-sacks to hide the rents and keep out the air. A section of stove-pipe protruded through the roof, through which smoke curled, showing that it was inhabited, and an undue proportion of gunny-sacks at one place indicated an entrance.

When I struck it I had no idea that it was the object of my search, but thought it advisable to inquire. As I dismounted and approached the entrance, however, some one thrust the gunny-sacks aside and what I at first took to be a man appeared in the entrance. It was dressed in overalls and held a large hand in front of its face, peering into the sunlight.

When the hand was removed the absence of hair on the face indicated the sex, but otherwise she might have been the original for the caricature of the Russian Bolshevik that one sees in the daily Press. In the other hand she held a tin pan, which she was about to use as a gong to proclaim the hour for dinner, when perceiving me, a stranger, she waited for an explanation.

I made her a bow and told her that I had come in search of Mr. Cox. The announcement in itself was simple, but its effect was marvellous, for on the mention of his name she threw back her head, opened a mouth of extraordinary dimensions, and simply shook with convulsions of silent laughter. At first I thought she had been taken suddenly ill, and as I gazed into the cavity of her interior, with only one yellow fang to obstruct the view, I wondered what I could pour down it to afford her relief.

She came to without falling apart, however, and told me that he had been there the evening before, but had gone back to Cooney in company with Willis Shelhorn, and that she thought he intended to accompany old man Shelhorn over to Claremont, to recover some things left at his ranch. She added, however, that some of the miners would be in to dinner presently and that they could give me full information ; after which she beat a tattoo on that old tin pan which made the rocks resound through the entire Mogollon Range.

In answer to her summons some half-dozen prospectors began to drop in from different directions. Each of them carried specimens of rock and were loud in their praises as to the richness of the strike and the future prospects of the camp to be founded there. It was to outrival Leadville and all the other great camps in the United States. That was forty years ago and the outrivalling has still to come.

One of the prospectors, named Mike Tracey, was known to me as a friend of Old Charlie's, and he confirmed the story told to me by the lady conducting the establishment. I had now to return to Cooney, with the almost certain prospect of having to proceed from there to the Shelhorn Ranch, which was nearly twenty miles farther up in the mountains, and as I jogged back over the hills the crime of desertion began to look very black in my eyes.

On reaching Cooney I met the young man Willis, and he told me that his father, Cox, and his young brother Rob had gone to the ranch, five or six miles beyond Claremont, early that morning, and that he really did not know when they would be back, but thought they would probably travel at night on account of the Indians. I also gathered that his father was rather hard of hearing, and that if I held much conversation with him I would have to talk loud.

Armed with all this important information and mentally cursing all deserters, I started off on my journey to Copper Creek and the Shelhorn Ranch. There was a two-mile climb out of Cooney Canyon, over the most awful apology for a trail that it is possible to imagine. At one point it passed over the apex of an arch that might have represented the Gothic entrance to a cathedral several hundred feet in height, and came so close to the edge that when one's horse's hoof kicked a little rock it dropped over the side and there was a pause of many seconds before one heard the dull sickening thud below.

When I got to where it was possible to make better time the shadows were getting long, and my thoughts reverted to the Apache and his playful habit of waylaying unwary travellers. Then, again, I had never met the elder Shelhorn, and rumour credited him with a Puritanical disposition, his principal discourse relating to Biblical subjects and the upbringing of youth. It even went so far as to accuse him of carrying a copy of the Gideon Society Bible around on his person, which, if not exactly a crime, waś an unusual circumstance on the frontier of those days. I was weak on the subject myself and I wondered how I would get along if called on to quote Scripture at the top of my voice. Altogether it was not a cheery outlook.

It was nightfall when I suddenly came on to the Şhelhorn Ranch, a substantial log house. My friend Cox was outside the door, chopping firewood, and I hailed him with a cheery 'Hallo'! He demonstrated that the visit was unexpected by turning quickly, brandishing the axe, but immediately lapsed into a smile on recognizing me.

On my acquainting him with the situation his language was both disrespectful and mutinous, and not at all what was to be expected from a non-commissioned officer who had the maintenance of good order and discipline at heart. He swore volubly at the authorities in Washington, D.C., and expressed a wish to come in contact with the individual who had lodged the information. I suggested the advisability of his lying doggo and keeping out of sight till the military moved out, and after he had finished swearing, he intimated that he would take it under consideration.

Anyway, my conscience felt relieved and I said no more about it. Then followed inquiries as to my intentions for the immediate future, and I intimated that some refreshment for man and beast might not be out of place. This appealed to his sense of hospitality, and he got busy taking care of my horse, as became a true frontiersman.

After that we went into the house and I was introduced to Mr. Shelhorn and his son Rob, the latter a smart boy about twelve years of age. On the way he explained to me that they intended starting back to Cooney about midnight and hoped to reach there before the Indians got busy at dawn.

I was rather diffident about approaching the old gentleman, who looked at me suspiciously over a pair of horn-rimmed glasses of the old-fashioned type. He was reading a well-thumbed book by the light of a kerosene lamp and his infirmity was apparent from the start. I had great difficulty in explaining my name and place of residence—in fact, would have failed entirely had it not been for the assistance of Rob, who came to my rescue from where he had been lighting a fire in the stove, and, making a trumpet of his hands, yelled it into the old man's ear.

When he got it pat he smiled affably and asked if I had not come from England. I nodded assent and he remarked in his thunderous tones that the first settlers in Massachusetts came from England. Not being in a position to dispute the fact and suspecting he probably alluded to the gentlemen known as the Pilgrim Fathers, I did not tell him I thought the country was well rid of them, but merely smiled and tried to look wise.

There were several more futile attempts at conversation, and I tried to explain to him that I had met his son Willis, who had directed me there, but the name was evidently all that he understood, and he informed me that Willis was a good boy and well brought up. He then pointed to Rob, whom he had evidently brought along to attend to his wants, for he was demanding his services every other moment, and said that he also was being trained in a godly manner and was entirely different from the uncultivated youth of the frontier.

This was intended to be *sotto voce*, but in his vibrant tones reached the object of his remark, who, though busy at the stove, immediately turned and, taking advantage of the old man's diverted gaze, thrust his tongue in his cheek and gave a knowing wink. Supper being announced shortly afterwards, and Cox having joined us, our efforts at conversation were superseded, much to my relief.

After supper Rob and my red-headed friend left to attend to chores, while the old gentleman and I retired to a back room and, seated on some up-ended pine logs, made ourselves comfortable in front of a log fire. Here I took refuge in my pipe and listened to a homily from the old gentleman on the training of youth. He quoted frequently passages from the Scriptures and verified them from the well-thumbed volume which he carried with him. I merely smiled and nodded, expressing acquiescence when he came to a pause, and, lost in my own thoughts, allowed him to go ahead without interruption.

I was comfortably dreaming and enjoying my tobacco when I was brought down to earth by a stentorian shout of 'ROB!' It appeared the fire was getting low and the old gentleman wanted some more wood. I offered to go and fetch some, but the old gentleman wouldn't hear of it, saying that Rob would be along presently, and I should sit still. However, wherever Rob was, it was not until the old gentleman had nearly lifted the roof off the house with his cries of ' ROB ' that he put in an appearance.

He then burst open the door very hurriedly, demanding what was wanted ?   In very solemn tones the old gentleman said : ' ROB ! go and get some wood.'   I was prepared for a grumbling acquiescence on Rob's part, but not for what followed ; for Rob's reply, in distinctly audible tones which might even have penetrated the hearing of a partially deaf man was : ' Go and get it yourself, you old son of a b——h ! '

Talk of rank blasphemy.   My hair almost stood on end and my thoughts reverted to the *Ingoldsby Legends* and the ' Blasphemer's Warning.'   I seemed to see the little stony Saint Romwold, Sir Alured Denne, and the wedding guests in the church :

> Nay, many averred he half rose in his niche,
> When Sir Alured, always in metaphor rich,
> Called the priest ' An Old Son of —— ' some animal, which
> Is not worth the inquiry—a hint's quite enough on
> The subject. . . . For more I refer you to Buffon.

I certainly half rose from my seat, but was immediately floored by the old gentleman, who turned to me, his smiling face aglow with satisfaction, and remarked in self-congratulatory tones : ' There !   That's the way to bring a boy up !   Prompt obedience and respect is what I like.'

The rest was lost in confusion, for I missed the log as I tried to resume my seat and fell prone upon the floor.   It was necessary to go through all sorts of contortions to conceal my laughter, and I had to get busy with the overturned log to assure the old gentleman that I wasn't hurt ;   I had scarcely succeeded in suppressing it when Rob returned with an armful of wood and tipped me a wink, which started me off again.   The old gentleman was quite concerned over my accident, and for the rest of the evening it was necessary to listen in silence to his successful methods.

Before he got through I had stretched out on the floor with my saddle for a pillow and had gone to sleep.   About midnight I was roused by Cox, who said they were ready to start, so I saddled up and accompanied them.   The old gentleman and Rob took the lead and Cox and I followed, driving two milch cows.   He started in congratulating Rob on his exemplary behaviour but raised his voice so loud that we were compelled to admonish him and call his attention to the fact that there might be lurking Apaches in the vicinity, whereupon he beamed proudly on his offspring and relapsed into silence.

At Claremont I parted company with them, as there was a more direct way to the ranch, and reached home about daybreak. While in his company Cox had confided to me that he intended to take refuge in the new camp on Silver Creek, and probably would be heard from through the medium of the lady who ran the boarding-house or tent, or whatever designation she applied to it. He was loud in her praises and impressed very strongly on me the fact that she was a real lady. I did not argue the matter.

On reaching the ranch I told Old Charlie all about my trip, and was surprised to learn that he knew all about the new prospects on Silver Creek and that he had a share in a location there, along with his friend Mike Tracey. When told that our friend Cox intended to seek a haven with the lady of the smile, Old Charlie said that he'd ' bet the old rascal would wind up by marrying her, so that she might support him '; and he proved a true prophet, for they were duly joined together shortly after the Indian trouble ceased.

It was too late to get much sleep after I got back to the ranch, but I was pretty stiff and tired, and as I was dozing on the porch that afternoon I became aware of the soldiers starting out in search of the Indians reported by Elliott. There was Maddox's tall figure, always a conspicuous object, riding a big buckskin horse alongside of Cabell, who looked short in comparison. There was Kinney the scout, riding a little in front on a sorrel with a conspicuous star on its face, and there was Fountain, looking pretty ill, on a big grey which he had lately acquired to take the place of a black which he called Diamond, and which we had induced him to sell to me.

They stopped off for a few moments to say ' Hallo ! ' and drink success to the expedition, and I was induced to tell them the story of Mr. Shelhorn and his son Rob. It was really too good to keep, but came near leading me into trouble, for Fountain asked me significantly if I had seen anything of Cox when up at Cooney. I said that he was not there when I passed through, but that I understood he was leaving the country. Whereupon he mumbled something about an accessory, but I shifted the conversation to the forthcoming expedition and drank success to it, and there was no further opportunity for inquiry till we parted.

We had great hopes that they would meet with some decided success and capture that portion of the hostile band which had been dismounted. But late the following afternoon, while Wilson and I were talking together, we saw a soldier riding hurriedly up from Alma, and when he reached us he handed us a note from Fountain.

Wondering what it could be we tore it open. It ran somewhat as follows :

Troop ambushed on Dry Creek Hill. Maddox and five others killed. Would you kindly send up a wagon to help to bring up bodies.

CHAPTER IX

THE AMBUSH

THE messenger knew nothing more and had to return at once. His departure left us dumbfounded. We just looked at each other and said nothing. The catastrophe had been so sudden and so tragic that words seemed totally inadequate. Fortunately there was need for immediate action, which came as a relief. It was well on in the afternoon and a team had to be rounded up. When everything was ready a Canadian boy named Bob O'Brien and I left for Dry Creek, where we arrived almost as soon as the orderly.

All the way there we kept wondering how such a thing could have happened. The Dry Creek Hill mentioned in the note was less than two miles from the Siggins Ranch, and if they had camped there, as they intended, the attack must have taken place immediately after they had broken camp. They had been accompanied by a considerable body of Navajo scouts, and altogether it seemed inexplicable.

On arrival we were met by poor Fountain, who looked very ill and run down and had evidently received a severe shock. We shook hands in silence and accompanied by an orderly with a lantern moved over to the tent where the bodies had been laid. They had been covered with wagon sheets, but we just lifted the corner to look at them. Poor Maddox lay by himself at one side, his tall figure extending the full diameter of the tent. He had a jagged bullet wound at the corner of his mouth, as if the bullet had made an exit there.

Fountain thought it inadvisable to leave the bodies on the ground during the night, so we drove the wagons—a Government wagon which they had procured from the infantry camp higher up the creek, and ours—close to the tent, and having spread some blankets in the bottom loaded them on. Four bodies were spread in the Government wagon and the doctor and Collins in ours.

Having secured them carefully from all possible molestation we went to the camp-fire for a cup of coffee. Here we met Cabell, who was in conversation with Kinney the scout.

One of Cabell's hands was bandaged, and we learnt that he had had the top of his little finger shot off in the fray.

While we were waiting for Fountain to relate how it had all happened, Mr. Siggins and Old Man Elliott came down from the house and invited us to go up there and stay for the night. Fountain wanted to remain in camp, but he really was so ill that we all joined in urging him to sleep under a roof, at least for one night, so after considerable hesitation he turned the camp over to Cabell and came up with us to the house.

Here, sitting by the stove, he was induced to tell how the calamity had occurred. I might relate that the only road past the Siggins Ranch ran up Big Dry Creek for half a mile or more and then, swinging out in a semi-circle to the right, led after another half-mile to a jagged steep hill, clothed with cedar and other brush on both sides. It led up this hill to a narrow saddle, which divided Big Dry from its neighbour Little Dry Creek. Then, doubling back on its tracks, it followed a short draw for nearly another half-mile into Little Dry Creek. It then turned sharp to the left up Little Dry Creek, thus forming a letter S, with elongated curves.

In this way, although the space between the two creeks was rather less than half a mile, owing to the nature of the country and the steepness of the hills, it was necessary to travel several miles to encompass it.

Fountain commenced by saying that for some unknown reason the Navajo scouts who accompanied them, and who were under the immediate control of one of their own non-commissioned officers (my friend the White Chief being otherwise employed), were inordinately slow about leaving camp that morning. For this reason, and also because he was suffering from an attack of dysentery, he had remained behind, allowing the others to start out ahead.

It took him fifteen minutes or less to get a move on the Indians, and then he had ridden as hard as he could to catch up with the others. He had been uneasy owing to Elliott's account—in fact, so much so that they had mounted guard over their horses, an unusual proceeding so close to home ; but though he expected to meet the Apaches he had never dreamt of an ambush so close to the camp as this one was.

But he had only got a little way beyond where the road

turned out from the creek when he heard the firing in front of him. Putting spurs to his horse, he had almost reached the foot of the hill when he met some of the troop horses running loose down the road. These were followed almost immediately by some of the men, from whom he learned that they had been ambushed two-thirds of the way up.

They did not know very well just what happened, but, thought that the doctor, Lieutenant Cabell, and Kinney the guide were all killed. Rallying them as they came along, he had dismounted and extended them round the base of the hill to the left, while he dispatched the Navajos, who were now coming up, up a draw to the right, with instructions to head off the hostiles if possible. He had then got his men spread out for an advance up the hill when he met Cabell and Kinney and learned from them what had really taken place.

Kinney was in the lead and the doctor and Cabell riding alongside each other a few paces behind. For some reason they had no thoughts of coming in contact with Indians until they got nearer the mountains, but the Apache was a wily creature, and when they were about two-thirds of the way up the hill they were met by a volley from in front and from both sides.

Everything was in confusion for a time. Kinney's horse was shot, and evidently saved its rider by the quickness of its eye, for it must have seen the flash or a glint on a gun barrel and thrown up its head, receiving the bullet squarely between the eyes. Cabell, as has been mentioned, had his finger shot off, and poor Maddox, whose commanding figure no doubt caused them to look upon him as the leader of the troops, was shot through the body immediately under the right breast.

Maddox dismounted along with Cabell, telling the latter that he had been hit. The order was given to take cover. The only possible way to do this, for those in front, was to retreat down the left side of the road, which meant crossing an open space for thirty or forty yards. While crossing it the doctor was again hit, this time in the back of the head. The bullet came out at the corner of his mouth. It killed him instantly.

The others had been killed at the first volley and were all in the leading sections of the troop. Several of the horses had been killed as well as Kinney's. The bodies completely blocked the road, preventing anything like an immediate advance on horseback. As quickly as he could rally the men and collect the loose horses, most of which had been caught by the Navajos coming on behind, Fountain took up the pursuit, leaving Cabell with a party to gather up the dead and clear the road.

It was all done in record time, but the wily Apache had managed to get the guns and ammunition of the dead soldiers before clearing out. He was disappointed, however, in his attempt to get fresh mounts, which had evidently been one object of the ambush.

They persevered with the pursuit till well into the afternoon. There was little or no probability of catching up with them after that, as the nature of the ground they made for was impracticable for horses. Then they returned to camp and sent the messenger to us.

It was a sad story, and poor Fountain was almost heartbroken as he related it. Besides his natural grief at the loss of his friend and companions, he blamed himself for having stayed behind in camp, overlooking the fact that his presence there was necessary and utterly ignoring his physical condition. He really should have been in bed, as he was overstraining himself to the breaking point. But when such a course was suggested to him he waved it aside impatiently.

The road had been cleared while they were in pursuit and the carcases of the horses rolled over the edge, where, being completely frozen, they dried and withered up. There they remained for years as a landmark to be pointed out to strangers when the story of the ambush was retold. From that date this particular hill has been known as Soldiers' Hill. I believe subsequent investigation showed that the ambush had been carried out by Nana in person.

As I walked back to the camp with Fountain that night he talked over the final disposition of the bodies, and expressed a wish to bury them in our little cemetery. He said that both Maddox and he had always admired its situation, and he was sure the poor doctor would like to be buried there, even if it was only a temporary resting-place. So it was arranged.

It was nearly noon the next day when we broke camp and left in solemn formation on our sad errand. Kinney the guide was in the lead, as he had been when the attack was made, mounted on a horse belonging to Mr. Siggins. He was followed immediately by Fountain and Cabell, riding side by side. They were followed by several files of soldiers in the formation of threes. Then came our wagon with the bodies of the doctor and Collins, followed by the doctor's big buckskin horse, led by a trooper. Then came the other wagon containing the dead soldiers, with their two surviving horses, led by troopers immediately behind. They were followed by the rest of the soldiers in regular formation, and then came the baggage train, while the Navajos brought up the rear, an irregular but picturesque group.

As we started out we passed the regular stage and sent word by Al to all whom it might concern that the regular funeral would take place about two o'clock the following afternoon at the W S Ranch. Passing through Pleasanton the entire population turned out and accompanied us for several miles along the road. At Whitewater there was a halt for an hour, during which the men fell out and had something to eat.

At Alma we picked up two of the coffins which had been sent for, and the whole population turned out in respectful silence. When we reached the ranch it was almost light, so we left the bodies in the wagons and backed them into the buggy-house, while the troops went on to Camp Maddox, as it was formally named after the funeral.

The next morning, shortly after daylight, a fatigue party arrived from Camp Maddox, and having selected a suitable site in our little graveyard under a spreading cedar, which the sun reached only in the late afternoon, we prepared to dig the graves. This was by no means an easy task, for the soil, though loose and stony for a few inches on the top, consisted below that entirely of hardpan. This came away only in small chunks, even with the aid of a pick, and it was slow, tedious work.

However, by adding what forces could be spared from the ranch we managed to complete two graves by the time allotted for the funeral. One was the ordinary size, about three feet by six, close to the foot of the tree, and the other, a large one, a little lower down, in which to place the five men. The doctor we put in the upper grave by himself, as it was expected his people would wish to remove the body as soon as possible and have it shipped to his home. In regard to the others, Fountain was not at all sure, as many of them had enlisted under assumed names and it was doubtful if their relatives could be located.

As for the coffins, they were just pine boxes. When we had nailed them down and written each man's name and regiment on the lid, the question arose as to flags to cover them with. Fountain had only been able to raise two, but we fortunately had a large one, which had been kept for Fourth of July celebrations, and with it we covered the doctor. The other two were sufficiently large to spread over the remaining coffins, and as they were all to lie in one grave it had to suffice as a military honour.

It took three wagons to bear them from the corral to the graveyard, and in this way we divided the flags, so that each should go to his last resting-place under his country's flag, in whose service he had lost his life. It was considerably after noon before everything had been arranged, and the people from the surrounding country had been arriving for some time. From appearances it was evident that we were going to have a large concourse. They came from every side and from all distances, with their wives and families down to the infant in arms, and I was surprised, not only at the number, but also at the possibility of their having received news of the disaster so quickly.

It looked as if the fiery cross had been sent round, and many riders must have spent the night on the road to bring together so many strange faces. Till then I had no idea there were so many people in the country, and some of them must have come a distance of sixty or seventy miles. They had brought not only their wives and families, but also their dogs, and they were the strangest collection of canines I have ever seen.

They were still coming as we went in to lunch. They had brought their provisions with them and were settling down to await the ceremony of a military funeral. After a hurried meal Cabell and the rest of the troop arrived. They were all turned out in their best and made a brave display, despite the fact that they had only their field kit. The procession was soon formed up, a firing party of twelve men told off, and the rest with arms reversed fell in, and with Fountain at the head, followed by the three wagons, we marched solemnly to the graves.

The trumpeter had first sounded the assembly, and the crowd fell in in solemn procession behind the soldiers

There must have been nearly two hundred of them. It was the small grain of comfort in the otherwise sad ceremony, and I think both men and officers felt grateful that the settlers were not in accord with some of the criticisms of the local Press.

The graves had been lined with cedar branches, and their aromatic odour reached us as we lowered the coffins, until they were almost entirely hidden in the green boughs. Fountain read the Burial Service over them, in a clear distinct voice, which carried to all who were present, and every one stood with bowed heads, making a solemn and impressive scene.

When we had covered them up three volleys were fired in the air. The trumpeter sounded the ' Last Post ', and we all moved sadly away.

We returned to the house and sat silently brooding for the short time before the soldiers left us. Poor Fountain was very ill and Maddox's death had been a great shock to him. We also missed him sadly, for he had always been the cheeriest of companions, and his personal magnetism would have rendered him popular in any society.

Two hours after the funeral the ranch had returned to its normal state of quietness. The soldiers had gone back to camp. The crowd had dispersed in silence, much impressed by the dignity of the simple service. All felt as if they had lost a near and dear relative. Our little graveyard was growing fast. It had begun with one occupant the previous May. Now there were seven, all victims of Geronimo and his band.

There was quite a stir amongst the military authorities after the ambuscade, and reinforcements of infantry were sent to all the permanent camps. More cavalry would have been sent, no doubt, had any existed, but the entire mounted force was already in the field. It was really totally inadequate for the task they had undertaken. They could run the Indians from place to place and keep them on the move only by keeping the field till men and horses were exhausted. It was an utter impossibility to surround them in that wild country and force them to surrender.

More Indian scouts were employed, and the White Chief, who had moved farther north, returned to Camp Maddox. He told us that the Indians had at first gone east, to the San Mateo Mountains, where they must have managed to raise a mount of fresh horses, for he thought they were heading back for Old Mexico.

After that the reports of their presence gradually became more remote, until we had to seek knowledge of their movements in the weekly press. The soldiers, however, stayed on until Geronimo finally surrendered in Old Mexico. They made frequent excursions into the mountains, as they had done since they came, and kept a vigilant watch at all points, as it was never known whether the Indians might not break back. But as the months rolled along into summer everything gradually dropped back to normal.

The White Chief was now a fixture, and I had many opportunities of renewing my acquaintance with Slim Jim and Bow-legs. They had taken me to their bosom since I had come through with the stakes. It was some time during the following summer that, seeing me limping from the effects of a long ride, they instigated the White Chief to propose my partaking of an Indian sweat bath.

Wilson had returned to England at the time and Cook was away, so that having no one at hand to tell me what it was like, I rashly consented and told him I would be ready at any time he and his Indians got down to the river by the ranch.

A week or two later, when I was busy over accounts, I was rudely disturbed by an Indian poking his head in through the open window and saying ' Ugh ! ' The day had been extremely hot and I was busy with a lot of slips of paper representing sales of beef, and was transferring the contents of same to a book. My time was fully occupied between fighting flies—for in those days the luxury of window screens had not penetrated to our remote region—and rescuing the slips which were being blown about by the wind. So when the interruption came I was so taken by surprise that I jumped into the air.

My first impression was that Geronimo had come himself to pay me a visit, but before I could retreat I was reassured by the grin on the Indian's face. He had by that time thrust his head and shoulders through and was more occupied in admiring the furnishing of the room than intent on his message, so that I had plenty of time to return to the normal. When my heart ceased fluttering I grunted back at him, and when I had eventually gained his attention he thrust forward a crumpled piece of paper on which the White Chief had scribbled a note saying that he and his following were down on the creek and awaiting my presence to invest me with the ' Order of the Bath.'

I wasn't very sure that I wanted to be invested, but the day was hot and the flies maddening, so I summoned up my Spanish and said : ' *Poco tiempo* ' (pretty soon), till the Indian apparently understood and took himself off. I then tried to put my accounts in order, but the flies renewing the attack with increased vigour, I finally clapped on my hat and prepared to face the ordeal.

I hadn't the vaguest idea of what was in store for me, but recollected I had promised the White Chief to go through with it, and he had pronounced it a sure cure for rheumatism and all stiffness of the muscles. I found them on the other side of the creek, about a quarter of a mile from the house, close by where a deep hole had been washed in the river bed, which at that time was about the only place in the creek which held water enough to hide a tadpole.

They were prepared for action. Most of the Indians were stark naked and the White Chief himself was sitting on a log devoid of all clothing except his pantaloons. They had two tepees, and the naked Indians were busily employed gathering stones and carrying them into these tents, where they piled them around the edges. I noticed they were particular about gathering only the surface stones which had been lying in the hot sun, and that they carefully examined the lower side of them, so I asked the chief what they intended doing with them.

He told me that they were preparing the Turkish bath, and that they were careful about selecting only those stones which were heated through and had no signs of moisture on the lower side.

The tepees themselves were just the ordinary Indian affairs, conical in form, with the pole or stick standing out through the top for a foot or more and somewhere around six feet in diameter at the base. They had evidently been long in use and were far from inviting. In addition to the dirty canvas the Indians had hung old saddle blankets and portions of their discarded clothing over them.

This, the chief gave me to understand, was to keep in the heat, so that they might derive full benefit from it. About that time I was taken in hand by Slim Jim and Bow-legs, who by signs and grunts indicated that it was time to remove my clothing. I wasn't so enthusiastic, so I dallied over the disrobing while I acquired further particulars from the White Chief. He explained that the temperature in the tepees was what it would be in the hot room of a Turkish bath ; that they would cover up all openings, so as to exclude all air ; that the last to enter would secure the entrance, and there they would sweat for as long as they were able to stand it.

It did not sound inviting, but he said that he was going into one of the tepees and that Jim would look after me in the other. He also added that he found it superior to any Turkish bath as a cure for rheumatism.

I didn't doubt his word, but at the same time I had no rheumatism. However, I was under the impression that I was going in alone with Jim, and as the White Chief was going to brave it in the other tepee I felt bound to go through with it. I soon divested myself of all clothing, much to the delight of Jim and Bow-legs, who prodded me all over to see if I was in condition and accompanied each prod with a grunt and ' Bueno ! ' ' Bueno ! ' and the other Indians who were not elsewhere employed stood around and grinned.

It was quite an ordeal standing stark naked before a crowd of grinning savages. The entrance to the tepees had been closed with blankets, and anyway they were so small that one had to go down on hands and knees to enter. I was given the post of honour, and when I had pulled aside the blankets and thrust my head in I thought of the Black Hole of Calcutta.

Jim was close behind me and more than half-way through before I got my feet clear, so I kept on past the centre before I turned and sat down. When I did so I discovered that there were others crawling in after him. They came one after the other in a continuous string, while I kept moving back till I struck the wall of the tent and was eventually crowded on to the hot stones. Still they kept coming, and to allow more room I was compelled to stand up. It was impossible to stand erect, but I got on my feet, and to this alone I ascribe the fact that I escaped suffocation.

I counted thirteen Indians crawling through the entrance into that small tent, and after that my head began to swim and I could count no more. That several more worked their way in before they sealed it up I judged by the sound, and then the atmosphere became so thick that I was oblivious of their presence. As each one came in he tucked himself away somewhere, for none of their heads were on a level with mine. How they managed it I really don't know.

They kept up a continuous chant that sounded like ' Heyah, heyah jing-a-jing jing,' which never ceased all the time they were in there. A few moments after the place had been sealed up they began to sweat, and then the atmosphere of Indian that assailed one's nostrils was indescribable. To say that the atmosphere was thick gives but a faint idea. I felt as if I could climb on to it.

How long I stood it is but a memory. I thought at the time it was more than half an hour, but believe it was considerably less than ten minutes. I groped vainly for the pole to pull the damn thing down, but couldn't reach it. Then I tried to scratch my way through the canvas, but that proved futile. In desperation I pushed the stones away with my bare feet, and catching the bottom of the tent in the soft sand I literally burrowed my way to fresh air and freedom.

How the denizens of the inferno took it I don't know. Once my head was in the air I thought of nothing but filling my lungs with the blessed ether and trying to expel the raw hide taste from my mouth. That they filled up the hole and went on with their chant was self-evident, but whether they invited any one to take my place I didn't wait to see, and I very much doubt if they could have squeezed another in.

I rushed to the creek, and getting down under the high bank where the water was deepest lay down in it, thinking what a happy relief it would be to drown. However, after a time I recovered, and with the aid of a pocket handkerchief and the sun I dried myself and resumed my clothes.

To relieve my feelings I filled a pipe and tried to smoke it, but it tasted of Indian and smelled of raw hide. For weeks I was unable to get rid of the taste—everything I touched and smelled was Indian.

It must have been fully half an hour after I got dressed before any of the others put in an appearance. Then an Indian crawled out who looked as if he had been dipped in oil. He rolled himself in the hot sand till he was entirely covered with it, then retired to the creek to wash it off. It reminded me of the days before blotting paper had been invented, when they sopped up the ink by throwing sand over it.

He was followed in a little while by the White Chief, who looked as if you had boiled him and taken him up before he was quite done. He rubbed the sweat off himself and also took to the water, omitting the sanding. I stalked over to the bank and sat down to watch him. I wanted to be sure that he was really alive and to find out by what agency he had managed to survive. When he had spat the water out of his mouth and I could get him to talk he said he enjoyed it and that it was really fine.

I didn't contradict him, but I thought that if he really meant it he could afford to be as wicked as he pleased ; for hell could have no terrors for a man so constituted.

About a month or more before the final surrender of Geronimo the White Chief received an assistant in the shape of a young cadet from West Point, who on receipt of his commission had been posted to the company of Navajo scouts. Knowing the chief's prejudices in regard to West Point, we wondered how they would get along. It was merely the inexperience of youth, but when we had settled down after dinner he expressed his views rather emphatically about the simplicity of being able to find your way through the country. He remarked that the employment of Indian scouts was entirely unnecessary. He said there were white men enough in the country to do all the scouting that was needed, and as for finding one's way through the mountains, why, to a man of intelligence, it was as easy as finding your way down Fifth Avenue.

This was a sore subject with the chief, for he was fond of his scouts and very proud of them. He bridled up and fairly snorted, while Fountain and I could scarcely suppress a smile. We tried to throw oil on the troubled waters and divert the conversation, but our young man was fairly started and not easily turned from his course. He gave us a long dissertation on the improvement of modern methods and the futility of being bound by fossilized traditions.

The chief held himself in check till I thought he was going to burst a blood-vessel, but at length he stood up and said : ' See here, my friend, I don't believe you could find your way back to camp without some one to guide you. Why, if I turned you loose in those mountains you'd starve to death in the midst of plenty, or you'd die of thirst within reach of water.' This only caused the young man to smile loftily, and he said he always carried a map of the country about with him and could find his way anywhere.

The upshot of the business was that the chief bet him five dollars that they would take him out, anywhere in the neighbouring mountains, and that if he allowed them a ten minutes' start, from the time of breaking camp, he would never catch up with them or even get sight of them before they got back to Camp Maddox. He added that the chances were they would have to send out and find him. After some further discussion a paper to this effect was drawn up and signed by both of them.

A week after that, when I was returning from a long day in the broken country on the east side of the river, I saw the chief and his scouts coming off a long, narrow *mesa* that divided Deep and Copper Creeks. I overtook them, and after the usual greetings to all my friends as I passed them rode up alongside the chief and asked what he had done with his ' strategist '. He grinned and asked me if I had been out in that country all day, indicating the land behind him whence he had just come. I said I had been back and forward through those hills the greater part of the day. He then wanted to know if I had seen anything of the cadet. I told him no. This appeared to afford him great satisfaction, and he told me that that morning when they broke camp he had proposed to the cadet that it was a favourable opportunity of putting his knowledge to the test. The latter had gladly acquiesced and agreed to give them ten minutes' start ; after which, if he succeeded in catching sight of them before they reached camp, he, the chief, was to forfeit the money.

The chief, on his part, had promised not to travel faster than the usual shuffling gait which the Western pony adopted when he had a long day's travel before him. He said that he had fully expected that the cadet would catch them up within an hour, but that they had been going steadily since early morning and so far had seen nothing of him. He had questioned me because he thought it possible the cadet might have been lurking behind them, in order to give him a surprise just before reaching camp, but he knew that if he had been waiting until they got off that long *mesa* he would have to show up immediately afterwards, and I would probably have seen him from the high ground on which I was riding. He now believed that he might have lost his way, and he thought it served him right, he was so damned cocksure : even asked him what his favourite brand of cigar was, as he proposed to treat when he had pocketed the stakes.

I accompanied them the rest of the way to camp, and on leaving promised to bear witness to the fact that the cadet had lost his bet. The conclusion we came to was that his horse had fallen lame and that he was obliged to continue his journey on foot. The chief hoped it would knock some of his fool theories out of him, and I ceased thinking about it and went on home.

It was late the following afternoon when, having nothing in particular on hand, I thought I would ride over to the camp and find out what had really happened. I found the chief looking a bit worried. He told me the cadet had not shown up. He didn't suppose he could have got really lost, but thought he might have strayed into Cooney or the new mining camp, Mogollon, and elected to stay there till he got rested.

I volunteered to go to Cooney for him and find out if he had been there or at Mogollon, but he said to wait a bit, as it was getting late and the Indians proposed to make medicine after it got dark and find out what had become of him. In the meantime he said he would probably show up and could superintend his own horoscope.

I stayed with him for supper, and when it was quite dark we walked down to the banks of the creek, where his charges had built a great fire and were busy in their preparations for making medicine. They had been preparing for some time, for they had built a small brush corral, which enclosed two moderate-sized cotton-wood trees. They had built a great fire, and immediately over it, some six feet from the ground, had run a bar with the ends resting on each of the trees. From this they had suspended a chain, and as we came down there were three men in the enclosure hanging a great camp-kettle so that it was immediately over the flame.

Then two of them retired to the fence, one on each side in line with the fire, and squatted down on the inside of the fence. The third man remained standing by the fire with a discarded stove poker in his hand, and with this wand he every now and again stirred the contents of the cauldron, peeping into it to see if it was working right.

The other Indians were all on the outside, completely surrounding the place three or four rows deep. Under Slim Jim's guidance room was made for us to get close up to the fence, but he intimated that no one was allowed inside except the man in the centre, who was to make 'Big Medicine' and his two assistants, who were sitting down by the fence.

There was a solemn hush over the audience. Every one watched the Medicine Man with bated breath. As the cauldron began to simmer he stirred it gently with his poker, and began a kind of chant very similar to the one I had heard while endeavouring to take the Indian bath. I don't know what they had put in the cauldron, but as it boiled up its aroma was wafted to our nostrils, and from what reached me through the folds of a handkerchief I had little difficulty in determining that it must have largely consisted of portions of the offal which they had brought away from the ranch, no doubt mixed with other filth in an advanced stage of maturity and of a particularly sacred character.

I recollected reading about the Augurs of old predicting the future from the entrails of freshly killed animals, and wondered if the tradition had descended to the Navajos. No doubt it had, only they didn't need them fresh.

The Medicine Man had painted his face with streaks of white and red and blue, and as the light of the fire flickered on them he looked a fairly respectable demon. As the stuff boiled up and its fumes spread, he used his little short poker with vigour, and his chant arose and increased in pace till it became a regular wail. Sometimes the two assistants joined in like well-trained acolytes, repeating the responses, and sometimes the entire congregation joined with a chorus which ceased as suddenly as it began and made one feel the hush that followed.

Despite our unbelieving souls the chief and I were more deeply impressed than we would care to acknowledge. As it boiled up, a greenish scum came to the top, which the Medicine Man raked off with his wand and distributed over the coals and towards his assistants in a kind of asperges. This was kept up with a few variations for about twenty minutes, when, the contents simmering down in the kettle, he peered closely into it, and raising his voice in a final chant waved both arms wildly in the air.

This was a signal to the acolytes. They rose immediately

and began throwing handfuls of sand and earth into the cauldron. This caused a great steam, which, fortunately, owing to the stillness of the night, went straight up in the air ; otherwise our position close against the fence would have become untenable. As it was, the weirdness of the proceedings had quite got hold of us, and like the others we looked on in silence, wondering what was to come next. This, however, was evidently the end of the ceremonial preparations, for the Medicine Man waved to his assistants, who immediately left the corral, and a gentle prod in the back from Jim and a grunt from the chief indicated that we, along with the rest of the congregation, were expected to disperse.

A final whiff from the savoury mess hastened our departure. We sought shelter to windward on the banks of the creek, where we sat down to smoke, while the Indians glided away like shadows in all directions. It was a lovely night, with the stars shining as they can shine only at that elevation. As we lighted our pipes I asked the chief in an awed whisper what His Eminence was going to do alone in the corral with that awful camp-kettle ? He said that he didn't know, but thought that when he had scattered the contents he had some way of telling what had happened, or was about to happen, but that, at any rate, he would let us know the result as soon as he was through.

Before we had finished a second pipe we got news of the result of the augury. His Eminence did not communicate personally with us, but sent us word through Jim, with the orderly as interpreter. He said the Señor, as he called him, was lost. That he had started from the camp ten minutes after the main body, as arranged, but had missed the trail and got into a wrong canyon, where, getting confused, he had travelled towards the sun instead of away from it, meaning that he had gone east instead of west ; that later on, getting off his horse, to climb down to some water, he had been unable to find him again, and was at the time wandering through the mountains on foot ; that though he had food in his pockets he was very hungry. He said that if he was to be found, they would have to look for him on the east side of the mountains, and that this was all he had to tell.

The whole thing sounded like a fairy tale, but in the light of after events it was uncanny.

At the time neither the chief nor I were inclined to pay much attention to it.   I promised to go and look for him the following day at Mogollon and Cooney, while the chief said he would go back to Devil's Creek with some of his Indians and try to trail him up.   The following day I rode to Cooney and Mogollon and hunted up all the prospectors and outliers, in those camps, amongst them my friend Cox, whom I found on sociable terms with the Scandahoovian widow, but nowhere could I get any tidings of our lost cadet.   I went out of my way when returning, to take in Camp Maddox, but found the chief had gone out to Devil's Creek and had not as yet returned.   Fountain and his men were also out somewhere, so that I had to return to the ranch with my ill success unreported.

I couldn't sleep very well that night.   I was constantly thinking about the cadet and what had become of him.   It was getting pretty serious.   It was the third day now since they had left him, and if he hadn't made his way to some settlement he was liable to starve to death or perish from thirst.   Though there was plenty of water in those mountains it was very easy to miss it if you didn't know where it was located.

My thoughts led me to recollect that there was a prospector named Zuk who had a camp somewhere up there, nearly due east of Pleasanton, and I decided to go and hunt him up the following day before reporting to the chief.   In pursuance of this I made an early start, and although I thought I had located the smoke of his camp-fire while crossing Whitewater in the early morning, it took me nearly all day to find him.

When I did find him he had seen nothing of our lost sheep. After our interview he directed me to a trail which led directly to Pleasanton, and which was much easier going than the one by which I had come.   On reaching Pleasanton I struck the stage road and was jogging along when I was attracted by the noise of wheels, and, looking round, discovered the stage.   I pulled up to hear whatever news Al brought from Silver City.   When he got alongside the first question he asked me was whether we had lost any of the soldiers from Camp Maddox.   I told him how the cadet had disappeared and that we were still hunting him.   All the time I was wondering how Al could have got track of him, as his route was entirely out of any course one could possibly expect him to take.

When I had finished explaining Al told me that a bedraggled individual in the last stages of exhaustion and with the shoes worn off his feet had come to the L C Ranch the evening before, shortly after he, Al, got there. He had been unable to give an account of himself. In fact, as Al expressed it, he was ' nutty '. They had taken him in and given him coffee and put him to bed. From his clothes, which were almost in rags, they came to the conclusion that the Government had some claim on him.

Up to the time Al left he was more or less delirious. He talked of having to live on pine bark, which Al thought funny, as they had found a piece of stale bread, as hard as a rock, in one of his pockets. From my description of the man we were looking for Al said that it might be him ; but he was so emaciated it would be hard to recognize him. I, however, felt sure that it must be him, and hurried as fast as I could, not stopping at the ranch, but going straight to Camp Maddox to apprise the chief.

The latter had just returned from his trip. He was much relieved, and agreed with me that the wanderer who had turned up at the White House must be the cadet. He then told me of their own efforts. He said they had followed his trail from where they left him for some fifteen or twenty miles. They had found his horse ten miles or more from where he started. The latter had evidently been tied by the bridle rein and had escaped, as the rein was broken.

The Indians said that he had been scared by a shot, no doubt fired by his owner to try to attract attention, or for some other purpose. In proof of their statement they had produced an empty cartridge case picked up in a nearby canyon. The trail had led them in all directions, and back and forward over the same ground, as if he had been endeavouring to find the place he had started from. They had found where he had got a drink and where he had lain down for a while, they presumed, to sleep. Also they had found where he had cut great strips of bark off the pine trees. The chief thought at first it had been done as a guide to any one following him, but the Indians showed him the marks of teeth on the inside of some pieces thrown away, and no doubt it had been done to satisfy his hunger.

They had eventually lost all track of him on the rocky ridges which overlooked Gila Valley and were obliged to return home. It was on the way home that they picked up his horse, which had evidently rolled with the saddle on, for the latter and the canteen attached to it were all crushed and broken.

All this coincided with Al's story of the wanderer's eating pine bark and still more closely with the account of the Medicine Man, deduced from his filthy pot of boiled offal. I asked the chief what he thought of it and of this making medicine. He said he didn't know. That those Indians were crafty rascals, and that no doubt they knew pretty well what a tenderfoot would do when he got lost in the mountains. But I pointed out that our friend the seer had said that he was hungry and had food in his pocket, and that Al's statement of their having found a piece of stale bread there was more than a mere coincidence. He scratched his head and said he gave it up, and we let it go at that.

We both agreed that despite his being fresh the lad must have had good stuff in him, for it was no joke getting lost in those mountains and making your way over forty miles to a place of refuge without food and probably without water. The chief said that as soon as he had forgotten all they tried to teach him at West Point he would be all right ; but I judged him to be slightly prejudiced on this point and did not pursue the subject.

The next day the chief went off to the White House to identify him, and stopped at the ranch on his way back three or four days later. He said that he had found our friend in bad shape, but they had taken him to Silver City, and after a few days' rest intended sending him to San Antonio, Texas.

He had been unable to explain his wanderings, further than that he had got lost and that he thought his horse must have broken loose and got away when he was down in a canyon looking for water. After that he had climbed the highest point in an effort to locate himself, and the only open country he could see was the Gila Valley. From where he stood it looked almost beneath his feet, but evidently it had taken him a long time to reach it, for after that he lost all track of things till he found himself in bed at the White-House.

He recollected eating pine bark, both to allay his thirst and because he was very hungry ; but he didn't know that he had bread in his pocket, and supposed he must have put it there before he left camp. The chief said that his greatest trouble was to keep him from paying the five dollars he had lost, and the only way he could pacify him was by promising to have a bottle at his expense after he got well. That the boy was all right he gave ample proof in later years, for I recollect seeing his name prominently mentioned about the time of the Chino-Japanese war.

And that was the last I saw of Rogers. I was away when new orders came, and he left a little note saying he had to mizzle away with his Indians but hoped we'd meet again. I missed him sadly. He was a cheery companion and has always occupied a warm place in my memory.

It was shortly after that the news came of Geronimo's surrender in Old Mexico. We had a farewell dinner and a silent toast to our departed friends. Altogether it was a sad little affair, though we tried to be cheery. Those soldier boys had come into our lives in stirring times and created an epoc in our humdrum existence. They had been with us for nearly two years and had borne their part like real men despite a lot of unjust and adverse criticism. I have always looked back to the time they spent with us as the pleasantest period of our long experience on the frontier.

CHAPTER X

LIFE at the ranch was rather lonely and depressing after the departure of the soldiers. For them it must have been a godsend to get back to comparative quietness and civilization from their long sojourn in the field ; but their presence, besides insuring protection, had lent a social zest to our otherwise rather solitary existence.

That summer of 1886 we were busy improving the exterior of the ranch, setting out trees in an ornamental way as well as establishing an orchard. All summer it was exceptionally dry. Great black clouds that looked as if they must develop into a deluge came up every afternoon, but just as they seemed about to break the wind would get up and everything would end in a cloud of dust. The water in the river was a bare trickle, less than an inch in depth, and one could cross it dryshod anywhere. When things were at their worst Ed had taken a lay off, saying the cattle were so poor it was impossible to do anything with them, and that we would be fortunate if we did not lose the entire herd. When the rains came at last there were on the ranch with me only Old Charlie, Henry, Indian Jack, and a man named Jasper Thomason, who answered to the name of Jap.

Many strange things came to my notice during that drought. I had heard of cattle climbing trees, but was disposed to regard it as an exaggeration, till one day I saw a great lanky steer, five or six years old, standing on his hind legs, with his forefeet resting on a cotton-wood limb, eight or nine feet in the air. While in this position he was hooking down with his horn branches which still held a few green leaves within his reach, and devouring them.

So intent was he on his work that he paid not the slightest attention to me. I waited for some time to see if he would pull himself up any higher, but he didn't. I shouted to encourage him, but he only dropped to his feet, snorted, and ran away. That was the nearest I have seen of any cattle climbing trees, but he was doing his best, and since then I have been more credulous.

Just prior to the rains some of the outlaw cattle from the

hills had been coming to the river for water. They never approached the river except at sundown, and then only in ones or twos. They drank hurriedly, suspiciously, like wild animals, and disappeared as soon as they were full ; but by watching for them we succeeded in putting the W S brand on many a maverick that might otherwise never have been tallied.

Now, however, everything was changed ; grass was springing up everywhere and what had been a sandy waste was in a few days covered with verdure. The cattle, which had been merely living skeletons, within a week began to grow sleek and shed off their ragged coats. I did not think it possible that such a transformation could come about in so short a time and doubt if it could be done on any other feed than gramma grass. A more succulent food would have bloated and killed them. The change was almost miraculous, but I have seen it occur several times under similar conditions during my forty years of ranch life.

We were now reinforced at the ranch by our friend Cox, who was anxious to earn sufficient funds to celebrate his approaching nuptials with the fair lady who ran the boarding-house. We readily found him a job, as there was now plenty of water for irrigation, and he claimed to be an expert at this method of farming, having gained his experience amongst the Mexicans.

We had at this time a pet cinnamon bear called Ned, and also a pet deer, of the black-tail or mule variety. The latter had been made much of by everybody until he became a regular nuisance. It was almost impossible to keep him out of the house. Shortly after his arrival he took up with Mr. Cox, sleeping with him at night and accompanying him through the day at his task of irrigation. If Cox went in a wagon, the deer followed it, dropping behind every now and again, then breaking into a run to catch up. If he felt like riding, he jumped into the wagon and tramped over everybody till he reached Cox.

When it came to irrigating he accompanied Cox to the alfalfa field, and while Cox leant on his shovel, contemplating the spreading waters, the deer amused itself by nipping the tender shoots and occasionally bounding around and endeavouring to attract his attention by playfully butting at him. These little attentions were generally received good-naturedly, but if persevered in were apt to be resented.

The fact is, Cox was contemplating his approaching wedding, and when his thoughts were too rudely disturbed he would attempt to ward off the intruder with the shovel. The deer looked on this as part of the play, and as Cox never succeeded in hitting him there was nothing to disabuse his mind ; so the merry game went on from day to day, according to the mood of the actors, and might have continued for all summer had not their relations become strained.

I don't think that Cox intended to work for very long, in any event, but his stay was brought to an abrupt termination through the following incident.   He and the deer had gone off to the alfalfa field as usual, and were apparently on the best of terms until the latter got hold of a piece of sacking that Cox had nailed to a stick in order to assist him in making temporary dams in the irrigation ditch.

He employed several of these devices.   They consisted of old gunny-sacks split in two and nailed to a strip of wood which, when laid across the ditch, allowed the sacking to drop loose into it.   In this way it held the earth and prevented it washing away while the dam was in course of construction.

This particular piece of sacking had been taken off a side of bacon (known as sow-belly), and being thoroughly impregnated with salt had attracted the attention of the deer.   It tasted nice and juicy and he hadn't had a good feed of salt for some time, so he promptly appropriated it and walked off contentedly chewing it.   Cox needed it and promptly pursued him.

The deer looked on this as a new phase of the game and easily avoided him.   He led Cox several times round the field and reduced him to a state of frenzy before he finally dropped it.   By this time it was compressed into a ball, but evidently still succulent, for he stood over it on the ground and turned to face Cox and to renew the game when the latter got close enough.

Cox, now too much exhausted to continue the pursuit, threw the shovel at him.   This caused him to bound lightly to one side and Cox rushed in and secured his head-gate.   He carefully smoothed it out and having recovered his shovel walked back to where he had been irrigating.

Old Charlie and I, who had been watching and enjoying the scene, thought that it was all over, but we had reckoned without the deer.   The latter evidently was not prepared for the loss of the juicy morsel, for as soon as Cox had departed he came back to where he had left it on the ground. Not finding it, he looked up, and seeing something flutter in the latter's hands, as he spread it out, went slowly in pursuit of him, bent on its recovery.

By this time Cox had got back to his irrigation, and having unfolded his head-gate prepared to put it to use. He carefully surveyed the ground till he had selected the highest point, and placing the stick across the ditch allowed the sacking to drop loosely into it. He then threw in a shovelful or two of earth, but the spread of the sacking not being to his liking he went down on his knees and bent over to arrange it.

This necessitated the use of both hands. He laid the shovel beside him while, with his head completely immersed, only his hinder portion was visible above the stalks of alfalfa. By this time the deer, who had observed the whole proceeding, was within ten or twelve feet of him, and seeing his advantage lowered his head and struck him like a battering-ram. He struck him with such force that he carried on over the ditch for some fifteen or twenty feet before he could turn around and study the effect of his manœuvre.

When he did so Cox had disappeared entirely from view. The deer stamped his forefeet on the ground, as if preparing to renew the assault. There was no immediate response, however, and Cox was so long putting in an appearance that Charlie and I, who were almost overcome with laughter, hastened to his rescue. Before we reached him, however, his head, streaming with mud and water, appeared above the alfalfa.

To say that he was angry would convey but a feeble idea of his mental state. His face flamed under the rays of the sun like a torch. Entirely ignoring our proffers of help, he got on his feet and seizing the shovel went for that deer with murder in his heart. The deer, assuming it to be part of the game, jumped nimbly out of his way and showed a disposition to rescue the coveted sack from the ditch.

In this, however, he was foiled by another furious attack. Then perceiving that matters were serious, he bounded briskly away, followed by Cox in a rabid state of mind. The deer made straight for the corral, and Cox, failing to reach him, hurled the shovel after him, and disdaining to pick it up made his way to the bunk-house. Thither Charlie and I followed him, striving to control our laughter.

We found him endeavouring to rub the mud and water out of his eyes with a gunny-sack. He could see nothing funny about the incident ; in fact, he was hurt by our want of sympathy and declared his intention of quitting. Being in no mood to reason with him I got him his cheque and he left the same evening for Mogollon.

Shortly after the rains ceased Mr. Cox returned with his bride and found everything in readiness. He was followed later on by Wilson, who came out from England about the end of October. Then we were all a happy family again assembled at the ranch.

Nothing particularly exciting occurred that fall. Perhaps the greatest event was shipping our pet bear to the Zoological Gardens in Philadelphia. The wherefore of this takes us back to the days prior to the Indian raid when a Professor Cope and other celebrities had been touring New Mexico in search of bugs. They had stayed at the W S Ranch for a short time when the bear was a tiny cub, and duly admired him. The question arose as to what kind of a pet he would make when he arrived at years of maturity. They expressed a wish to have him shipped to Philadelphia rather than have him destroyed, and said they would be responsible for all arrangements and expenses in connexion therewith.

Afterwards the whole thing was forgotten, but Wilson had run across some of them on his way out from England and they had inquired about the bear, reminding him of his promise. As a matter of fact, the bear was getting rather unmanageable, so Wilson decided to get rid of him. In a way we were sorry to lose him, for in his amiable moods he was quite companionable, but he had his bad spells. One could generally detect when these were coming on by the persistent manner in which he kept sucking his paw, and while thus engaged it was judicious to leave him severely alone. When otherwise employed he rather liked being petted and scratched, and if he became too demonstrative with his teeth was easily brought to terms by seizing his lower jaw and wrapping his own heavy chaps over the teeth. In this way one could keep a hand in his mouth, and as he was unable to squeeze it without detriment to his own lips he at once became gentle.

The shipping of him to Philadelphia was not such a simple

matter as one might think. To begin with, he had to be hauled to Silver City in a wagon, a trip which at that time took fully four days. For this purpose a cage had to be constructed, and it was necessary that the cage should fit the wagon bed, as well as leave ample room for Bruin.

In course of time a dwelling was constructed which for weight alone was unparalleled and later drew caustic remarks from the employees of the Express Company. It was fitted with a drop door which fell like a guillotine when a peg was pulled out, and could only be raised with the aid of a crowbar. The inside was fitted with a trough for food and the half of a kerosene can nailed to the floor for water. That it never did hold any was entirely due to the bear being uncultured and chewing up the can before one had the chance of testing it.

When all was in readiness it was conveyed to the corral, and set down a short distance from where Ned was chained so that he should have a chance of inspecting it and growing familiar with it. Then a day was set apart for sending him off, and Jap was told off to drive the team and take him to Silver City.

As became a young man from the country about to pay a visit to the town Jap was dressed in his best and was exempt from the more menial task of putting the bear in his cage. This we would have readily forgiven him, had he confined himself to his legitimate pursuits, but when he saw fit to perch himself in security on the top of the gate and laugh at us when we were having difficulty with our friend the bear, why, we felt more than recompensed at the Nemesis which eventually overtook him.

But I am anticipating. When the corral gates had been securely closed and we were all inside we approached Ned in the friendliest spirit. He was in a tolerable frame of mind, and though somewhat surprised at the number of his visitors inclined to meet us on friendly terms. He sniffed around for expected titbits while we unchained him, and when satisfied that he was loose made a determined rush for the gate, with visions of the garbage-can flashing through his brain.

He was hampered somewhat by half a dozen men hanging on to the chain, and was only brought to a halt with difficulty before he reached the gate. He was then manœuvred and coaxed around to the front of the cage, into which a piece of meat had been thrown as an inducement. It looked good to him all right, but he seemed to think it could be reached more readily through the bars than through the open doorway.

When finally got in front of the door his suspicions were aroused, and while refusing to enter he reached for it with his front foot. Advantage was taken of his doing so to pass the chain through the cage and through the bars at the back, where it was taken hold of by every one who found space to grasp it. Then all hands tugged, while those that were behind put their shoulders against his back and pushed with all their might.

Ned lost interest in the decoy and braced himself to resist with all his formidable strength. There was a moment of intense strain, and then the strap around his neck to which the chain was attached gave way and he fell over backwards. In doing so he brought all those behind him down in a heap, where they mauled each other violently in their endeavours to regain their feet and get out of the way.

Ned, after the manner of bears, continued his backward roll till he came on to his feet. When he did so he was fighting mad, and it might have fared badly with some of those on the ground had not two dogs which lived on the place created a diversion. One of these was a liver-coloured pointer called Patsy, the other a nondescript animal called Chug. Patsy was the first to arrive and, to his astonishment, received a cuff which knocked him half-way across the corral, where, picking himself up, he ran off howling and took no further part in the proceedings. Chug, however, was made of sterner stuff, and taking advantage of the cuff delivered to Patsy, dived in behind the shoulder, from which he retreated immediately with a mouthful of hair.

From thenceforth Ned devoted himself entirely to him, and they growled and snarled and rolled over until they finally brought up in a corner of the shed which was used for hanging meat and storing rock-salt. Here poor Chug would probably have had his life squeezed out had we not come to the rescue. Cook had seized a raw hide *rietta*, and followed by several of us he climbed on to the pile of rock-salt, and from this point of vantage diverted Ned's attention by attempts to lasso him.

The place was confined and he found it necessary to make several attempts before being successful. It was a simple matter getting the rope over his head, but quite ineffectual, for every time it tightened up he scratched it off with his paw. But at length by a deft turn of the wrist Cook managed to get the noose over one of the forefeet as well as the neck and thus in a position behind the shoulder from which Ned was unable to pull it off. As soon as the noose was in position we all seized the end of the rope and began to pull on it with all our might, hoping to drag the bear into the open.

We might as well have pulled on a rock, but the tightening of the rope was uncomfortable, and hoping to escape from both it and the dog he came right over us of his own accord. He came with a rush, and this unexpected manœuvre prostrated us all in a bunch. We hung on to the rope, or most of us did, and he pulled us about like a bunch of flies before we were able to regain our feet.

The progress over the lumps of rock-salt was decidedly unpleasant and over the floor of the corral not exactly comfortable, but what seared us, as Mr. Kipling puts it, ' like a white-hot brand ' was the unseemly laughter and jeers of Jap from his point of vantage on top of the gate.

When we managed to get to our feet we were sadly out of breath and unable to express our thoughts in any intelligent form, but we gritted our teeth and paid strict attention to the matter in hand. I don't know how many of us were attached to that rope, but the last ten or twelve feet of it was sadly congested, and the competition to move closer to the front and create more room was not what might be called keen.

That bear dragged us all over the place as if we were chaff, and all the time Jap kept up his infernal badinage. However, all things have an end, and in the course of time the bear, more by his own will than by our guidance, came sufficiently close to the cage to enable us to pass the rope through the doorway and out through the bars at the back. By taking a turn in the rope we were able to hold him till help came rushing to our aid.

Now that we had brought the beast to a standstill all the boys who had been unable to catch hold while we were being whirled around and around jumped from their perches and joined in, so that by sheer weight of numbers we dragged Ned unwillingly to his doom. As we brought him slowly round Chug joined in and nipped his heels. This annoyed

him, and he covered the last few feet with a rush. Some
one pulled out the peg and the door came down with a run.

Ned was now secure, though in the worst of tempers. It
only remained to get the cage, with him inside, on to the
wagon. The gates of the corral had been thrown open, but
the team refused to approach the cage, so it was necessary
to back them up as near as we could get them, and then,
so to speak, to take Mohammed to the mountain.

This was a matter of levers and rollers. During the
operation Jap continued his ribald remarks. He insinuated
that we were delaying him from reaching the Siggins in
daylight, where he had hoped to make a proper display of
himself and his captive.

However, Ned was soon to take the matter in hand and
requite us for our self-control. With the aid of planks we
got the heavy cage at last on the wagon bed, and putting
a roller under it we ran it up to the front end till the back
of it rested against the driver's seat. All the time this was
going on Ned had been too busy reducing to infinitesimal
fractions the fixtures which had been installed for his
comfort. Now that his water-can, which had afforded some
gratifying resistance, was reduced to indistinguishable pulp,
he looked around for fresh worlds to conquer.

There was nothing in front except the empty length of
the wagon-bed, so he swung around to survey matters from
the back of the cage. Here things were more favourable,
for his hated prison served as an additional rest for the
driver's back. The very respectability of Jap's garments
must have been an insult to him, for without the slightest
warning he reached through the bars and getting his claws
in Jap's collar literally ripped the clothes off his back.

Our first intimation was an unearthly yell from Jap,
followed by an attempt of the team to break away. The
latter was quickly checked, and then we had full liberty to
admire Jap, standing up in front of the seat with his beautiful Sunday suit ripped from collar to tail. The bear had
made a clean job of it and not only taken the vest and shirt,
but even caused a slight abrasion to the skin. As for poor
Jap, all his debonair manner had fled and he was the most
abject creature one could possibly imagine.

Lord, how we laughed ! If it had not been for the
necessity of looking after the team, which had become restless, we would have simply rolled on the ground to relieve

the paroxysm. As it was, we were just helpless, and every time we looked at Jap it broke out afresh. He stood on the front of that wagon for fully five minutes while he examined each mutilated garment in detail, and then remarking that some people were very funny he jumped to the ground and retreated ignominiously to the house.

When Jap returned he was clothed in a long overcoat which had seen much service and was in strong contrast to his former gallant display. We admonished him to take good care of the bear and deliver him over with all the necessary pomp and circumstance due to his rank, but he disdained to reply, and gathering up the reins drove off without a word. We felt amply avenged and a holy calm descended on our previously outraged feelings. Ned was delivered to the authorities in due course, and arrived at Philadelphia without mishap, where it is to be hoped he led a happy and uneventful life, for beyond an acknowledgment of his arrival we never got any further news of him.

When Jap returned he had a new suit of clothes, which were duly admired, but for the sake of the peace of the outfit it was not considered good form to allude to them, except in his absence.

That we missed Ned, after his turbulent departure, goes without saying. We still had the deer, but we were compelled to look with disapproval on his depredations, now that we had become sufficiently civilized to raise a garden. Nothing was sacred to him. We could have forgiven him for eating our lettuce and annuals that could have been replaced by seed, but when it came to perennials and shrubs that had been imported from England our hearts were hardened.

He had endeared himself to us in many ways, and despite the fact that he had grown fat and succulent we hesitated to slaughter him. At first we had endeavoured to give him away, but our attempts were unavailing, for he always returned as soon as he got loose. This meant that he usually arrived back at the ranch in the middle of the night and woke up the household, tramping round the porch and endeavouring to effect an entrance. When successful, he either stuck his cold, slimy nose into your face, before you were fully awake, or jumped into bed with you and lay on your chest. Then, being an early riser, he was liable to devour your socks or some more necessary portion of your raiment before there was a chance of rescue. All this and other minor offences we might have stood ; but when it came to browsing on our cherished rose-bushes we rose up and condemned him, without a dissentient voice.

Having acquired a sort of military complex, through our long association with the soldiers, we tried him by court martial, and as he offered no defence he was promptly condemned and turned over to the provost-marshal, in this instance Mr. Cook, for execution. It was intended to carry out the sentence *in camera* the following morning, but the deer broke away on being returned to cells, and Mr. Cook, who was a noted marksman, ended his career with a ·22 bullet : a rather novel weapon in those days and a remarkable shot—in the centre of the forehead at almost a hundred yards.

This was almost Cook's last official act, for he and Wilson agreed to part very shortly afterwards. The assumption of family cares called for a more domestic way of life and they parted with mutual esteem and respect.

After he had gone a good many of his duties fell to my lot, and Ed having come back to us resumed his position as range foreman. Wilson stayed on at the ranch until well into the following spring, and I attended my first Cattle Convention in Denver some time during the early part of the year. There were a number of young Englishmen there, all more or less interested in the cattle business, amongst them being Wyndham-Quin and a young fellow named Ogilvy, who carried a very big stick. I also met a man named Maude, who had been in the 71st Highland Light Infantry, some of whose brother-officers I had known before coming to America, and we had a good time together.

It was there I also had the pleasure of meeting for the first time both W. J. Tod and Murdo McKenzie, who at the time, I think, were connected with the Prairie Cattle Co. Also poor Francis Clutton, with whom I was to come in contact more frequently in later years. Another surprise was a man named Theodore White, whose brother Cecil White, of Carrick-on-Shannon, County Leitrim, Ireland, might almost be termed a neighbour of ours in Ireland.

In regard to the business of the convention itself, things did not seem to be much in harmony, and they accomplished practically nothing, beyond paving the way for a closer co-ordination of the stock interests, to be worked out in future years. Gillett, as he had threatened through the newspapers prior to the convention, entertained us with a long speech, in which he undertook to cure all the ills that live stock fell heirs to, provided we entered into a combine after the manner of the Standard Oil Co. and formed a trust which would include all the cattle, sheep, and swine in the United States and Canada.

The stock was to be apportioned *pro rata*, according to the number of cattle owned by the investors, and they were to receive bonds in lieu of their lands and amount of invested capital. It was a large order and not without hope for those in a position to manipulate and control a majority of the stock. He wound up with a fierce denunciation of the Chicago packers, who were alluded to as the ' Big Four '. He claimed that failure to comply with his schemes would result in all the cowmen of the country becoming bondsmen to the packers, and sat down amidst absolute silence. Evidently recognizing from the lack of applause that the sympathy of the assembly was not with him, he jumped to his feet again and announced that he was going to quit the business. The company didn't seem interested and his final remarks were almost lost in a hum of conversation.

The convention was presided over by Colonel Dick Head, known throughout the range as Dick Head and at that time looked upon as the beau-ideal cowman. My friend, G. L. Brooks of Socorro, was also a conspicuous member of the assembly, attended by his faithful henchman Slickery Jim, and represented the Fourth Estate from New Mexico. The interest of the delegates seemed largely concentrated in a rumour that Congress was about to pass an Act appropriating the sum of three million dollars for the suppression of foot-and-mouth disease, an epidemic of which had broken out somewhere in the East and threatened to spread to the range country.

In company with Maude, who enjoyed the sobriquet of ' Daddy Long Legs ' and was familiar with all the ropes, I did the town and enjoyed a sumptuous repast at Tortoni's. We also visited a Scotch gentleman a short distance from the city and saw some prize shorthorns, also sampled some excellent Scotch whisky. Alfred Rowe and Harold Carlisle entertained me at the Denver Club, and, taking it all in all, from this point of view, I was inclined to look on the convention as a decided success.

On returning to the ranch I had nothing in particular to report to Wilson, except the failure of the convention to appreciate Mr. Gillett and his stupendous scheme, which he agreed with me had great possibilities for an ambitious speculator. Ed at the time had not yet returned to us and we were without the services of a regular foreman. Nevertheless cattle were bringing a fair price and it became necessary to do something to put some of the W S steers on the market.

A visit from Montague Stephens of the S U Ranch, who had returned with me from Denver, led to an arrangement to throw our forces together and ship a mixed train-load from both herds to Kansas City. The foreman of the S U was a boy named R. A. Jones, who had been a W S hand and had taken over their outfit at a time of stress and difficulty, so that he was well acquainted with both ranges and in a position to do justice to both outfits. The cattle were in fine condition after the plentiful rains of the previous summer, so that altogether the shipping of our first train-load to market took place under favourable auspices.

We all worked like blacks and were quite exhilarated and full of admiration for those big four- and five-year-old steers with their sleek coats and long, keen horns. We got them off early and they came on the market about the beginning of May or end of April. They were in fine condition and made a ready sale. It took nearly a week for the telegram sent us by Stevens, who accompanied them, to reach us, and when we realized that they had brought us three dollars per hundredweight the very morning of their arrival we were duly elated.

This was quite a big price for Southern cattle in those days, and Wilson at once resolved to gather another herd, hoping to dispose of them before there was any break in prices. The outfit was away on the S U range at the time, and by the time they got back to the W S it was nearly the end of May. Also the steers were not so plentiful as when we threw the first herd together, so that, what with one thing and another, it was well into July before they were ready for the road.

They were a good-looking lot of cattle, however, not quite so heavy as the first shipment, but mainly threes and fours with a few long twos to fill out. The market had been going off a little, but as yet there was nothing like a break, and our hopes of their bringing a good price ran high. If anything they were in better flesh than the first lot and we hoped they would bring us at least three dollars ten cents.

Wilson had decided to return to England about this time and aimed to reach Kansas City about the same time as the cattle, but something turned up to delay him, and when we got to Silver City the cattle had already reached Kansas City. As he got on the train he got a telegram from there saying they had an offer of two dollars ninety cents for them and requesting a reply by wire. Neither of us thought this good enough, and as the train was about to move out he got me to wire saying to hold them till he got there.

This was practically my first official act as general manager and superintendent of the W S Ranch, the duties of which I took over automatically, there being no specific agreement between Wilson and myself with regard to the matter.

From Kansas City I heard from him that they had been unable to sell the steers, the market having gone from bad to worse. They had, however, made arrangements to pasture them in Kansas, and he had come to an agreement with the commission firm to put them on the market, should there be any improvement in the current prices.

Despite the predictions of the stock journals and the commission men, however, no improvement occurred and prices got lower and lower. When the summer was over an arrangement was made through the commission firm to winter them, with the understanding that they were to come on the market the first thing the following spring. All predictions were in favour of an improved market at that time, and as there was plenty of hay and shelter, everything seemed satisfactory.

I was looking forward to the receipt of a nice fat sum the following April or May to meet expenses, but was doomed to be sadly disappointed. Some time in late December I received a wire from the commission firm to say the people who were pasturing our cattle had gone into bankruptcy, and wanting to know what they were to do with the cattle. Not realizing the full extent of the disaster I wired back to hold them. To this they replied in a lengthy message, which explained that although the creditors could not touch our cattle they had got a court order sequestering the feed and that it was necessary to come to a decision at once.

Some further exchange of telegrams brought out the fact

that it was impossible to find any other place to transfer them to, as the feed was more valuable than the cattle. The result was they had to go on the market and were bought up by some of the packers for rather less than a dollar a hundredweight, and when the proceeds were realized they failed by forty cents to cover the expenses.

This was our first experience of marketing cattle, and though we had done pretty well with the first train-load we had managed to get rid of some four hundred head of fully matured beasts in the second instance without realizing a cent. It so disgusted me with the market that fully ten years or more elapsed before I could be induced to ship another animal there, and it was the only instance in my experience where an entire train-load of cattle failed to bring in even one cent to the producers.

Wilson took it like the philosopher and gentleman that he was, and told me to go ahead and forget it.

CHAPTER XI

THE year 1888 brought news from Wilson that he was about to get married, and this gave rise to considerable discussion amongst the boys as to the upbringing of the bride and whether her tastes ran to country or city life. Also there was fierce rivalry as to which of them would have the honour of furnishing her a horse from his mount.

When it became known that they intended to visit the ranch on their bridal tour the polishing of spurs, saddles, and other accoutrements would have done credit to a British regiment about to embark on foreign service. Even Old Charlie came into competition, and having spent an entire day polishing up Pow-a-Sheik, our recently acquired thoroughbred stallion, even oiling his hooves, was anxious to know if I did not consider him a perfect lady's mount. But at last it was generally conceded that the most suitable animal was a little black in my mount known as Chinuk.

Besides carrying off the competition in the furnishing of a mount my personal contribution to the coming reception took the form of the construction of a wedding-cake. The recipe was extracted from the pages of Mrs. Beeton, a copy of which had been sent to Wilson by his sister prior to his leaving for England. The time and labour devoted to his exploit could have been used by an expert to construct an entire bakery. But when it was finished, it was quite a respectable-looking cake, with several inches of almond icing on the top, all hand-made and the almonds pounded in a mortar filched from a drug-store in Silver City.

When word came about the middle of January that they had landed in New York and were actually on their way out West the excitement became intense and the necessity for sleep seemed superfluous. Without a dissentient voice it was decided that the indignity of having to stay over at the White House must be eliminated from the journey from Silver City. We had eight dandy horses at the ranch, and with four hitched up to a light buggy and a change of teams half-way, the eighty odd miles between daylight and dark did not seem an impossibility, despite the evil condition of the roads.

So far it had never been accomplished, or attempted as far as I know ; but if we had claim to being pioneers, what did that amount to ? We resolved to drive them through in one day between daylight and dark. Some genius suggested that if we made arrangements with the livery stable in Silver City we might have two relays on the road and thus be independent of the muddy roads. I went to Silver City, made the necessary arrangements with the livery people, and sent our own span back to the Gila, with a whole twenty-four hours to rest up.

Mr. and Mrs. Wilson made their appearance in due course and, having rested for a day in Silver City, we made the memorable trip in something under ten hours. The last fifteen miles were made at a hand-gallop and the distance covered in less than an hour and a half.

It must have been an uncommonly rough trip for Mrs. Wilson and her maid, who occupied the back seat on the buggy, but she was delighted with everything she saw and never complained. Wilson and I, who occupied the front seat, were rather anxious to convey the idea that this was our usual method of getting to the ranch, but whether we succeeded or not I never knew.

The boys had intended to form an escort and shepherd us in for the last mile or two, but we made such good time that we actually arrived an hour before they expected us As for Mrs. Wilson, everything was new to her and she was delighted. The comforts of the ranch after her long journey were much appreciated, especially a bath-room, with hot and cold water turned on, which we had installed in the new wing.

When the wedding-cake was produced—our *pièce de résistance*—she was gracious enough to partake of some without demur and without fatal results. Their arrangements had already been made to go on to Australia, and to our great regret they only stayed with us for a couple of weeks. Those were two memorable weeks, however, in our ranch life. Her presence and graciousness created an entirely new atmosphere, and we on our part did all in our power to make her stay a pleasant one. The whole ranch was sunk in gloom after their departure, and all sorts of schemes were suggested that might induce them to take up their permanent abode there.

About this time our friend Jap, in whom the bear had taken such an interest, got into trouble.

Jap had been the original owner of a portion of the land and some of the cattle which Wilson had bought when first entering the cattle business, and he had worked as a hand on the W S since its initiation. When Wilson left and I took charge, however, he decided to quit, ostensibly for the purpose of getting married. He had been paying attention to one of the young Meader ladies, who were our immediate neighbours. All the other boys on the ranch also paid attentions, but he seemed to be a favoured suitor.

It was therefore a surprise to us when we heard some weeks after his departure that the young lady had married another gentleman of the name of Potter. All sorts of rumours were afloat as to the pressure that had been brought to bear on her by a belligerent mother; there was no denying that Mr. Potter, though endowed with worldly goods, had no pretensions to compete with the debonair Jap in personal appearance.

The first intimation I had of the tragedy was meeting with Pa Meader. He seemed to be in a dilemma, and confided to me in a whisper that Jap was in trouble, saying that he had killed Potter and that it would stand him in hand to have his friends rally to his assistance.

The old gentleman was badly rattled as to what course he should pursue under the circumstances. Potter was his son-in-law, but he had known Jap since he was a baby and thought a sight of him. We had a little talk and he left me in a better frame of mind, saying that he would just be a looker-on, but thought Jap would need all the help he could get if he was going to come clear.

It seemed a nasty business and I hated being mixed up with it, but Jap was under arrest at Cooney and it behoved me to go there and try to find out what had really occurred. When I got there I found Jap was not in durance vile as I expected, but rather in open arrest under the care of a deputy, and they were both refreshing themselves at the local saloon.

As far as I could learn from Jap's own story and from several of his friends he and the lady had not been exactly discreet. He had taken her for lonely rides on several occasions when Mr. Potter had been absent, and the latter had cautioned him to desist or he would kill him. As to the actual killing there was a strong divergence of testimony. Jap and his friends declared that Potter had come after him with a gun and that he had killed him in self-defence, while the other side as vehemently declared that Jap had hidden behind a log and potted Mr. Potter as he came along.

The next morning the hearing came off before the local justice, who was a mining gentleman of erratic habits. We had considerable difficulty in finding him when the time set for the hearing approached. He had not slept at his usual place of residence and it was only after a prolonged search that we discovered his honour asleep in a trench which had been dug for the foundations of a new mill. Somebody said that he had been up late employed in a poker game, but no doubt that was malicious.

When he was waked and made to understand that his presence was needed in a judicial capacity he washed himself in the creek, and after drying himself with a large bandana handkerchief, mentally clothed himself in a wig and gown and assumed an air of dignity which was quite impressive. He strode in front of us into the room as if he had just arrived in haste from his office, and having rapped sharply on the table with a hammer desired his attending bailiff to open the court with due formality.

All this having been gone through in a very formal manner his honour read the indictment in an impressive voice and called for the witnesses. These were heard in due order, those for the prosecution being heard first, and it appeared to me that they made the most impression on the bench. Anyway, his honour's moral sense appeared to be disturbed, not so much by the actual killing, which was a more or less common event, but by the events which had led up to it. He reminded me of Bret Harte's hero :

> Mr. Jones, Lycurgus B.
> Whose one peculiarity
> Was Conjugal Fidelity.

Anyway, I remembered him as Lycurgus for ever afterwards. In summing up he dwelt on the enormity of disturbing the home and the seduction of innocent females, and wound up by binding Jap over to the grand jury at the coming Session of Court in Socorro, also consigning him to the custody of the sheriff till such time as the court opened, and refusing bail on the ground that bail was not admissible in cases of wilful murder.

He ordered the prisoner to be taken to Socorro overland, on the ground of saving expense to the taxpayer, which was a worthy move, though I was inclined to look on it with suspicion till I consulted Jap. It was a lonely road and the opportunities for an ambush and rescue or lynching of the prisoner many ; but Jap said that several of his friends were going along and that he would be all right. With this assurance I left him, promising to be on hand when the court opened.

In the fall I went to Socorro on Jap's behalf. I had never seen an assize court in session since coming to the United States and I was particularly interested. The judge who presided at this trial, to the best of my recollection, was named Brinker, an able man who maintained the dignity of the court in every respect and was treated with due deference by the various attorneys, who struck me as being a scratch lot. The only thing that seemed to me out of gear was that the proceedings were conducted in two languages, Spanish and English. As far as I could judge, neither the Bench nor the Bar understood the former, while the jury was entirely ignorant of the latter.

The Bar had chairs placed for them inside the rails, but sat about promiscuously wherever they pleased, not disdaining on occasion to use the rails themselves, and their frequent interruptions were met with dignified contempt by the Bench. One rather rickety chair on the right of the Bench, and between it and the jury-box, was kept for the witnesses, and there seemed to be no objection whatever to the use of tobacco, either in the body of the court or within the sacred precincts of the Bench, which gave a sort of social atmosphere to the proceedings.

When Jap's trial was brought to a close, after occupying the best part of two days, the evidence was of the same conflicting character as was heard before our friend Lycurgus. The same moral stress was laid on it by the opposing attorneys. In face of a rather favourable summing up by the judge, the jury, after a brief recess, brought in a verdict of ' Guilty of murder in the first degree.' I think they recommended life imprisonment, but am not positive. Anyway, the death penalty was not popular at the time, except at the hands of a vigilance committee.

So Jap was sent up for life and I bade him good-bye before leaving Socorro. He seemed a little disappointed, but in no way depressed. Two years later he was pardoned by Governor Prince, as the result of a petition circulated by his mother, which I had the pleasure of signing. It also bore the signature of Judge Brinker. The only man in our section who refused to sign it was Lycurgus, and he didn't mind about the killing, but the ' conjugal infidelity ' stuck in his gizzard. Personally I was much grieved over the result of Jap's trial, and the only tangible impression left on my mind through the brief observation of the jurisprudence of the assize court was the unworthy suspicion that if one should get into trouble through coming into conflict with the law it might be advisable to cultivate the friendship of the interpreter.

The following spring Ed left us. He was a good fellow, but naturally of a quiet disposition, and the elements in our neighbourhood were of a stormy character. They worried poor Ed a great deal, especially their unlawful method of acquiring cattle, and he told me confidentially, a short time before, that he didn't think he would be able to stand it. He said we needed a fighting man, and I was disposed to agree with him. His logical successor was Henry, but when I sounded him on the matter he said that naturally he was too cranky and he didn't want no boss's job. Moreover, his trip to Wyoming had brought him back to his old stamping-ground and he had an offer of a job there whenever he was willing to take it, and he said that if Ed was going to quit he would prefer to go along with him.

After talking the matter over with Ed we both decided that the best man for our purpose was a man named Golden, who had come to us a few months previously as a broncobuster. Fred was a big, stout fellow, of rather a rollicking disposition, and was a marvellous hand with horses and an accomplished rider. When I spoke to him about taking charge of the outfit he said that he thought he could handle it.

Fred's first duty on taking over command was to prepare to fill a contract we had made for a number of bulls by gathering and shipping a herd of steers. We anticipated no difficulty in this matter. The outfit was well mounted, as he had been breaking horses for several months, and we had added quite a number to the *remouda*. Everything was shipshape, and we were about ready to move into camp when, a day or so before starting, we received a visit from one of those gentlemen known throughout the West as ' Chuck-liners '. I believe they call them Sundowners in Australia, but the name known to us was evidently derived from their custom of trading on the hospitality of the different ranches for food and fodder.

This gentleman said that his name was McNeil, and beyond the fact that he had red hair and brought four head of horses with him there was nothing in particular to excite our suspicion. The horses were considerably larger and heavier than the usual cow-pony, and they bore the Hashknife brand, which was known to be the identification mark of a large outfit west of Albuquerque. But this, he explained, was because he had been working there and when he left he had asked them to give him his remuneration in horseflesh.

His preference he ascribed to a natural weakness for speculation, which might have induced him to blow the amount in at the first faro or poker game that he came across. The fact that the brands were unvented he explained by saying that he had come away in a hurry (which was probably true) and that he did not like to scar the animals, as it would reduce their value. It sounded a bit fishy, but then he had his redeeming points. He played the mouth-harp and he was an expert clog-dancer, and in view of these unusual accomplishments we accepted him without demur, and he entertained us mightily.

When we went into camp we left him at the ranch under the watchful eye of Old Charlie and the farm-hands and thought no more about him, beyond an occasional reminiscent smile due to the amusement he had brought us. It only needed a day or two to gather the steers necessary to pay Captain Hurst, and we had them all gathered and ready to move into the ranch, where the captain was to be on hand to pass them on. They were about a day's drive from the ranch, and Fred had gone on ahead of us to see that everything was in shape.

We were drifting along peaceably with the cattle, never dreaming of anything unusual, when Fred, accompanied by a boy named Payne, came flying towards us and startled me with the news that our thoroughbred sire Pow-a-Sheik had been stolen out of the stable the night before. I was dumbfounded. I knew Old Charlie always kept the stable locked and guarded Pow-a-Sheik like the apple of his eye

It seemed that Charlie had locked the door as usual before retiring, and when he woke up in the morning he still had the key in his possession. But when he went out to the corral the door of Pow-a-Sheik's box was open and the horse gone. The clog-dancer who had been entertaining them the night before was also missing, so the connexion was apparent. Charlie, without waiting for his breakfast, had saddled up a horse and gone in pursuit. At Alma he had met Bud Payne and sent him with the news to camp, and the latter on his way thither had met Fred, who had turned round and accompanied him.

This was all they knew about it, and they related it as we returned at full speed. When we got to the ranch Charlie was still absent, and an examination of the lock showed that it had been opened with a key and not forced. It was an ordinary lock and probably any skeleton key would have opened it, but it tended to show that our friend McNeil had other accomplishments beside clog-dancing.

I tried to study out the best method of circumventing the thief, but could think of nothing except organizing posses to hunt him down and offering a reward for his capture. The latter proposition was all right, but in regard to the posses, I was rather short-handed, on account of having to deliver the steers in Magdalena. Anyway, I drew up a proclamation and before I got it finished Old Charlie got back.

He had no further information to impart, beyond what we had already discovered, but he had learned, probably from the individual himself, that our friend had other names besides McNeil, one of them being James Howe. He had been unable to get any definite trace of which way he had gone after leaving the ranch, but thought he had gone across the Mogollons, and expressed his determination of following him as soon as he had secured a fresh horse and got something to eat.

I drew up my proclamation, offering a reward of one thousand dollars for the arrest of William McNeil alias James Howe, giving his description and the nature of his crime, with a description of the horse. This I dispatched to Silver City, to our lawyer there, Tom Conway of the firm of Conway, Posey & Hawkins. I asked him to get several hundred copies printed and to wire an editor friend of ours, Slickery Jim, asking him to insert it in his paper.

I also asked him to insert it in all the local papers of the bordering counties of New Mexico and Arizona.

This was promptly attended to and a sheaf of notices sent to the proper authorities of all the neighbouring counties. Also our friend Slickery Jim filled one whole sheet with it and wrote an editorial, urging the capture of McNeil and denouncing all cattle and horse thieves as public enemies. When Fred got back we had to arrange about posses and the most likely direction to hunt in. After stripping the cow outfit to the lowest possible point the best we could do was to muster about eight men, i.e. six beside ourselves.

We then turned the cattle over to a boy named Tipton, while Fred and I, each in charge of a posse, undertook to scour the country in search of McNeil. As for Charlie, he had decided to play a lone hand and was already on his way across the Mogollons.

In regard to our hunt none of us was successful. Charlie, on his lone trip, created more excitement than an Indian raid. He held up every ranch on the Gila and the Sapello, by popping suddenly through the door after nightfall with his gun at the ready and saying, ' Hup, fellows ! ' After scanning every man closely with their hands in the air he would explain his errand and apologize for the inconvenience he might have caused. But he didn't find McNeil, because he hadn't gone that way.

Fred took his men up the Frisco to the plaza and then up the Negrete, where he sequestered a man called Stuttering Bob and in company with him rode out on the plains and back *via* the Tula Rosa. I took the other direction and followed the Frisco down to Clifton, where we found that we were more in disfavour than the horse-thieves. We could get no information from any one, not even the constituted authorities.

We kept on our way, however, having a hunch that we were on the right track, and after some seven or eight days, covering from thirty to forty miles a day and sometimes more, we arrived in the vicinity of the Tonto Basin. The inhabitants of this section were few and far between, and the few we met regarded our inquiries with marked suspicion. Failing to find any trace of our man and our horses being decidedly jaded, we thought it advisable to return home, more especially as we had been given to understand that owing to the customs of the country we might be raided, and the prospect of being left afoot in that benighted spot was not attractive.

We got back to the ranch after an absence of eighteen or nineteen days, just about as wise as when we started. My mail, however, was awaiting me in stacks, the outcome of the proclamation and the newspaper publicity. There were letters, I think, from nearly every petty officer in the territories of Wyoming, Utah, New Mexico, and Arizona. Each one of them had Mr. McNeil located, in the possession of a horse exactly fitting the description of Pow-a-Sheik and were only awaiting the necessary papers to seize his person and collect the thousand dollars which was displayed so prominently at the head of the proclamation as a reward for delivering him into custody.

Having arrived at the conclusion that he could not be in so many places at one and the same time I began tossing them into the waste-basket, as I took them off the pile, merely glancing at the postmark and headline. Amongst them was an envelope which had almost escaped my notice. It had either been mailed in a very dirty post office, or had been carried about in a very dirty pocket for a considerable time before mailing, and the writing was primitive, like that of a very small boy.

I noticed that it bore the Clifton, Arizona, postmark, and moreover, it excited my curiosity, for it was fat and clumsy. When I opened it I was astonished to find one of my own proclamations and no other communication. My first thought was there had been an omission of some kind, but a second glance showed that it was merely an alteration The name of William McNeil alias James Howe had been erased and mine substituted for it. Also at the foot, where I had signed it on behalf of the W S Ranch, my name had been erased and that of William McNeil alias James Howe substituted : all done with very indifferent ink, a decrepit pen, and a very primitive hand. It now read that a thousand dollars reward would be paid for the custody of my person and the payer was to be William McNeil alias James Howe. Verily, our friend the clog-dancer was not devoid of humour, and my soul went out in sympathy to him, and from thenceforth I felt less hostile to him. Incidentally it showed me we had been on the right track when we took the road to Clifton.

Old Charlie was not so easily pacified. He laughed

heartily when I showed him the notice, but he had a theory that McNeil had kept the horse hidden somewhere and would not venture taking him out of the country till we had all gone off in pursuit of him. This sounded reasonable, and it was arranged that he should go and hunt in the neighbourhood of Webster Springs while I answered some letters, and if he found anything tangible he was to come back and let me know. I told him about the old Indian trail we had discovered when in camp with the soldiers and he said he knew where it was, though he had never been over it.

When Old Charlie came back he said he had discovered a single horse-track on the old Indian trail. He wasn't able to make much of it, but that it appeared to be barefoot and about the size that Pow-a-Sheik would make, but he wasn't very sure about it, and altogether it looked an odd kind of trail to him.

Whatever it was, we decided to investigate it and started out the following morning. We found the horse-tracks all right and I ceased to wonder why Charlie had been puzzled. They were the size and shape of a horse's foot all right, but the imprint was perfectly flat and smooth and looked, as Charlie said, as if he had been shod with moccasins.

The trail itself was interesting, and, like all Indian trails I have come across, its construction was a marvel of ingenuity. It appeared to lead up against a bare impassable bluff, but just when one would have thought it was about to lead into the open, where one would be exposed with the cliff as a background, it dived into what looked like an impassable crack and wormed its way round the peak. When unable to avoid a place that was open and devoid of timber it disappeared altogether, and at such places the Indians must have scattered out and only crossed singly and when they were sure they could not be observed from the plains. On the other side of those spaces one would pick it up again, sometimes after considerable search, and find it worn several feet deep from years of travel. The peak it ascended was known as Bullard's Peak, and though the summit appeared to be blocked by an impossible bluff, the trail found a way round and over the divide on to the other side. Neither Charlie nor I had ever been over it before, and we wondered how our friend the clog-dancer had come to know of it ; but this we were never able to solve.

We didn't have the least idea where it led to, but knew

that it must either strike the Frisco or the Blue, and Charlie said that if we didn't catch up with McNeil before night we could make our way to the residence of a gentleman named Stuttering Johnson who had a cabin on the Little Blue.

The funny-looking tracks showed up from time to time where the nature of the ground was favourable. They led us over the divide and down a long sidehill track for fourteen or fifteen miles, which was almost impassable in places. About a mile or more before reaching the bottom it passed over a shelving rock for forty or fifty yards and tested the sure-footedness of our ponies to the fullest extent. At this place our queer-footed friend seemed to have had trouble, for the ground was all ploughed up as we entered it, and one could see the scars on the rock where he slid. Our own ponies shuffled and scrambled and gave us all we could attend to, and the ground being hard we soon lost sight of those marks and thought no more about them.

Shortly after reaching the bottom we got into the narrowest canyon it has ever been my lot to enter. It looked like a tunnel, and though it extended for some two or three miles there was no single place in which two horsemen could ride abreast. For almost the entire distance you could spread out your arms and touch the roof on either side. We sincerely hoped that it would not rain while we were in there, for the drift-wood was jammed across the canyon from seventy-five to a hundred feet over our heads. The top must have been fully a thousand feet up, for although it was not very late in the afternoon the stars were distinctly visible.

As the sun was setting we got on to the Little Blue and arrived at the abode of our friend with the loud stutter in his speech. He received us hospitably and invited us to get down. At least that is what we supposed he intended but we had dismounted and almost unsaddled before he came to the end of his speech.

As was the custom of the frontier he made no inquiry as to our business or destination, leaving it to our own goodwill to take him into our confidence or not. Consequently it was not till we had finished supper and settled down to tobacco that the subject of our errand was broached. We said that we were after a gentleman named McNeil and several other names, one of which was Howe, and that he had stolen a valuable horse from us and that it would be a source of gratification to have a personal interview with him.

He listened to us patiently till we had finished, and then he drew a deep breath and screwed up his face until I thought he was going to explode. It was only a preliminary effort, however, and he stuttered out a query as to whether the gentleman in question was what he called a ' Red-headed Rooster '. Charlie informed him that he was.

He then got up and produced a saddle, bridle, and blankets from an obscure corner of the cabin. Charlie immediately recognized them as the property of our friend the clog-dancer, and we were beginning to grow exultant. However, Mr. Johnson's next speech, when he managed to get it out, was rather a damper. It was simply an advice, tendered in a fatherly manner, to turn around and go home again, coupled with an intimation that we were not likely to recover our horse, and that although Mr. McNeil had been afoot when he had last seen him, it was more than two weeks ago and we had little or no chance of overtaking him.

A demand for further particulars brought out the facts. Our friend McNeil had turned up there two weeks previously, late at night and carrying his saddle and bridle. He had informed Johnson that his horse had fallen over a bluff and broken his neck and that he had removed the saddle and bridle and carried them till he was about to give out. Mr. Johnson had taken him in, like the good Samaritan he was, and catered for his wants.

He said that McNeil was a cheery soul and entertained him with excellent music on the mouth-harp, which he produced from his pocket as soon as he had satisfied his more material wants. He didn't know that he was a clog-dancer, and in all probability he was too tired to exhibit his accomplishments on that occasion. During his sojourn he had gathered from him that his horse had become sore-footed and cast his shoes, and that he had killed a calf and shod him all round with the fresh hide. Charlie slapped his thigh and muttered that that accounted for the moccasin track. Stuttering Johnson went on to relate that the horse had got frightened at a certain portion of the trail which passed over a shelving rock, and that when he had tried to lead him he had reared up and fallen backwards over the bluff. The drop was about a hundred feet and from there he had rolled some seven or eight hundred more, till brought up in a clump of brush at the bottom.

He further told us that when McNeil had made his way down he found the horse dead, and stripping him of the saddle and bridle had made the best of his way to his place. The following morning, not having the wherewithal to purchase a fresh mount, our friend had sold him the saddle and attachments and gone on his way rejoicing.

The next morning Mr. Johnson took us back over the trail we had come fully ten miles or more and showed us the carcase of Pow-a-Sheik. It was lying at the bottom of the canyon seven or eight hundred feet below the shelving rock, where we had noticed the ground ploughed up on the previous day. So ended our dreams of improving the stock of cow-ponies.

After we got back to the ranch some two months or more had passed when I got a letter from a sheriff's office in Utah, enclosing a photograph, and asking if that was the man who had stolen our horse and for whom we were offering a thousand dollars reward. It was undoubtedly our friend the clog-dancer and I wrote back to say so ; at the same time I explained that we had found our horse dead and had later withdrawn our offer of a reward. They wrote back to say they had arrested him for train-robbery and were holding him for the grand jury to return a true bill, but they thought that if we wanted him it could be arranged to take him to New Mexico and try him on the horse-stealing charge, and if he was turned loose they could re-arrest him for the train robbery.

I wrote back declining to have anything to do with it and returned them the photograph. After that I heard no more for several weeks, and then was enclosed a clipping from a newspaper saying that he had been found guilty on the train robbery charge and sent to the Penitentiary for twelve years. I felt rather sorry for him. He had fallen a victim to his ambitions, and this time he had brought off something. His photograph had the same devil-may-care happy grin on his face and he held one hand in his pocket, no doubt nursing his beloved mouth-harp. I never heard what became of him—whether he died in prison or served his time out. If the latter, I bet he came out playing his mouth-harp, and danced a double shuffle on the pavement.

CHAPTER XII

IT was in 1888 that poor Old Charlie was murdered at Cooney. It was the first really great tragedy we had at the ranch since I had taken over the management. It came with a suddenness that was entirely unexpected, and the thought of it even now, nearly forty years afterwards, gives me quite a shock.

Old Charlie had a mania for investing his money in mining property, and must have had a prospect in every mining camp in Socorro and Grand Counties, not to mention the adjoining counties of Graham and Apache in Arizona. When the first strike had been made in Mogollon he had grub-staked his friend Mike Tracey, and between them they had several claims in that camp, amongst them an extension of the Last Chance, which was afterwards absorbed by that company.

I don't think that Charlie himself ever worried much over their value, being content to leave that to his partners, but he liked to have claims in all regions, having a blind faith in the certainty of some day striking a bonanza. In this way he let Mike attend to the Mogollon properties, but looked on him as especially under his protection and guardianship. Now Mike needed relaxation at times, and the town of Mogollon not being as yet fully established, he came over to Cooney for it.

In this town of Cooney was a notorious resort run by two men named Penny and Shelton. The resort, which they were pleased to call a saloon, had an unsavoury reputation, owing to the fact that when they had drained a customer of all his savings, if he was sufficiently inoffensive, they usually beat him up before throwing him into the street. Of course this method of expressing their disapproval of a customer whose resources had petered out sooner than they expected had to be exercised with great caution and could only be put in execution when the victim was hopelessly intoxicated. After that they trusted to loss of memory and a peaceful disposition to evade the consequences. Now, Mike had not drawn on Charlie for some time and his visit to Cooney was partly for the purpose, but as he had not had a drink for a long time the temptation to fill up before coming to the ranch was irresistible. Messrs. Penny and Shelton being convenient, he dropped in there.

Notwithstanding its evil reputation the place was well patronized. Mike soon got all he wanted and perhaps a little more. He rapidly forgot the object of his journey and remained there for the rest of the day and a good part of the following night. Now, Mike was an inoffensive creature who never carried a gun and, unlike most of the patrons of the place, was too good-natured to take offence easily, so as the night progressed and he became too drunk to be any longer a source of profit the enterprising proprietors bashed him over the head with a bottle and threw him out in the street.

At the time they had no idea he had any connexion with Old Charlie or they would probably have treated him with more respect, for Charlie was not a man to be trifled with ; but considering that it was only Mike Tracey, a scar on the scalp and a mud-hole to sleep in were good enough for him.

Mike would probably have forgotten all about it when he woke up in the morning, and would have ascribed his wounds to other causes, had he not still been suffering from thirst and rashly gone back and applied for another drink. This time he had nothing to offer and he barely escaped the empty bottle as he fled through the door. Hence, having bathed his head in the creek and wrapped it in the semblance of a handkerchief, he sought his burro and with throbbing temples and a chastened spirit made his way to the ranch to lay his troubles before Charlie.

It was late in the afternoon when he arrived, but as he and Charlie retired to the corral in secret conclave no one inquired as to his business or where he came from. He stayed at the ranch that night and in the morning, when he left, Charlie accompanied him. Neither of them said where they were going and beyond a few remarks as to the resemblance between Mike and his burro, who looked as if he had been wintered on a diet of pine-cones, nobody gave them a thought.

The boys were all out on the range and Charlie was frequently out all day, so I had no cause to worry. Arthur Burr from the S U Ranch dropped in, and it was just as we were about to sit down to supper that a messenger rode in from Cooney saying that Charlie had been killed there two hours previously.

We hastily accompanied him back to camp. On the way he related to us all he knew, which was not very much, as he was not present at the killing, but said that Uncle Billy Antrim, who had been in the saloon at the time, had sent him off to bring us word. We lost no time in getting to Cooney, and when we got there we found Uncle Billy waiting for us, and he immediately brought us round to a little outhouse where they had carried Charlie. The poor old fellow looked perfectly natural and must have been killed instantly, as his features were perfectly calm, but I noticed that just over his heart, where he had been shot, his shirt and the skin underneath were all burned and powder-marked, as if the gun had been up against him when the shot was fired.

He still wore his chaparejos and spurs and had his cart-ridge bent around him, but Uncle Billy said he had taken the gun out of the scabbard as it got in the way when they laid him out. He also confided in me that when he had done so it was tied in there and he had great difficulty in undoing the knot. I asked him about Penny and Shelton and he said they had closed the saloon and gone home ; after which he invited us over to his cabin to talk the matter over.

When we got there he told us that Charlie and Mike Tracey had come to the camp in the forenoon and that they had at once gone to the saloon, where Charlie had told both Penny and Shelton what he thought of them and abused them roundly for their treatment of Mike Tracey. He said they endeavoured to make out that Mike had been quarrelsome and that they had been obliged to handle him roughly to put him out. After some talk between them, Charlie had ordered drinks and invited all present to join him, and they had all gone up the bar and the conversation ceased for the time being.

After a few more rounds of drinks they had all left the saloon, and Charlie and Mike had gone to the hotel for their dinner and he didn't see any more of them till well on in the afternoon. There was no doubt, however, that they had been paying frequent visits to the place, for Charlie was very drunk and Mike was not much better. He had gone into the saloon with them then, and Charlie wanted

him to have a drink, but he had declined, and he described
Charlie as being so drunk that he had fallen down when
endeavouring to adjust his pants, which had been slipping.

Charlie himself seemed to recognize his condition, for he
spoke of getting his horse and going home.   While he was
there both Penny and Shelton had spoken up and said they
were sorry for having beaten up Mike and promised to
make amends in some way for it, and this seemed to satisfy
Charlie, who said he was willing to forget it.   After that he
and Penny had shaken hands and they all had a drink on
the house and he supposed the matter had ended.

He had left them all chatting in the saloon and gone over
to his cabin, and it must have been about an hour later that
he saw Charlie come out of the saloon accompanied by
Penny.   The latter was assisting Charlie, who, he thought,
was still very drunk, and they both went over to where
Charlie's horse was tied in front of the saloon.   Here Penny
assisted Charlie to mount and spent some time arranging
his belt and putting his pistol in the scabbard, from which
it appeared to have come out.

After that they had talked some more, and Charlie had
got off his horse and gone back to the saloon with Penny.
He didn't know at the time what they had gone back for,
but they had been in there for less than five minutes when
he heard a shot and immediately ran over to see what had
happened.   His cabin was not over fifty yards from the
saloon and it took him only a few seconds to get there.

When he got there Penny was standing up with a pistol
in his hand, alongside a small round table, and Charlie was
lying face down on the same table with both his arms under
him.   There were several others in the place who had been
engaged in a card game at the far end of the saloon, amongst
them Mike Tracey, but he thought that he was really too
drunk to realize what had happened.

The others had all got on their feet and were crowding
down to the scene of the tragedy as he entered, and Penny
had at once declared that he had shot Charlie in self-defence
and was corroborated by Shelton, who was behind the bar,
and declared that he had seen Charlie put down his hand
and go after his gun.   Billy didn't see how he could have
gone after his gun and still have both hands under him
when he had fallen forward on the table.   Moreover, he
said that his gun was securely tied into his scabbard with a

hard knot and not the usual slip-knot which cowboys use to prevent its jumping out when riding on the range.

The others in the room said they had not taken much notice, but that when Charlie and Penny had come in the latter had invited him to take a farewell drink and they had both sat down at the little table, facing each other, while Shelton had prepared to serve them from behind the bar. As soon as the drinks were ready he had brought them over and set them on the table and then went back behind the bar. He could no more than have arrived there when they heard the shot and they had all jumped to their feet.

Uncle Billy had taken charge of the body and they helped him to carry the corpse over to the little outhouse where I had seen it and laid it out as best they could. He then had put Charlie's horse in the stable and sent off the messenger to me. I asked if Charlie had been very abusive, and he said not more so than lots of people who had told Penny and Shelton what they thought of them. It occurred to me to ask if any attempt had been made to place Penny under arrest. Uncle Billy thought not, and said it might be a good idea to attend to it, as otherwise he might skip out. The three of us accordingly went in search of the local justice. Our friend Lycurgus had left and gone to reside in Silver City, and this man was an entire stranger to me and I fail to recall his name.

We found him in bed and had some difficulty in waking him up, but when we mentioned official business he made haste to let us in, no doubt scenting a fee. When he understood the nature of our business, he said he had heard of the killing and intended holding an inquiry the following day. He didn't see what we wanted to arrest Penny for, as there was little danger of his skipping out and, from what he had heard, he understood the killing was perfectly justified.

We told him that our version of the story, as told by eye-witnesses, put an entirely different aspect on the case and that we thought it was a cowardly murder. Anyway, we said we had come from the W S as friends of the deceased and wanted to see justice done, and thought it only right that the perpetrator should be in custody. He made all sorts of objections, such as being unable to get any one to execute the warrant at that time of night and being responsible for the safety of the prisoner and such like, with many more that were entirely irrelevant.

Finally our patience was exhausted, and it was only on the threat to take Penny into custody on our own responsibility that he consented to issue a warrant. He cautioned us that we would be responsible for the safety of the person, and then deputized Uncle Billy and myself to execute it.

We had no difficulty in gaining admittance to Penny's house, as he was not in bed, but when we marched in with our guns still in our hands and made known the nature of our business his wife made a great outcry. She felt sure we had come to take the law into our own hands and refused to look at our warrant, which she declared to be a forgery. I feared at one time that she would arouse the camp, which was probably hostile to us, but at length Penny himself assisted us in quieting her and declared his willingness to come along without any further trouble.

He seemed surprised at being arrested, but, I think, was little troubled regarding the outcome. His wife, however, was not so confident, for shortly after we left, she sent a Mexican boy after us, and he followed us up to the boarding-house where we proposed to spend the night.

When we got there Penny seemed desirous of unbosoming himself, but we were not in the mood to hear him and told him he had better reserve anything he had to say for the preliminary hearing, which was scheduled to take place at ten o'clock the following day. After that Uncle Billy went home and Burr and I undertook to guard the prisoner during the night. We laid out blankets on the table as being safest from invasion, and, it being well after midnight, I undertook the first watch, telling Burr I would call him about four a.m.

Our prisoner went to bed and fell asleep; he was the least perturbed of the party, and had acted throughout as if a killing was an everyday affair with him. I think he really expected that the charge would be dismissed the following day, and thought he was only humouring us by remaining under arrest. Burr settled down on the table and eventually fell asleep, but my intention of arousing him at four a.m. failed to materialize as about that time I fell asleep myself in the chair on which I was sitting. I had, however, taken the precaution of locking and bolting the door after Uncle Billy had gone, and had the key in my pocket.

I was dead to the world for the next two hours or more,

and then was brought to my feet by a persistent pounding on the door. As soon as I regained my faculties I took in the situation, and my first impression was that Penny's friends in the camp had come to take him away from us. I could hear a number of feet shuffling outside the house and a woman's voice talking volubly. I supposed that Mrs. Penny had gone around amongst her friends and was urging them to take him away from us.

I roused Burr hurriedly and told him what I thought, telling him to get his gun and stand by me while I answered the door. The pounding still continued, and whoever was there was evidently getting impatient, for he began to use his foot. I shouted to know who was there and what they wanted, and gasped with relief when I heard Fred's voice in reply. It was only a matter of seconds to dig up the key and admit him, and in answer to his inquiries I pointed to the bed where Penny, awakened by the noise, was rubbing the sleep from his eyes.

He told me Mrs. Penny was outside and anxious to see her husband, so we withdrew while he called to her to come up. He told me they had come off just as soon as they got the message, but all that they had heard was that Charlie had been killed and that Burr and I had gone to the camp. Not knowing what the conditions might be, when they had got to the mouth of the canyon they left their horses and came on foot, thinking it possible they might have to fight their way into camp.

As they passed Penny's house, Mrs. Penny, who had not gone to bed, spotted them, and rushed out begging them not to kill her husband. She told them where we were, and to assure her they had told her to come along with them. It was her voice I had heard, as I thought, haranguing the crowd. He said she had thrown herself on the ground and clasped him round the knees, as she was certain they intended to lynch him.

We went outside to the boys, who surrounded the house. In the grey light of morning, with their unshaven faces and loaded down with guns and ammunition, they looked quite capable of carrying out a lynching bee. As a mere matter of ethics it would have been a public service if they had, but I could forgive Mrs. Penny's distrust.

After that we turned the prisoner over to Fred, and Burr and I got a bed and had a couple of hours' sleep. Now that we had a backing we did not feel so isolated, as up to then Uncle Billy was the only friend we had in the camp. I felt very grateful to Burr for the gallant way he had stuck to me in what was really none of his fight. We had gone into what was really a hostile camp, where not a soul except Uncle Billy had come near us, and if we had not kept a stiff upper lip might have got into trouble; but Burr never batted an eye, and acted as if he had a thousand men at his back.

At ten o'clock the court convened. I suppose the justice in virtue of his office could have held an inquest, but this was not an inquest. There was no jury and the corpse was not in evidence. The procedure was rather new to me, but it seemed to be a sort of preliminary inquiry that might be held before the issue of a summons. There were sixty or seventy people there besides our crowd and the sentiment seemed pretty evenly divided.

Quite a number held the killing was justified, but the majority, I believe, came with an open mind, prepared to hear the evidence. All those who were present in the saloon at the time were sworn, and also Uncle Billy, who had come on the scene immediately after the shooting. Shelton swore that Charlie had gone after his gun but failed to explain how his hands came to be on the table after he was shot. The others swore as to the position of the hands and that they had not seen Charlie make any hostile movement and also that he was helplessly drunk at the time. Uncle Billy testified that the smoke from the discharged pistol was still hanging over the table when he got there, and that Penny was on his feet calling on those present to witness that he had shot in self-defence. He also swore to the position of the body, and gave it as his opinion that it was physically impossible for Charlie to have got his hands where they were if one of them had been employed in reaching for his gun.

After this the belt, scabbard, and gun of the deceased were produced and Uncle Billy demonstrated how the gun had been tied into the scabbard, saying it had taken him several minutes to unfasten it. This was corroborated by three or four of the others who had assisted him in carrying out the body. When the evidence was all in, Penny, who was represented by a sort of Jim Crow lawyer, held a sort of consultation with him, and the latter made a motion to dismiss the case on the grounds that the evidence tended to show that the killing had been done in self-defence.

The justice, who seemed to be of the same opinion, but was evidently guided by the sympathy of the audience, said that the evidence was conflicting, but he thought the prisoner should be turned loose. He was about to make out an order to this effect when I interrupted him and said that it mattered little whether he turned him loose or not. If he did we would re-arrest him and take him to Socorro anyhow. This statement was received with mixed feelings by the audience, but Penny's friends by no means had it all their own way.

Charlie was very popular, and while the trial was going on his friends had been dropping in from the various sections of the county, so that though the body of the room received my statement with cries of dissent, we had a pretty strong backing at the rear end of the room. His honour, who seemed to be in the habit of keeping his finger on the public pulse, hesitated, and he, Penny, and his lawyer held a little private consultation in the neighbourhood of the Bench.

The result was that the prisoner agreed to waive an examination and go before the grand jury. The question then arose as to who was to take him there. There was no regular deputy available, and it was necessary to deputize some one to take charge of him and turn him over to the prison authorities in Socorro. I did not contemplate taking any part in these proceedings and was about to leave the room when some of Charlie's friends became rather demonstrative at the back of the room.

There were several volunteers for the job, but some one called out indiscreetly—I think it was my friend Bob the artist from Pleasanton—that if he was going to Socorro it was up to them to see that he never got there. This candid statement put a new complexion on the case, and the prisoner, who up to then had been apparently indifferent, collapsed like a paper bag. He turned a palish green and threw himself on the protection of the court. His quondam friends began to leave the room, and for the first time he seemed to realize that he was up against something.

The question now was, who should take him to Socorro. His friends had slunk off and there was apparently nobody willing to take charge of him. I consulted a bit with Fred and then told him that I would be willing to see he got there safely, asking him whether he preferred going overland or round by rail from Silver City. He decided without hesitation in favour of the latter, and so it was arranged.

I had to be sworn in and get the necessary papers from his honour, after which we took the prisoner over to his house to say good-bye to his wife. Here we had another trying scene, and to satisfy her I offered to take any one she named along with me to look after the safety of the prisoner. She selected the medico with the shaky reputation, and so we had him sworn in and properly deputized. After that we all adjourned to the ranch, taking poor Old Charlie's remains along with us. We buried him there the same evening.

Burr had stuck to me like a brick all through this trying period, and I was deeply thankful to him. At one time, when poor Charlie's body was taken out, just before leaving for the ranch, it looked as if we really would have to fight to save Penny's neck, but beyond a threatening demonstration there was no actual attempt to take him away from us. Things looked so threatening, however, that I got Fred to attend to the funeral arrangements while Burr and I spirited the brute away ahead of the rest.

We buried poor Charlie that afternoon, and there was quite a large attendance from the surrounding country. When the grave had been filled up and the ground smoothed over every one departed in silence, but the boys were in an ugly mood, and we thought it better to keep Penny out of their sight, so we had him locked in a room during the ceremony. We kept him there all the time he was at the ranch, but I was decidedly uneasy as to the outcome after we had got him started on the road. This preyed on my mind to such an extent that I thought it advisable to pretend that we would take him to Socorro overland, despite the fact that we had previously arranged to take him *via* Silver City. I accordingly gave out the idea that we would not start till the medico arrived the following day, as he was coming down from Cooney on the stage.

That night, after I had gone to bed, my friend Bob the artist came up and asked if I intended to put up a fight should an attempt be made to take the prisoner away from me. I said it was a disagreeable task, but I didn't see how I could do otherwise than defend him to the best of my ability. Bob said that was ' a hell of a note ', but made no further attempt to dissuade me.

He had spoiled my night's sleep, however, and long before daylight I got Fred to slip down to the corral and saddle a couple of horses. When he had led them out and brought them up to the house I hastily aroused the prisoner and told him to come along with me. I then told Fred to meet the stage in Alma and tell the medico to stay on it until we joined him at some point on the road. I also told Fred we would leave our horses there and he could follow us up until he found them. In this way we slipped away from the ranch and rode down to Whitewater, some five miles below Alma, where we waited by the side of the road till the stage came along a few hours later.

I never really knew whether any definite attempt was planned to take the prisoner away and hang him, but it seemed desirable to get him out of the way. When the stage came along the medico was occupying the back seat, so we put the prisoner between us and sat one on each side of him. It rained that day, and the roads got so muddy that it was quite late before we got to Silver City. All the way the medico and I regarded each other with suspicion. He was evidently imbued with the idea that I had designs on the prisoner's neck, while I rather suspected that he would connive at his escape should the opportunity occur.

When we arrived in Silver City we had some difficulty in getting accommodation. Every place seemed to be occupied, and at length we had to be content with what they called ' The Bridal Chamber ' at the Timmer House. This was a palatial apartment with a huge bed, heavily draped. It was sufficiently large to hold the three of us, but I demurred at lying down with the prisoner, saying I would sit up and stand guard, while they could sleep if they wanted to.

This proposal was looked on with suspicion and resulted in all of us agreeing to sit up ; it was then after midnight and the train left at six o'clock the following morning. To assist in passing the time we got hold of a pack of cards and invested in a flask of whisky. The only three-handed game I knew was ' seven-up ', and we spent the rest of the night at that intellectual pastime. Not deeming it orthodox to play for money in the circumstances, we compromised by allowing the winner of each game to have a drink while the losers were privileged to smell the cork.

When we got on the train in the early morning we took possession of the small smoking compartment, where we all three fell asleep and did not wake up till we got to Deming, where we had breakfast.

It was an uncomfortable trip ; we were stared at everywhere and I had the feeling I was regarded as the prisoner by the lookers-on. This was no doubt due to my rather hang-dog appearance, as well as to the fact that though I carried all the papers necessary for the committal I had no weapon of offence in sight. My *compadre* the medico had borrowed the very largest forty-five and the most conspicuous belt of cartridges that he could find, while I had only a little thirty-two that I carried in my pocket.

The prisoner acted as if he was used to it and always walked ahead as if showing the way. It was with a great sense of relief that I turned him over to the warden that night in Socorro. The committal papers I took to the District Attorney, and told him all I knew about the case, urging him to combat any attempt to release him on bail. He was of opinion that bail was not admissible as the charge was wilful murder.

As it turned out, the prisoner was not anxious for bail, as he considered himself much safer in jail in Socorro than in his saloon at Cooney. The upshot of it was that he lay in jail for nearly a year before the grand jury met and brought in a true bill against him. His friends, however, had not been idle and had secured Mr. Ferguson of Albuquerque to defend him. Mr. Ferguson at the time had the reputation of being the best criminal lawyer in the territory and was noted for his defence of notorious criminals.

In addition, I strongly suspect that in his saloon days Penny must have held a corner on votes and delivered them to some of the local politicians, several of whom took a marked interest in his trial. He was tried before Judge Brinker, the same who had presided at the Jap Thomason trial, and his was one of the first cases called when the court convened.

We had brought a host of witnesses besides those who had been subpœnaed and who had actually witnessed the killing. The District Attorney had them all up in his office for several days before the actual trial and seemed very confident of securing a conviction. When the actual trial came on there was considerable delay in securing a jury, and the whole proceedings took up nearly a full week of the court's time.

The evidence was practically the same as had been given before the justice in Cooney, with a number of others testifying to Charlie's benevolent disposition. There was only one witness for the defence, his partner Shelton, who swore, as he had done previously, that Charlie had gone after his gun. He could not account for the position of his hands underneath him on the table. The belt and scabbard were produced, and Uncle Billy demonstrated how the pistol had been tied into it, and this was fully corroborated, as it had been previously.

The summing up of the judge was strongly against the prisoner ; in fact he told the jury that if they believed the evidence they had no alternative except to find the prisoner guilty. The interpreter got in his usual work, and the jury after retiring for about twenty minutes brought in a verdict of ' Not guilty ! ' The Court scratched his head and regretted that he had not any alternative except to discharge the prisoner. Great was the power of the interpreter.

Personally I was astounded and swore I would never seek justice in a court again. I rather regretted that I had not been more amenable when approached by my friend Bob the artist. As for Penny, he had turned over all his property to his lawyers and others and did not deem it advisable to return to Cooney. The last I heard of him he had taken up his residence in Bisbee, Arizona, and that enlightened community had elected him justice of the peace.

Poor Old Charlie having died intestate it became necessary to dispose of his property according to the laws of the territory, and it was suggested that I should act as administrator for his estate. Having no objection to offer, I was duly appointed by the probate judge, or whoever it was that was authorized to act in that capacity. All that was needed was to post a bond which was large enough to cover its assumed value, and this I had no difficulty in complying with.

His visible assets consisted of a couple of old plugs, which Charlie had valued more from old associations than from any present use, and these, with his saddle, bridle, blankets, pistol, scabbard, and belt I offered to purchase at whatever value the court was pleased to put upon them. These comprised what were classed as chattels and were easy to dispose of, but when it came to his mining claims, which were classed as real estate and were scattered all over New Mexico and Arizona, we were completely at sea.

Neither the court nor I had the faintest idea what they might be worth. To me a mining claim was a hole in the ground with a pile of dirt outside, governed as to size by the depth and diameter of the hole and in professional parlance termed a 'dump'. His honour the Court, besides labouring under the disadvantage of being unable to speak English, had been raised on the banks of the Rio Grande and was unfamiliar with mining phraseology in any tongue.

To assist us we called in Uncle Billy, who claimed to be a mining expert and, what was more to the point, had a certain knowledge of the Spanish tongue, which enabled him to make himself understood by the court. The result was that Uncle Billy was named official valuer for Charlie's mining property, it being understood that I was to compensate him out of the proceeds of the estate.

After several weeks we had hunted around and found most of the holes with their attendant dumps which were assumed to be Charlie's claims, and looked them over professionally. To me they were just rocks stained with what they used to call verdigris in the days of my childhood. Uncle Billy pronounced them rich in copper. He was not quite positive, however, and said it would be necessary to take samples and have them assayed. In the light of later experience I don't think that Billy's knowledge was so profound, but he could look wonderfully wise and was very impressive. I was inclined to take the highly coloured green samples, but Billy discarded them in favour of a rusty red with black streaks in it. Mine were prettier to look at, and I put several of them in my pocket, but discarded them on the way home as they bumped against my leg.

When we returned to the ranch Uncle Billy left me, saying he would report on the specimens as soon as they were assayed. My impression is that he threw them away as soon as he was out of sight, for he returned the next evening saying they were valueless and advising that the claims be abandoned. I accordingly reported the same to the probate judge and enclosed him a small balance remaining in my hands after compensating Uncle Billy. All efforts to discover any relatives of poor Old Charlie's had proved useless. No one knew where he had originated, and from his own statements he had lived in every frontier State in the Union.

This was my first and almost my last attempt to become interested in mining. I was evidently not intended for the game—lack of imagination probably—for Charlie's claims afterwards turned out valuable. The ones in Mogollon resulted in what was later known as ' The Last Chance ' mine, a considerable producer of both gold and silver, while the Morenci claims, when taken hold of by the Phelps Dodge Company, were considered rich enough in copper to induce them to build a railroad to it. But in those days it was as Uncle Billy remarked : ' Who wanted copper anyway ? ' Was it not sticking out of the rock in sheets near Silver City and nobody could be induced to take hold of it.

Shortly after this mixture of tragedy and comedy we settled down to the usual routine at the ranch. The next anxiety came in the shape of a Federal land inspector. This gentleman was named Walker, and he surprised me considerably one morning by turning up at the ranch alone and on foot. He impressed on me that he was the special commissioner appointed to inquire into the land titles in New Mexico, and that point being conceded he wanted all the information I could give him about the holdings in the neighbourhood. I could not enlighten him as to our neighbours, as it was none of my business, but I gladly gave him all particulars as to the acquisition and titles of the W S lands.

Two or three months passed after Mr. Walker left us, and I would have forgotten all about him had he not made himself notorious. The favourite occupation at the time for the man who proposed to get something for nothing was ranch-jumping, which meant filing a claim to any piece of unoccupied land that controlled water and then offering the neighbouring cattleman a quit-claim deed to same for a fabulous price.

Sometimes he got it, but more frequently he was told to go chase himself, and as a quit-claim deed conveyed no title but merely gave the owner an uncertain prior right to obtain one, it can easily be seen that he had not much to offer. But Mr. Walker had gathered all this class of gentleman about him and was accepting their statements as evidence of fraudulent entry on certain lands by some of the most respectable cattlemen in the country.

They were all receiving notices from the Land Offices in Washington that their claims were being contested and were summoned into the Federal courts to prove title to lands acquired in the ordinary course of commercial transactions. This naturally put them to heavy and unnecessary expense and in some cases made the proof of the original title very difficult, owing to death and the itinerant habits of the frontiersmen who had first located them.

Mr. Walker apparently hunted up witnesses of his own volition as a means of preserving the nation's heritage. After a while he worked up a case against the W S. Wilson had been a stranger to the people he had bought out and there was no chance of proving collusion. But Mr. Walker may have got a tip through finding out that Jasper Thomason was in jail under life sentence for killing Al Potter. As Jap was a convict he could not be produced to give legal evidence, and there were a hundred and sixty acres in the possession of the W S which had been purchased from said Thomason. Furthermore, he, Thomason, had been in the employ of the W S for several years after its establishment, and that seemed to have made the circumstances seem suspicious.

This was the actual substance of the case against the W S, and I have no doubt that most of the cases started by Mr. Walker (they ran into hundreds) were of a similar nature. Anyway, I received a notice in due course that it would be necessary to appear at the Land Office in Las Cruces, with two competent witnesses, residents of New Mexico, who could testify that Jasper Thomason had lived upon his land for the required period and made the necessary improvements to entitle him to a patent from the Land Office of the United States at Washington, D.C.

It really amounted to my having a little over twenty-four hours to hunt up the necessary witnesses before taking the stage for Silver City and making my way to Las Cruces. It so happened that I found two comparative strangers who willingly and smilingly did me a service which entailed their absence from their families for a week or more and I don't know what other inconveniences. Small wonder I should feel grateful. Apart from their kindness there was no other way out. I read the darned paper over and over again, but the notification was absolute. It was what the boys called a ' groundhog ' case—either show up with your witnesses or lose the land. The best we could expect would mean a lengthy lawsuit, with no assurance of success unless, on our obeying the immediate summons, the case might happen to be dismissed.

At the White House Ranch, where we stayed the first night on the way to Las Cruces, we were overtaken by Captain M., of T-Bar Ranch, and an unattractive, sinister-looking individual known as Dick Deadeye. They informed us that they were also on their way to Las Cruces, in connexion with some of the suits instituted by the Federal Government in their investigation of land titles. They were in fact Government witnesses.

It seemed that Dick had been picked up by Mr. Walker in Chicago and taken along to ferret out the wickedness of the Cattle Barons, and owing to some indiscreet talk of Captain M.'s, who was boastful in his cups, he had fastened on to him as likely to be of assistance in proving their theories. They had already been at a previous session of the court and the case was now due for rehearing.

M., who was rather elated, was full of his former experience, and was amused because they had already threatened to indict him for perjury. He said, however, that he was not in any way uneasy, as he was a good friend of Judge Henderson, who was trying the case.

When we retired at an early hour they put us into one room, while M. and his friends occupied another, so that we saw no more of them until breakfast next morning. But I noticed that although the weather was warm M. carried a heavy sheepskin coat, which he kept rolled up and close beside him while entertaining us and carried off to bed with him when he left. Thinking it contained something of extra value, I asked him why he did not give it to Mr. Lyda, the foreman, to lock up for him, and he told me it was only medicine, which he said he was compelled to carry to stave off attacks of what he called ' typhoid-malaria.'

The next day we went on to Silver City, and as we arrived there nearly an hour ahead of M. and his party we were fortunate enough to get the only room that was vacant at the Timmer House. The roads were several inches deep in dust, so that we felt grateful for having the opportunity of cleaning ourselves, and when M. and his party arrived one could hardly distinguish them from a dirt pile.

Not finding any space at the Timmer House they tried several other places, but without success. It looked as if they might have to spend the night on the sidewalk. This prospect did not please Deadeye, however, and he said the Exchange Saloon was good enough for him ; he promptly rolled out of the buggy and betook himself thither, and we saw no more of him till train-time next morning.

M., however, felt that he had a position to keep up, being impressed with his dignity as a Government witness, and was not quite so happy over the situation. I came to his relief by telling him to go and find shelter for his team and in the meantime I would see what could be done about having a cot put in our room. I also offered to take charge of his ague medicine, but this he declined, saying he never knew when an attack might occur and it was safer to have it with him.

The livery stables were evidently not in the same congested condition as the hotels, for he quickly returned with no other baggage than the sheepskin coat and said that he was ready to go and change his things. I asked where was his grip, which was the usual Western term applied to all shapes and sizes of hand luggage, but he said the coat was all he had, so I led the way to our room.

All the time I was vaguely wondering where his change was to come from, and concluded that he must have the necessary shirt wrapped round the bottle inside the coat. I thought that in accordance with Western custom I had curtailed the necessities of the toilet to the smallest possible space, but he had evidently gone me one better, and I was anxious to see what he could produce. Before very long I was destined to get what the cowboys called ' a new wrinkle on my horn ' in the most direct method of changing linen.

When we got to the room I expected him to unroll his coat. but instead he only fastened it tighter and placed it carefully in a corner. Then he took off his dusty outer garments, rinsed his hands in the basin, and splashed a little cold water over his face. So inadequate a wash was it that he had to dig into his eye-sockets with a dry towel to remove the dust.

He then looked at himself in the glass and said he thought it would be necessary to put on a clean shirt. To the onlooker it looked as if it might have been necessary a week or so previously, but this was an afterthought and I thought : 'Now I will see how he manages to carry things about with him.'

He stripped off an old cardigan jacket, a waistcoat, and

what we call a jersey, but which was more familiarly known in the States as a ' sweater ', before he came to the shirt to be discarded.

I ceased wondering why he had found it unnecessary to unroll his sheepskin coat ; but I was lost in amazement when he pulled the soiled garment over his head and disclosed another shirt underneath. It was not quite so dirty as the one he was taking off, but it was evident that it had not been to a laundry for a considerable time. He claimed to have several more underneath that. Small wonder he was unencumbered with baggage.

We all arrived at Las Cruces without mishap and betook ourselves to the hotel—I think the only one in the place. There we left M. and his party while we went to the Receiver's Office, which was situated close by. There were four of us, including Tom Conway our lawyer, who had accompanied us from Silver City. He was *au fait* with all the necessary proceedings, and when we found that Mr. Sheilds, the gentleman before whom we were to appear, had left that morning, he reassured us by saying that his presence was unnecessary and that we could make our declaration before his assistant.

There was something funny going on, for the assistant had not volunteered us this information at the start, and had Conway not been with us we would probably have gone away and waited for the return of Mr. Sheilds. Anyway, we filled up all the necessary papers and swore to their contents, after which the assistant said he would issue the necessary receipt and have Mr. Sheilds sign it as soon as he returned When all was over I asked Conway if there was anything further, as if not we could catch the train back to Silver City that afternoon.

As we were about to leave the office, however, the assistant called Conway back and held a whispered conversation with him. He was an old friend of his and we paid no attention to the matter, but went on our way back to the hotel, where we proposed to refresh ourselves before catching the train. When Conway overtook us, however, he said it would be necessary to change our plans, as the assistant had confided to him that we had better not leave Cruces before the Land Office closed officially for the day. He said he had told him no more, but he surmised that some person or persons unknown meant to file a contest as soon as we had left town. As a contest meant more expense and further proof we decided to stay over and frustrate the attempt. On arriving at the hotel we had some lunch, presuming that our friends M. and Deadeye had gone out. Before we had finished, however, the latter came in and told us that M. had been arrested for perjury and taken to the Housegau.

Dick said that he was trying to find bail for him, as they had put him under bond for a thousand dollars and refused to turn him loose unless he could find two substantial citizens, residents of Donna Anna County, to stand good for him. Dick was in a quandary, as he said he was unknown to any of the residents of the county and M.'s friends were all in Grant or Socorro Counties. The same objection applied to us, but Tom Conway supplied a solution, saying he would call on his friend Numa Raymond, who was the wholesale merchant of the town, and get him to furnish surety.

Conway and I went down to see Numa Raymond and he laughed heartily when we told him of M.'s plight, but said that he would get him out right away. He said that M. had been there as witness before, and all Las Cruces closed up their places of business and adjourned to the courthouse to hear him whenever he was on the stand. He came down with us to the Housegau, an adobe building with a very high wall enclosing a sort of corral at the back. Raymond said that it came in handy for holding the alien voters who came over from Old Mexico at election time. Whichever side captured them would put them in the pen, and hold them there till election day, when just before the poll closed they would lead them out and vote them in a body. In this way you could generally foretell the result of an election, according to whether the inmates of the pen were Democratic or Republican prisoners. Sometimes the opposing party broke into the jail and carried off the inmates, whom they held as voters, for their own side, thus upsetting the apple-cart, but this led to violence and was frowned upon by the more respectable members of the community.

We found M. inside sitting on the floor in company with a few tough-looking citizens. They were mostly Mexican peons—Spanish-American citizens at election time. M. seemed to have given up hope of being released and was settling down for the night still nursing his sheepskin coat. They might deprive him of his liberty, but he couldn't be separated from his typhoid-malaria medicine.

A few words from Numa Raymond to the *hombre* in charge sufficed to set M. free, and he gladly accompanied us back to the hotel. He said that he had almost despaired of finding any one to bail him out, as Deadeye was not to be depended on and was probably now in some dive and had forgotten all about him. We saw no more of Deadeye that day and M. stayed with us at the hotel.

On the following morning we all went over to the court-house together. The land cases were set for ten a.m., and the judge and jurors were all in their places and ready to proceed when it was announced that the Federal district Attorney, a dignified gentleman from Virginia, had missed his train at El Paso and could not put in an appearance till the afternoon.

The judge, a learned gentleman named Henderson, seemed in a quandary, but after a short consultation with the members of the Bar present announced that as there were no other cases before the court he would adjourn the same until such time as the district attorney was able to attend. He at the same time cautioned the jurors and witnesses not to leave town as he intended to hear the case, if possible, that day, he having to open court in some other district a day or two later.

The audience were much disappointed, but the jurors and witnesses were jubilant and left the courthouse like a lot of boys released from school. Amongst them was M., who seemed much relieved at not having to give evidence, and went off with his friend Dick to celebrate the occasion. We adjourned to the hotel, to pass the time as best we could until our train went out that evening. We sat around and smoked and yarned, and had almost decided that the best way of passing the time was to go to bed and try to sleep, when somebody brought the news that the district attorney had unexpectedly arrived on a freight train and was now in communication with the judge at the courthouse.

This was followed almost immediately by bailiffs and other myrmidons of the court rushing wildly around announcing that the court was open and searching everywhere for missing witnesses and jurors. We hurried over to the place so as to secure good seats. At the courthouse we found them all waiting for M. and Deadeye, whom, so far, they had been unable to locate.

We started out to assist in the search, and at length dug

them up in a little Mexican barber's shop, where M. was preparing to get shaved. Dick hurried off at once, but M., who was pretty well primed, was inclined to take it easy till a couple of bailiffs seized hold of him and, thrusting him into his clothes, dragged him off ignominiously, paying no heed to his attempts to explain the situation, but hustling him along, while we followed in his wake.

When they arrived at the courthouse they pushed him up the stairs and into the court room, thrusting him up the aisle till he came to a halt at the witnesses' chair. Here he mopped his brow with a large red handkerchief and looked dazedly around the court before taking his seat. He was the star witness for the Government and everybody had been waiting for him. The district attorney was inclined to be fretful, but the judge smiled indulgently on him and bade him good day.

The others had kept a seat for me in the front row, and I squeezed into it as the court was formally opened, after which everything was as still as in church. The gentleman from Virginia was a trifle shaky, but very dignified, and he opened his case in a most formal manner. He first produced several bundles of papers, which he sorted carefully and placed in their order on a table before him. He then cleared his throat and the case was called.

It appeared that one Wheeler had filed a pre-emption claim on a certain tract of land with fraudulent intent and for the purpose of transferring his title to some other parties, in contravention of the laws of the country as set forth in chapter so, and so, etc., and it appeared that M. was called upon to swear as to whether he had actually ever resided on the place or not. The Virginia gentleman read it all from his notes, and when M. had been duly sworn and requested to sit down by the court, he turned to him and in his blandest manner began the examination.

In answer to his name and residence, M. came through without a fault, but when asked if he was familiar with the case he hesitatingly answered : ' More or less.' He was then inclined to enter into an explanation but was cut short by the judge, who requested him to reply only directly to the questions. Then the prosecuting attorney went on to ask him if he would not swear that on such-and-such a day a certain notice had been posted in such-and-such a place. He wrapped it up in a coating of legal phraseology, which made it more imposing than merely nailing a dirty scrap of paper to a cotton-wood tree.

This question seemed to stump M., and he pulled himself together and looked around for enlightenment. After considerable delay and scratching of his head he replied rather to the court than to the prosecuting attorney : ' No. your honour, I wouldn't swear to it.' This answer was evidently unexpected, for the prosecuting attorney looked puzzled and the judge suddenly became interested.

The former was not dealt with, however, and had a good many more questions up his sleeve, for, after consulting his papers, he shot a string of queries at M. one after another, to all of which, after mature thought, M. returned the same answer : ' No, your honour, I wouldn't swear to it ' with increasing emphasis on the word ' swear '. Finally the judge got a little testy, pounded his gavel on the bench, and said : ' Come, come, Captain M., what would you swear to ? '

M. looked at him pathetically, as if a valued friend had gone back on him, and, shaking his finger at him, said sorrowfully : ' Now, look here, Judge, if you had been indicted for perjury as often as I have you'd be damn particular about what you swore to .'

Some enthusiast on a back bench gave a whoop and the whole courtroom burst into a roar of laughter. The judge, who was *au fait* with M.'s experience of the previous day, stifled his mirth, and pounding loudly on his desk ordered his witness out of court ; whereupon he was immediately seized by the attending bailiffs and hustled out more ignominiously than he had been ushered in. The only one who seemed puzzled was the Government attorney, who immediately strode up to the Bench to consult with the judge.

We did not wait for the result as our interest in the case was over, as indeed was that of most of the audience, for they flocked out in M.'s wake. M. was contentedly seated on the edge of the sidewalk and had regained possession of his sheepskin coat, though where he had left it in the meantime has always been a mystery.

After condoling with him, as we had nothing better to do, we went back to the courtroom, where Deadeye was on the stand. His readiness to testify was in sharp contrast to M.'s, and he was making out rather a strong case against the defendant, or defendants—I forget which—till the lawyers for the defence got hold of him.

They completely ruined his reputation, for they got him mixed up with an attempt which it seems had been made to rob the grave of President Lincoln, and in fact exposed his career as a detective in such a rascally manner that his entire evidence was thrown out of court. The Government lost their case and withdrew their other prosecutions, and both Mr. Walker and Dick Deadeye disappeared from the country.

We travelled up to Silver City that evening in company with Judge Henderson, and he told us some of his other experiences with M. as witness. M. had been a great god-send to them and he regretted they had no further use for him as he relieved the monotony of the proceedings. As a sop to my foreign extraction he said they were not perhaps as dignified as the Old Bailey, but they had more variety and could combine amusement with business, which was certainly true.

We left his honour in Silver City to open the court in Grant County and I returned in triumph to the ranch, very much indebted to the two gentlemen who had helped me out.

CHAPTER XIII

HUNTING BEARS AND MEN

SOME time passed in regular routine, and I became considerably nonplussed as to how we were to carry on from a financial standpoint. We had plenty of cattle and our credit was good, and it might have been possible to borrow money from the banks, if the banks had had any money to lend ; but the only ones we had ever dealt with were in Silver City and our experiences with those had not been fortunate.

Wilson had already lost money in two of them, which took it into their heads to suspend payment when he happened to have fairly large deposits there. From one of them, which ran a grocery store in connexion with its banking business, he had been compelled to recoup himself to a limited extent by accepting groceries at retail prices, and the other had smiled graciously on him and paid fifteen cents in the dollar, which amount was only paid after some two years' delay.

As for shipping cattle to markets, so lowly had the cow fallen that it was doubtful if the railroad would accept them unless you were prepared to lodge the amount of the freight beforehand.

Under the circumstances I thought it advisable to take a trip to the old country and have a personal interview with Wilson on the matter. In addition, I was feeling home-sick ; I had been away now for a good many years and my time for personal correspondence was limited. The very thought of getting back caused a return of the same feelings that I used to experience when at school on the eve of the holidays.

I thought I had plenty of clothes, for the raiments of civilization were not of much use in the ranch, and I had laid them away. But on inspecting them I found the moths had been beforehand. So reduced was my wardrobe that it was with difficulty I managed to find sufficient to take me as far as New York. I was the possessor of a hat-box, and while I had not been rash enough to bring out a topper I had made use of it to hold a brand-new pot-hat, acquired in Dublin just before leaving.

The climate must have affected it, however, for when I

went to put it on it seemed many sizes too small for me.   One look at it in the glass perched on the top of my head was enough to make me discard it.   The only substitute I could rake up was an old cricket cap, which seemed rather out of place, but, I reflected, could be carried in the pocket till I had the opportunity of purchasing more orthodox head-gear.   I dare not wear it at the ranch or in Silver City except at the risk of having it shot at, but I could wear my cowboy hat till I got on the train, when I might send it back by one of the boys and go bareheaded till I got to the Missouri River.

I left in exuberant spirits and was having a fine time of it till I met my old friend John Reilly, accompanied by my sometime antagonist Lockhart, who joined us at Rincon. Our meeting at first was slightly embarrassing, but when Reilly explained to me that they had just entered into partnership it quickly wore off and we enjoyed each other's company till we got to La Junta.   There our Pullman took them on to Denver, while I had to change to go on to Kansas City.

We would have parted without comment had they not asked what I had done with my hat, and when I told them I had left it at the ranch, and pulled the cap out of my pocket, they thought it the funniest looking cap they had ever seen.   It was an old Phœnix Cricket Club cap, in red, black, and orange stripes, and no doubt did look rather startling on the platform at La Junta ; but they might have spared me the cheer they gave when they kept me so long admiring it that I had to run for my train.

The result was to draw every one's attention to the cap, and I hastily restored it to my pocket as I dived into the Pullman.   Travel was light in those days and there were few other occupants of the car, so that I lost it out of the window on the first favourable opportunity.   There was no further incident which dwells in my memory between there and Kansas City, which we reached the following evening and where we had supper.

I was agreeably surprised on getting on the train for Chicago to find my old friend Alfred Rowe, accompanied by his brother Vincent, whom I then met for the first time. We had a most enjoyable trip, and they brought solace to my soul by saying that they expected to be in the market for some steers the following spring.   They were anxious to know how many the W S could put up, and when I told them they said they would probably see me after I got back from the old country.

They envied me my trip, and I said good-bye to them in Chicago, as they were not going any farther and I was going straight through. I had a pleasant voyage, but met no other friends till I got to Queenstown. There I was cordially greeted by the sergeant of the Royal Irish Constabulary, who was on duty at the dock. I could not recollect ever having seen him before, but he apparently knew me, and I remembered that my brother John was the resident magistrate of that district.

Whether he recognized me from a family likeness or really knew me beforehand I was never able to learn, but whichever way it was he proved to be a godsend. I had brought back with me a miniature Express rifle and a shotgun for repairs, and a returned American bearing arms was not exactly a *persona grata*, even in those quiet days. The customs officials were regarding me with suspicion till he intervened, after which they passed them through without any trouble.

My interview with Wilson was entirely satisfactory, but my stay in the country was necessarily short, there being so many things to attend to. Before leaving Dublin on my return I had a chat with an old friend, Major Trocke, who was, I found, on behalf of his niece, the principal shareholder in the T-Bar Ranch. He was very much dissatisfied with the way things were going and begged me to take hold of it and sell the cattle and ranches and get what I could out of it.

I explained to him how things were, and how difficult it would be to find a purchaser, except at ruinous prices ; but he was insistent, and said that his niece had determined to take her money out of it, or as much as she could recover, and I would do him a personal favour by complying with his wishes. I did not like the idea of supplanting Captain M., with whom we had so much fun at Las Cruces, but he was really not making any serious attempt to run it, and I told Trocke I would do the best I could to secure some one to buy it, and he must not be disappointed if it went for a song.

His final instructions were to take whatever I could get, but to sell it or give it away, and with that I had to be content, as I had to leave the next morning to catch the steamer at Liverpool—as nearly as I can recollect it was the Cunard liner *Etruria*. Amongst the passengers were Madame Modjeska and her husband Count Bozanta, whose acquaintance I was privileged to make. In common with the rest of mankind I had long worshipped her as a Queen of Tragedy on the stage, and to meet her personally was unexpected bliss. Before landing in New York she presented me with her latest photograph, which she had kindly autographed, and to this day it is one of my most treasured possessions.

I also made the acquaintance of a gentleman named Wilde, from the ' county of broad acres', who, with his son, was visiting America for the first time. When we arrived in New York we agreed to seek quarters in the same hotel. It being his first visit, Mr. Wilde was desirous of seeing everything that was exclusively American, so we decided on the Murray Hill Hotel, which was run on the American plan—meaning that you paid so much per day, which included all meals, and you ate them there or not as you thought fit ; but in either case you had to pay for them.

The tariff was moderate and the rooms were comfortable and we were thoroughly satisfied—the only drawback being that we were intensely British and not fully broken in to American customs. The meals were served at stated hours, such as breakfast from six to ten a.m. and dinner from six to eight p.m., and after we had registered we each went about our separate business, agreeing to meet again at the hotel for dinner.

We took the announcements literally as we saw them, and as we were in the habit of dining late made no attempt to enter the dining-room till about ten minutes before eight. This apparent dilatoriness was entirely unintentional, but it did not coincide with the customs of the hotel staff. True, they had said they served dinner till eight o'clock, but this meant that every one was supposed to have finished his meal by that hour.

The consequence was that when we went in the place was almost deserted and the few waiters in sight were busily engaged in clearing away the debris. We seated ourselves at the nearest table which was still untouched. We were eyed unwelcomely by the waiters, but after considerable delay one of them approached us and wanted to know our business. We expressed a wish for something to eat, whereupon he produced a formidable menu, with succulent dishes listed under numerous headings. We decided on some soup by way of a starter, and he shuffled off, and after considerable delay returned with some lukewarm stuff which looked like dish-water. This was a sore disappointment to me, for I had been blowing to Mr. Wilde on the quality of the food and the great variety with which they regaled you for a comparatively moderate sum in the New York hotels. This stuff they brought us tasted even worse than it looked. We decided to pass it up, and looked around for our surly waiter to see if he could be more successful with something else.

He had disappeared, and all our endeavours to attract attention met with no result. We coughed and shuffled our feet, even descending to the atrocity of pounding the table and jingling our glasses, but failed to raise any one. I felt humiliated, and made a feeble effort to apologize to Wilde for having misled him. He was getting ravenous and paid no attention to me, evidently having come to the conclusion that my standards were derived from the wilds of New Mexico.

After some ten minutes or so we were relieved by a procession of attendants, who filed into the room, headed by the head-waiter, who, all deference and smiles, approached our table. He apologized for keeping us waiting, ordered our plates to be removed, and had the whole table reset with clean cloth and everything, even insisting on supplying us with fresh napkins. He then requested us to order our choicest viands and everything would be served without a moment's delay.

We were dumbfounded at the change and altogether at a loss how to account for it. Instead of the one surly waiter we were now being attended by five or six, who anticipated all our wishes, and if we showed the slightest inclination for anything assured us it could be prepared fresh without a moment's delay. We then enjoyed a most excellent repast, which must have occupied over an hour, and my reputation for veracity was fully restored.

We discussed quietly amongst ourselves as to what could have caused the transformation, and could only arrive at the conclusion that some of the authorities higher up had intervened in our behalf. But as we got up to leave the head-waiter whispered to me that there was a man in the kitchen who would like me to go round and see him. I did not grasp the idea for a moment, but asked the others to excuse me and I would join them outside later.

I went round to the kitchen and found there a man, grown rather stout, whom I had last seen as a small boy called Gilbert in the employ of my brother at a place called Lough Erritt, in the County of Roscommon, Ireland. That must have been nearly ten years previously. Now he filled the post of carver to the Murray Hill Hotel.

It seemed that as he was about ready to leave our surly waiter had approached him to fill our orders, and he had asked what was keeping him so late. He replied that as he was cleaning up three ' b—— Englishmen ' had come in demanding food and be d——d to them. What else he might have said was cut short by Gilbert's looking in through the opening whence they passed the dishes and recognizing me. The joy of recognizing some one from the old sod accounted for the rest.

Verily the borders of the County of Roscommon were of wide extent. This was the third occasion within a few years that I had been rescued from an embarrassing situation through the accident of my birth.

My stay in New York was short, as I was full of business and anxious to do all in my power to execute Trocke's wishes in regard to the T-Bar Ranch and get it over with. On my way to New Mexico I stopped at both Chicago and Kansas City, where I was introduced to bankers whom I hoped to induce to take an interest in the purchase of some desirable ranches and a herd of cattle at bed-rock prices. They all scoffed at the idea.

One plethoric gentleman shook a fat forefinger under my nose and said : ' See here, my friend, I'd just as soon think of investing my money in the purchase of a shoal of fish in the Atlantic Ocean as I would of investing it in a herd of cattle on the plains of the mountains or whatever you have in New Mexico.' I retired discomfited. On arrival at the ranch I took the earliest opportunty of going over to the T-Bar and explaining the situation to M. He agreed with me that it was a very inopportune time to attempt to sell, but supposed there was no help for it.

Things were about at a standstill there, and I brought Considine, the working manager of the T-Bar outfit, back to the W S with me. We had a talk over the situation and I put him in charge of the cattle and horses there till such time as I could make a sale, promising that he would be remunerated from the proceeds before remitting any of it back to the old country. In this state things remained for several months.

After a long and arduous debate I induced Black of the Y outfit to take the cattle. Later on Mr. Porter bought the ranches at a fair valuation, so that some of the investors got something out of it, but the small holders were left flat.

While turning over those T-Bar cattle another little border incident came under my observation which resulted in the death of three men. One of them, a boy named Grostette, was a really brave man and a loss to the community. The other two, who were brothers, and whose name I forget, got just what was coming to them.

The scene was on the plains between the middle and east forks of the Gila, not far from an isolated ranch belonging to a man named Cox (no connexion with our old friend of the Tula Rosa). I had not met Grostette up to that time, but knew of him through his brother Gus, who had been an employee of the W S on several occasions, and also was well acquainted with his brother-in-law, Jesse Pitts, whom I had known since the first year I came to New Mexico.

The other two I had never seen until the actual shooting took place, and after it was over there was no further opportunity of becoming acquainted. How the dispute arose or what it was about I am not very clear, beyond hearing from Jesse Pitts that the parties in question had made some derogatory remarks about Grostette's sister. Both he and Pitts at this time were working with the Y outfit, to whom we were turning over the cattle, and the offending parties were in the employ of the V-Cross-T or the D D-Bar, who were engaged in a like occupation and whose wagons were encamped about a hundred yards apart on the same water.

Considine and I were with the Y wagon, and our first intimation was Pitts informing us one evening after supper that Grostette had gone over to the other camp, and asking us to walk over with him as he feared the boy might get into trouble. He did not seem to think the matter very urgent, but told us that there had been words between his brother-in-law and those two brothers who were working there, and that the former had gone over to make them retract something, or offer to fight them. He wanted us to go with him and see that he got fair play in what one was led to believe was a hostile camp.

Anyway, we went along and reached the camp almost as soon as Grostette did. When we got there he was standing a few yards away from the fire, around which all the others were sitting, and although he wore a gun was offering to fight them with his fists, being willing to take them on one at a time, or both together if they thought they were not equally matched. That much of the conversation we overheard, and at the time Grostette was standing with his hands in front of him and made no motion whatever that would indicate he had any desire to use a gun.

The reply he got was a shot from one of the men sitting by the fire, followed almost immediately by another from a man who was sitting beside him. That Grostette was hit was evident for it swung him around on his feet, but did not disable him, for in much less time than I can relate it he had drawn his own gun and shot one of the men where he was sitting and got the other as he rose up to hunt for cover.

The first man stayed where he was and the other only staggered away a few yards before falling on his face, where he also remained till removed later. We ran over to Grostette and only caught him just in time to prevent his sinking to the ground. The whole thing only occupied a few seconds, and it was evident the men at the fire had determined to murder him before he got a chance to retaliate. Anyway, his markmanship had been better than theirs, for they were both dead, and we laid Grostette on the ground to see how badly he had been wounded.

Only one bullet had hit him, but it was a pretty close thing, for it had entered just below the heart. We never examined the other two, leaving that to their friends ; but as they were only a few feet apart it seemed fortunate at first that all the shots had not been fatal. The boy was quite calm, and as we carried him back to camp was able to assist himself somewhat, and at the time we had high hopes of his wound not being mortal. He said that he had no intention of using his gun if he had not been fired at, and wondered if he had killed them both.

At the time we really did not know, as we had come away

at once in order to try and secure medical assistance, but shortly afterwards we were informed that he had made a clean job of it. When we got to camp we made him as comfortable as we could and removed him to the ranch house, which was close by, in the meantime having dispatched a rider to Cooney or Mogollon in search of a doctor. These were the nearest places which boasted of a resident physician, and as they were some thirty miles or more from the scene of the tragedy we could not expect skilled advice before early the following day.

We bandaged him up and put him to bed, and he seemed fairly comfortable until along in the night, when he got a fit of coughing and, gradually sinking, died about an hour later. When the doctor came the next day he made a superficial examination and said the bullet must have grazed the main artery and the walls had given way under the stress of coughing. They took him away to the Tula Rosa for burial, and his opponents were also carted off in a wagon, but where they took them to I never heard. The rest of us went on with our work ; such little incidents were disturbing, but could not be allowed to interfere with the serious work of a round-up. Grostette was a whole man, however, and every one was sorry he had gone under.

When we got through turning over the T-Bar cattle Considine came back to the W S Ranch with me and kept me company for nearly a year. He was a great help to me in many ways, and besides the pleasure of his companionship was ready to turn his hand to anything that was needed. His stay at the ranch is associated in my memory with our joint attempts at carpenter work and the making of strange pets.

Amongst the latter was a ground squirrel, one of those little grey beggars that live in a hole and whistle at you aggressively. This one had wandered into a trap set for a larger animal. When I found him he was in dire distress with a badly broken leg. I gathered him up, released him, thrust him head first into my gauntlet, and conveyed him to the house.

The first thing he needed was medical attention, and Considine and I rendered him what aid we could. One held his head while the other set the injured limb, binding it up with heavy rubber plaster. Then fixing him a comfortable bed, we placed him in a deep box, out of which, owing to his crippled condition, he was unable to jump. Here he remained for several days, at first refusing all food and curling himself up into an incredibly small space whenever we approached.

As he got better the pangs of nature overcame his resistance and he gladly accepted milk or sugar, or raisins, or other delicacies from our hands. As his leg got better he came to welcome our approaches, and when it had completely knitted he allowed us to remove the plaster without resistance. After that we turned him loose, expecting he would return to his old haunts, but he was satisfied with his new quarters and took up his residence under the porch.

There he greeted us every morning, popping up in unexpected places and jibbering and chattering till we brought him something to eat. Then he filled his jaws till everything in sight was exhausted, after which he jumped about three feet in the air, turned two or three somersaults before reaching the ground, and disappeared into his hole chattering his approval.

He made free of the house whenever he felt like it, but never wanted to spend the night there, always returning to his quarters under the porch shortly after the sun went down. He was an early riser, however, and expected attention as soon as he got up, and if it was not forthcoming he went in search of it. He soon discovered where we were sleeping, and we were compelled to shut the door on him to prevent his sharing our beds at ungodly hours of the morning.

His pet aversion was the house cat, which insisted on looking on him as a member of the rodent family and making futile efforts to stalk him. ' Witty ', as we called the squirrel, looked on these attempts as a great joke. He usually took no notice of them till the cat was within bounding distance, when he would spring round, spread his tail out like a fan, and make a dive at the cat, chattering as if he was going to eat him up. Witty looked on it as a game, and whenever he felt inclined he used to hunt for the cat and place himself in a position to attract his notice, while he himself pretended to pay no attention. He would usually turn his back and feign to be busily occupied washing his face or nibbling at something held between his paws. The cat would also simulate and appear to ignore him utterly, while Witty would move a little closer, seemingly oblivious of his presence.

This game would sometimes last fifteen or twenty minutes, but the cat was always the first to give way and succumb to temptation. He would stretch out and yawn and make other movements to reassure himself that Witty was unaware of his presence, and then flatten himself out on the ground and proceed to make his stalk. With nothing apparently moving except his tail, which kept up a waving motion and seemed to propel him, he would gradually get closer till he arrived almost within striking distance. Witty in the meantime would have his back turned and feign to be utterly unaware of the danger. But his little eyes were prominent, and he apparently could see behind him, for he never allowed his opponent to pass the danger-line. All of a sudden he would spring to life, utter his shrill little chatter, and with outspread tail make a determined rush at his would-be captor. The latter was never able to stand it and would decamp like a shot. Then Witty would go through his performance, jump in the air, and with a chatter of triumph execute his ridiculous somersaults.

He was a natural born thief and was liable at any time to creep up and seize something you had just left out of your hand and disappear with it under the porch. This pernicious habit led to our frequently having to tear up the boards in search of missing articles. He had his Nemesis, however, for one day when I was nailing shingles on the roof I happened to be smoking and, without thought of Witty, took the pipe out of my mouth and laid it down beside me while I reached for something. I had no idea that the little beggar was anywhere near, but he had evidently been on the watch, for before I had realized it he had seized the pipe and scampered off with it.

I jumped to my feet in pursuit, but he was just disappearing over the eave when, finding it necessary to use his forepaws to climb down the pillar, he popped the bowl into his mouth. It was round and no doubt he mistook it for a nut, but it was also still hot, and the way he spat it out and disappeared chattering with all his fur standing out made me laugh so that I nearly fell off the roof. His tail was spread out like a fan and appeared to emit sparks as he disappeared from sight.

I think he actually knew his name, for we could always

get a response from him when we called it, even if he was too busy to appear in person. Poor Witty ! He was good company and beguiled many a weary hour with his antics, but he came to an untimely end. It rained one day, as it does at times in that country, something over five inches in less than half an hour, with the result of converting the whole country into a lake. The water was over a foot deep all round the house, and the ditches and dry *aroyas* were such torrents that it would have been impossible to cross them on horseback.

Everything that was loose was washed away or piled up in a heap and covered with sand and rubbish. When it subsided we were so busy clearing away and repairing that for a time we forgot all about Witty and his pranks. When we did think of him we wondered where he had gone and hoped he had been wise enough to seek a place of safety. We hoped, in fact, that he would return in search of food and continue the entertainment of ourselves and the cat. But he failed to show up.

That he was still under the porch, however, became evident very shortly, and we were forced to remove his remains. We tore up a large section of the porch, and after much probing amongst gravel and other debris Witty was produced on the end of a garden rake. He looked more like a disreputable dirty rag than our late playfellow, and he smelled abominably. We bore him to the garden and deposited him in the earth sufficiently deep to discourage aggression. The cat followed the procession looking sad and gloomy, and was evidently overcome with grief, but whether at the loss of a playfellow or a toothsome morsel we never were able to ascertain. Being merely humans we quickly forgot him.

One of our occasional pastimes in those days, and one that afforded us much excitement, was a bear hunt. These we enjoyed at the invitation of Mr. Tom Lyons of the L C Ranch. He had a motley collection of dogs which he called bear-hounds, and in company with his friend Dr. Barron of Tarrytown, N.Y., used to visit our section in pursuit of his favourite game.

It was a regular ' bobbery pack ' consisting of almost every known species of dog, from an English foxhound to about the tiniest specimen of a smooth-haired fox-terrier that I have ever seen. This latter answered to the name of

Gyp and made up in pluck and endurance for everything she lacked in size, with a large margin to spare. She was just a little bundle of steel wire, and I have seen her drag a skunk from under our barn through a hole that was hardly big enough for herself to squeeze into.

Those bear hunts were quite entertaining, and Mr. Lyons usually was well equipped with all the comforts to make the camp-life less arduous. At first he brought a Chinese cook, a nice intelligent boy named Jim who was an excellent cook, but lacked experience with horses ; so much so that after one or two experiences he was forced to leave him behind and substituted in his place a man named Trayler, who heretofore had gained a precarious livelihood as a trapper.

Now there is nothing necessarily antagonistic between cooking and trapping, and Trayler, though not to be classed in the same category as Jim, was a good enough camp cook, but one had to get used to him. His favourite pelts were removed from the skunks, and as skunks were plentiful everywhere he camped he employed all his spare time in capturing them, carrying them to a convenient place handy to his work, and removing their skins. The result was that everything and every one in camp became highly flavoured.

The particular bear hunt which took place about this time dwells in my memory somewhat, owing to the size of the quarry, but also from our unexpected proximity to it and the supreme impudence of Gyp, who ran it all over the country.

Every one who has visited the Rocky Mountain region knows how delightful the early mornings are. To be outside at sun-up, or before it, is to experience one of the joys of life. The air, though often cold, is balmy, and more stimulating than a vintage wine, and the pleasure of breathing it into one's lungs cannot be expressed in writing.

But on a certain morning when I stumbled on to the porch in *déshabillé* to inhale it and fill my lungs with a deep draught, my nostrils detected a faint odour. The sun was just showing behind the mountains and the air was balmy, but it was impregnated with something strange. I called Fred's attention to it ; he had just then joined me, and he raised his head in the air and took a whiff. He snuffed inquiringly for several moments and then said he thought it smelled of skunk.

Now there was nothing unusual in the smell of skunk in

our locality at that or any other time of the day or night, but this was different ; it also seemed to be impregnated with stale coffee grounds and frijoles and other edibles familiar to camp cookery. For a moment or two I failed to recognize it, but then it suddenly dawned on me that Tom Lyons and his bear-dogs were on the road. I expressed my conviction to Fred and he took another whiff and said : ' Sure ! and he has old Trayler along with him.' ' I wonder where they are ? ' I said. ' Probably camped on Dry Creek last night and got an early start.'

Sure enough they put in an appearance some two hours later, and incidentally they had camped on Dry Creek the night before. This description may seem somewhat exaggerated to those familiar with the locality, for Dry Creek was variously estimated at fifteen to sixteen miles from the ranch, but then the skunk was a long-range animal, and perhaps they were not familiar with Trayler. He had followed his profession for years and was not particular about changing his clothes.

Anyway, there was no doubt about their presence when Tom Lyons showed up and invited us to join him in pursuit of bear. Our country was a favourite habitat for Bruin, both the Mogollon Range and the mountains to north and west of us containing a goodly number. There was some debate as to the best district to try, which was shortly decided in favour of the head waters of the Gila in the vicinity of the West Fork, and thither Trayler and his assistant Bob Stubblefield were sent with all the dogs except Gyp to make camp, while Lyons with Dr. Barron and Gyp and I were to follow them later.

Bright and early the following morning they discovered some huge footprints and put on the hounds. But they led into a country that was practically impossible for horses, so we all took posts of vantage at different points, hoping they might get Bruin afoot and drive him to us. These posts, owing to the nature of the country as well as to the custom of the quarry, were necessarily far apart and usually taken with a view to covering the most likely place to be followed by a bear in his descent from the high mountains.

Bob Stubblefield took charge of Dr. Barron, and Trayler undertook to try and keep pace with the hounds on foot, while Lyons and I rode some miles ahead to the mouth of a large canyon which opened into a sort of mountain park.

We were accompanied by Gyp, who occupied her usual place of honour on the front of her master's saddle, and as we rode along we could hear the baying of the hounds several miles above us, near the top of the range.

It took us more than half an hour to reach our destination, and when we got there we found a wide, open canyon, with scattered timber and large clumps of oak brush lying fairly close together. The park into which it opened was thickly timbered with pines and pinon and cedar scattered in between. The mountains rose up almost perpendicular on all sides of it, and it looked an attractive shelter for a solitary bear.

There being nothing to do but wait, we took up our stations close to a clump of brush, and sitting sideways on our saddles beguiled the time chatting in subdued tones. Gyp, as was usual with her, jumped off and was skirmishing around the brush in search of chipmunks or anything that might interest her and help to pass the time. We paid no attention to her, and as we could still hear the hounds a long way off had no idea of the close proximity of a bear or any other large game.

Our surprise consequently can be imagined when there came crashing from a clump of brush, not over forty yards up the canyon, a bear that looked to me almost as big as a full-grown steer. He was smashing the timber and everything in front of him, and Gyp was in hot pursuit, nipping at his heels. What else he did I had not an opportunity to perceive, for our horses were if anything more surprised than we were. Lyons's horse gave a snort and swung round so sharp that it landed him in the middle of the clump of brush, while I only retained my seat by hanging on to the mane.

Both animals bolted, and mine ran fully a hundred yards before I was able to control him. As soon as I did I rounded up Lyons's horse and caught him, and then made my way back to the place where he had been unseated. As I did so I could see the bear away up the mountain smashing and crashing through all obstacles, while he rolled the rocks down behind him, and stuck to his heels was Gyp like a little white dot, yapping and snapping as if ready to eat him.

I had no time to take in any more for I had to go and see how it fared with Tom Lyons. I found him sitting up in the brush and enjoying himself hugely. His rifle, which he had held in his hand, was thrown to some distance, but he said that he was not hurt as he had come down softly in the brush, and the bear, which he described as being as big as a two-year-old steer, had almost brushed against him, but it was so busy trying to get away from Gyp that it took no notice of anything in its road.

As soon as we gathered up the pieces we went in pursuit of Gyp, but as the country proved so rough we were obliged to dismount and make our way on foot.

We did not find her till we had gone several miles, and then she was sitting on the trail licking herself, evidently being satisfied with having run Bruin out of the country. We hunted up the rest of the party and the hounds were eventually got together, but it was then so late that nothing further could be done that day and I unfortunately had to leave them as I had to go to Silver City to meet Vincent Rowe, who was coming to have a look at our cattle with a view to completing the deal we had spoken of the previous winter on our way to Chicago.

I regretted not being able to stay and see it out, for they put the hounds on the bear's track the following morning, and having brought him to bay after an exciting chase, killed him. I afterwards saw the hide, which was an extraordinarily large one, covering an astonishing number of square feet. The carcase weighed considerably over a thousand pounds. It was still in the possession of Mrs. Lyons when I had the sad duty of acting as one of the pall-bearers for poor Tom, who was foully murdered in El Paso some twenty years afterwards.

At the time he gave me a note to leave with his Chinaman Jim on my way to Silver City. They were at this time living at the White House, which had some time previously ceased to be a road-house, and the stage station was moved some seven or eight miles farther on to the banks of the Gila River. Lyons said that now having got hold of a cattle buyer it was advisable to stick to him, and if we felt like stopping over for lunch on our way back Jim would take care of us.

Some two days later I met Vincent Rowe in Silver City, and having sent a team in advance to the White House we drove through to the W S in one day We found lunch and everything prepared for us as we drove out, and to Vincent's great amusement Jim treated us to a bottle of champagne.

He said nothing at the time, but after we got started he would indulge in a hearty fit of laughter about every half-mile or so and twit me about the deplorable condition of the cowmen in New Mexico. I explained that it was merely the exuberance of our spirits at having really discovered a man who wanted to buy cattle, and that we were so fearful of his getting away that even the Chinese help had banded together to do him honour. It was the only prospect of their ever receiving any wages, and from that he might infer on what easy terms he could buy our cattle.

It was Vincent's first experience of a mountain country, and when I took him out on the range the day following our arrival he rode some nine or ten miles without comment. We were riding up a fairly open canyon, but like all others in that country it was thickly strewn with rock. At one portion of it we actually struck a smooth bit of ground, and Vincent was so pleased when we reached the end of it he turned round and rode back over it again. He said it was the only smooth bit of country in that section and he proposed to ride over it for the rest of the day.

When Vincent left us he said he was satisfied with the quality of the cattle but refused to commit himself as to contract of purchase, saying it was necessary to consult his brother Alfred.

Some three weeks later Alfred came out. He didn't bother much about the cattle, being satisfied with my statement and what his brother had seen, but he was very keen about the country, especially its geological formation, and we had many pleasant rides to different places. Before we left we entered into a contract in which to the best of my recollection I undertook to deliver him some three thousand steers—one-, two-, and three-year-old or over—free on board the cars at Magdalena, for which he agreed to pay the sums of seven, eleven, and fourteen dollars respectively.

We spent all the summer delivering those cattle, and the principal impression left on my mind during the transaction is that of being stampeded over and escaping without material injury. It came about through the innocent desire of the engineer of the train to entertain a friend. We had just got through separating the cattle in the pens and the train was standing by to load them. Two or three of us who had been on horseback were making our way out through the main gateway before returning to complete our task on foot.

As the last horseman passed through the gates I got down to close them and was reaching out to secure the iron hook in the spud when the engineer, to amuse his friend and show him how the cattle would run, blew off the steam on his engine. The next moment they struck the gate and I was lost in flying hooves. I must have been knocked some twenty or thirty feet, but otherwise not injured. I was in danger of being trampled to death, however, and instinct told me that safety lay in getting close to the fence and climbing up it.

It was impossible to see anything on account of the dust and the maelstrom of feet, so I crawled as best I could in the direction where I knew it lay. In doing so I struck into the heels of my horse, who had stood his ground and let the cattle stampede around him. As I bumped him with my head he lifted up a foot and tapped me on the nose with the calk of his shoe. The result was that he removed all the skin from the point of my nose to the roots of my hair. I didn't really know what I had struck, but I kept on my way till I touched the fence.

In another moment I had climbed up it, and suddenly appeared on top to the great relief of the boys who had been figuring on shipping my mangled remains back to the ranch. They gave me a great cheer as I appeared out of the ruck, and coming as it did, spontaneously and sincere, I felt duly grateful. I was a miserable object, however, for my face was grey with dust and the blood from my skinned features, aided by perspiration, cut channels through it. There was no time for investigation, however, for the cattle had to be attended to, and the boys rode off, still under the impression that though I had come out alive I was pretty badly chawed up.

The cattle were flying wildly all over the place, with two or three men in front of them endeavouring to hold them up. When the boys all got together they succeeded in getting them to milling, but it was fully an hour or more before they quieted down, and then they were some two miles from the pens. I got some men that were hanging around, and with the help of the train crew we tried to fix up the broken gates. One side had been knocked completely out and carried to some distance in the rush, but the bottom hinge on the other had held, causing it to swing to one side before falling flat.

Some seven or eight cattle had got piled up in it which later had to be destroyed, owing to broken legs and other injuries, but they undoubtedly had been my salvation, for they deflected the rush of cattle from running over me when they were coming through the gate so thick that I could not possibly have escaped their hooves. For the time being we just dragged them to one side, and as soon as we got the gates in such a state of temporary repair that they would stand I got my horse and joined the rest of the boys with the herd.

The poor engineer who had unwittingly been the cause was overcome with remorse, but we cheered him up by telling him that he had been able to stage a better entertainment for his friends than he had counted on. But the most trying part was to come, when I had to go home by train, for some forty different versions of the affair must have got about, and I was looked upon as the frightful example resulting from a cowboy orgy in Magdalena. When we got through delivering those cattle to the Rowe brothers there was more loose cash in Western Socorro County than there had been since I came into it, and my reputation as a cowman was established.

Returning from our last delivery we intended to devote ourselves to horse-breaking. In this, however, we were in some degree doomed to disappointment. We rounded up the following day and got a goodly bunch thrown together, and having cut out the colts needed got them safely in the pen, where Fred proposed to leave them until we got some more the following day.

We had scarcely got through, however, when we were invaded by three tough-looking strangers. They were heavily armed with pistols and saddle-guns, and the size and quality of their horses would have drawn attention in any frontier camp.

I watched them ride up to the bunk-house, and as they seemed uncertain as to whom they wished to address I left them to the tender mercies of Fred and went up to the house, where I got into clean clothes and sat down to my supper. Being both tired and hungry I quickly forgot all about them, and as soon as I had bolted my food returned to the office and sat down to enjoy a smoke and do some necessary writing.

I had scarcely commenced when they all three came up accompanied by Fred, who informed me that those three gentlemen, introducing them by name, were in pursuit of stolen horses—a grave offence on the frontier and still somewhat prevalent throughout the territory of New Mexico. In this case it was a notorious outlaw who went by the name of ' Black Jack '. He was commonly supposed to be a half-breed Indian and was the leader of a gang of desperadoes who plied their trade through the southern counties of New Mexico and along the borders of Texas and Arizona, not being above dropping in to Old Mexico when safety required it.

He had made a raid on a number of the ranchers in Lincoln County, New Mexico, and carried off a number of their top horses. He had been impartial in his depredation and some of his ill-gotten gains had been acquired from men whom, if report spoke true, had themselves in former days bordered on his profession. However that may have been, this time they had all got together and with all the resources at their command determined to recover their stolen property.

Knowing their business they went about it in a professional way, and selecting two of the most determined of their number had sent them along with another who bore a sheriff's commission, with instructions to follow the gang. No questions were to be asked as to the disposal of Black Jack or his gang, but on no account were they to return without the horses. They were mounted on the best animals that could be procured and, for the rest, were left to their own discretion.

They said they had followed the gang steadily for over a week and felt sure they were no more than a day behind them. They were probably on their way to Clifton, Arizona, and they would be under obligation if we could furnish them a guide, as the country was entirely unknown to them.

Now Fred declared that it was impossible for him to go— he had to get on with his horse-breaking and he didn't think he had a man in the outfit that knew the way except Tipton, and he could not possibly spare him. The upshot of it was that I reluctantly agreed to go with them and show them the way.

This being settled we all retired to rest and our Lincoln County friends and myself were on the road before break of day the next morning. I took them over the old Indian trail by which we had gone in pursuit of our friend McNeil, and we reached Clifton sometime between three and four in the afternoon.

Our researches there met with no result until we ran across an acquaintance of mine named Cipriano Baca, whom I had known as a peace-officer in Silver City. Cipriano told us he was holding down the office of town marshal in Clifton, and asked if he could be of any assistance during our stay. We enlightened him as to the object of our visit. He said that he was well acquainted with Black Jack, both professionally and otherwise, and that while he knew of his having a lady friend there he was positive that he had not come to Clifton either quite lately or within the last thirty days.

He advised that we go up the Blue and we might possibly get some tidings of them at the McKeen Ranch, near where the main trail crossed, and if we would leave one man with him to identify the stock and swear out the necessary information he would undertake to see that Black Jack did not get away should he in the meantime show up at Clifton. This sounded reasonable and we immediately accompanied him to the office of the local justice, where the necessary papers were made out.

There was nothing more we could do that night, so leaving one of our party with Cipriano, the remaining three of us got our horses and travelled up the Blue until it got too dark for further progress, when we made camp. It was pretty certain that if the outlaws did not intend to come to Clifton they would cross the Blue above the McKeen Ranch.

We reached the McKeen Ranch next morning before they had breakfast. Hugh McKeen was not at home, but Bob Bell was holding down the place and invited us to dismount, an invitation which was made doubly welcome by the smell of hot coffee from the stove. When we had refreshed ourselves and warmed up a bit we asked him if he had seen, in his vicinity, any one with a bunch of loose horses.

He said three men had crossed the creek the previous morning before daylight, following the trail to the Reservation. He happened to be out unusually early and had just seen them as they were watering their horses. They looked like Indians, and some of the horses they were driving had crossed the creek and were part way up the trail on the other side. It was on that account that Hugh had gone to Alma. Bob had told him that he was almost sure they were Indians and he was anxious to notify the people to look out for their stock.

I told him what Baca had told us about Black Jack having some kind of hold-out in the neighbourhood of the Reservation, and he said that he had heard of it and always understood that it was somewhere on a creek they called Rausensocker. It sounded Teutonic, and I asked him if he knew who had been responsible for its name. He said he didn't know whether it was Dutch or Hebrew, but it might be Mormon. There had been Mormons there till the Indians ran them out, and they might have got the name out of their Bible. Bob's theological ideas were a bit mixed. He said, further, that we would find a trail some fifteen miles west of the Blue which had a northerly direction and by following it we would reach Rausensocker.

With those instructions we left him and followed the main trail for what we estimated to be fifteen miles or perhaps a little more. Keeping a sharp look-out we discovered what appeared to be an unused trail leading in the right direction. He had described it as being very dim, and as the landmarks seemed to correspond, after a short debate we took it. Having followed it for a mile or more it played out. Here was further cause for debate, but time was pressing and we hated to go back, so we compromised by concluding that we had turned out too soon and decided to carry on, as by bearing somewhat more to the west we would be sure to strike the right trail in time.

This we did and let ourselves in for some very rough riding, but after some eight or ten miles we actually did strike the right trail and found it to be well worn and for that country pretty smooth riding. No doubt we had lost some time, but in the light of after-events we must have been guided by our good angels. Had we taken the right trail in the first place we would have run into Black Jack without our knowing it.

No doubt this was our object, but we wanted the element of surprise to be on his part and not on ours. With his Indian instincts he probably would have spotted us long before we were aware of it, and we might be there yet. As it was, we got in behind him, for he and one of his companions were on their way to Clifton, with the intention, as I understood afterwards, of visiting his inamorata.

As it was, we were glad of the smooth going, more especially as it contained fresh horse-tracks. We went on cautiously, keeping a sharp look-out. It was near sundown and our horses were showing signs of fatigue before we came to where it descended into a deep canyon, and as we could see cotton-wood trees at the bottom we decided that we had reached Rausensocker. Up to this I had been acting as guide, but here I turned matters over to the sheriff. He thought it wise to reconnoitre before descending into the canyon, and we agreed with him.

We tied our horses in the brush a little way from the trail and then spreading out a bit advanced cautiously on foot. We could descry a clear stream of water, and finding a place from where we could reconnoitre without being seen we sat down in the brush to have a good look. There was an old tumble-down cabin about a hundred yards up from the bottom of the trail, with a fairly good corral beside it, and though there was nothing in it at the time we could see some horses farther up the creek.

It was growing dusk and not easy to recognize them, but my companions seemed to be satisfied and we waited there for probably twenty minutes to see if any one was moving about the house. When we were about ready to give it up a man came out of the house and gathering up an armful of wood went back in again. We waited a little longer to see if any one else would show up, and then decided that he was alone.

This being settled we went back for our horses and led them to the point of observation, where it was decided that the sheriff and his companion would proceed on foot while I remained behind and looked after the horses. As soon as I heard a shot I was to hasten to their assistance and to keep a sharp look-out that the inmate of the cabin did not get away. If he bolted while they were getting down there I was instructed to take a shot at him, which, even if it proved harmless, would notify the others.

I carefully concealed the horses in a convenient place and squatted down behind a rock to watch the stalk. The sheriff and his companion disappeared into the brush and I did not see them again for nearly twenty minutes. Then one of them appeared crouching low about twenty yards above the house and began to wade across the stream.

He was evidently trying to keep a large cotton-wood tree between himself and the house, and after he reached *terra firma* broke into a little trot and squatted down close to the tree. This brought him within about fifty feet of the building and enabled him to command all that side of the house.

I was so busy watching him that I failed to observe his companion, who had crossed lower down and by creeping under an old fence had actually reached the front door. Here he was about to force an entry when its inmate saved him the trouble by returning after some more firewood. He found himself looking down the muzzle of a gun, and throwing up his hands backed into the room, followed by the gentleman who was holding the gun.

This I gathered afterwards : at the time it was brought home to me by seeing the gentleman under the tree jump to his feet, discharge his pistol into the ground, and run round to the front door. I waited a moment or two for any repetition of the shooting, and then mounting my steed and leading the other two made the best of my way to join them.

When I got to the cabin they were all three sitting inside, the lone inmate in the middle, where he had been answering questions in regard to the movements of Black Jack and the stolen stock. As I was about to dismount the gentleman who wasn't a sheriff came out and joined me. He said it would be a good idea to gather up the horses and put them in the corral before it got too dark.

While we were doing so he informed me that Black Jack and one of his companions had gone to Clifton, leaving the gentleman whom they had surprised to take care of the booty. He expressed disappointment at having missed them, but I was not disposed to agree with him and explained my reasons, which he seemed to think orthodox, but made no comment, merely remarking that ' Maybe it was as well '. The horses were all hobbled, and as there was plenty of good grass close by we had no difficulty in finding them, and in less than twenty minutes had them all in the pen, which was in tolerable good repair.

The question then was how we were going to guard them, as we did not put implicit faith in the statements of the prisoner. We didn't want Black Jack and his companion to come back and take us in as easily as we had done his henchman, when he would probably have disposed of us in short order. The best arrangement we could make was for the sheriff and his prisoner to sleep in the house while the other gentleman and I bedded down in the corral and took turns watching the stock.

After that we ate a good supper at Black Jack's expense and took up our respective quarters. My friend and I passed a more or less uncomfortable night with intermittent snatches of rest until it got so cold towards morning that we were compelled to light a fire, after which we were fairly comfortable till dawn. I don't know how the sheriff and his *compadre* fared, but Black Jack was well provided, and we found them fast asleep and coupled together on a pile of blankets when we went in at the first streak of day.

When we roused them he uncoupled the prisoner and he prepared an excellent breakfast, again at the expense of our absent host. We even trespassed on his hospitality to the extent of taking some of his food and fodder along in case of emergency, and then got under weigh as quickly as possible on our return journey.

There was some slight talk of how to dispose of the prisoner, and my companions evidently looked upon him as an unnecessary encumbrance, but eventually it was considered advisable to bring him along, and he was allowed to select his own mount while our friend the sheriff handcuffed him in front with sufficient play to allow his handling the bridle. Then the other gentleman and I took the lead, with the other two coming on behind and prodding up the loose horses.

There was no inspiring incident on the way back. We got started so early that we reached the Blue before noon. We were anxious to get home, and reached the ranch late that night, when I immediately went to bed and turned the rest of the outfit over to Fred. We had not got Black Jack, but we captured his henchman and, what was more to the point, recovered the stolen stock.

CHAPTER XIV

HORSE-BREAKING AND CATTLE-RUSTLING.

TO say that I was tired that night would but express it mildly. My next gleam of consciousness was next morning when Fred came into my room to tell me that the sheriff and his party were about to pull out and wanted to thank me for the assistance I had given. I noticed that the sun was high, but I told him to tell them that I was asleep and that I was glad they had recovered their horses, and immediately forgot all about them.

A little later I became more fully awake, principally urged by the thoughts of my neglected correspondence. This quickly brought me on to the floor, and I hastily dressed and had breakfast. During the meal another message from Fred came to tell me that they were breaking horses in the round corral, and that they had an old gentleman who had come in the evening before with a butcher's knife stuck in his boot who claimed he could ride, and the boys had christened him 'The Granger', and he thought they were going to have some fun with him.

I sent down word that I was busy writing but that I would come as soon as I could, and then proceeded to get busy and try to forget all about them. I had not proceeded very far, however, when the yips and yells coming from the corral sadly disturbed me, and I was tempted on to the porch to see if I could get a glimpse of what was going on. The walls of the corral were fully eight feet high, but I could see the form of the rider, and occasionally the back of the horse, appear and disappear at frequent intervals over it. Sometimes the back of the horse appeared without the rider, and then the cheering and yelling redoubled in volume, a sure indication of the failure of the rider to retain his seat.

I watched it for a minute or two, and then the temptation proving too strong, I let the correspondence slide and getting my hat hurried down to join them. The horse corral had large double gates facing each other, one opening into a series of picket corrals and the other leading into the open. Through the former the broncos were introduced to be saddled and broken, and when duly calmed were led out through the other and into an enclosure which contained the stables.

When I got down there were two or three in the corral in various phases of being roped and saddled with their prospective riders attending to them. The rest of the outfit were seated on the gate or in its neighbourhood, and amongst them I recognized the gentleman who had been christened ' The Granger '. He was a middle-aged man and a typical tramp from his battered hat to his run-down boots, with the handle of the butcher's knife sticking out of the top of one of them.

He didn't appear to be particularly interested in the proceedings, or indeed in anything else, and to the frequent invitations to get down and show what he could do merely jerked the tobacco juice out of his mouth and intimated that he was waiting for something that needed riding. The general belief was that he was merely bluffing, and after a time the boys took little or no notice of him.

The lot that were in at the time I came on the scene were fairly tractable and were duly ridden and led out to make room for the next batch. Amongst the latter was a big bay horse they called Bullet which at one time had been partially broken, but having got away and run wild amongst the mares he had proved difficult to catch and was for several years conveniently forgotten. He was now over eight years old and Fred had determined to make use of him, so this time he was duly rounded up and took his place amongst the colts.

All hands were eager to have a try at him, though most of them knew he was vicious, for I had related to Fred my experience of him, which had occurred before he came to the W S. When he had been brought in as a three-year-old and escaped they had bobbed his tail and I, on one of my excursions after the mares, seeing his bobbed tail had mistaken him for one of the regular saddle-horses. With great difficulty I had succeeded in corraling the whole bunch in a corral on the Thomason Flat, some miles from the Ranch.

Here, single-handed, I managed to separate him from the others and turned them loose. Then having got him alone in the corral I proposed to rope him and lead him back to the ranch. My rope was rather short, but I managed to get it on him without difficulty and then proceeded to lead

him. This was an entirely different matter, and to my
astonishment he dragged me around the corral for fully
twenty minutes.   Thus failing to get rid of me and finding
the tightening noose was beginning to choke him he changed
his tactics and came at me open mouthed.

I barely escaped him by climbing the fence, and then had
to run him to the ranch, where in order to recover my rope
we had to forefoot him.   After which we gladly turned him
loose   Since then, which was some three years earlier, he
had been unmolested, as, although he had been brought to
the ranch several times and some feeble attempts made to
handle him, he had always proved too much for his captors,
who generally connived at his escape.

There were three or four others of the same kidney, but
none of them so notorious as Bullet.   He came in towering
over the two or three broncos which accompanied him and
really looked magnificent as he snorted and pawed the
ground, as if to show fight.   The boys discreetly let him
alone while the others were being thrown and saddled, and
having ridden them for a few jumps, none of them giving a
remarkable display, they led them out.

Bullet was now alone, and he careered around the
enclosure, stopping every now and again to snort defiance,
and as soon as the riders came back they looked at him in
doubt.   Some were for throwing him, especially those who
did not pretend to be riders.   Others thought it advisable
to throw him back in the bunch till they had more time on
their hands.   Every one had forgotten about the old gentleman on the fence.   He was still chewing tobacco and
apparently not taking much interest in the proceedings.

Some one was about to open the gate when he held up
his hand and asked what was the matter with the bay.   He
was told that he was a pretty bad *caballo* and they thought
of tying a saddle on him and leaving him saddled up for a
day before attempting to ride him.   His only remark was
to spit the quid out of his mouth, slip down off the fence,
give a hitch to his old pants and say : ' Hell !   I'll ride
him.'

It took a minute or so for the observation to sink in, and
then it was received with an ironical cheer.   At first nobody
thought he was serious, but when he borrowed a pair of
spurs from Fred and proceeded to buckle them on it began
to dawn on us that he really meant to ride him.

Some caustic remarks were addressed to him in regard to his will and his choice as to the mode of burial, but of these he took no notice, merely indicating with his hand to go ahead and get the saddle on. The proud Bullet was fore-footed, and busted so hard that it broke his front teeth. Then it took all hands to hold him while he was hobbled fore and aft with the usual slip knot. A hackamore and blind was placed on his head and a saddle securely fixed before he was allowed on to his feet.

When he got up, although blindfolded, he still looked defiant, the more so on account of the blood from his broken teeth. He did all that a horse can do to get rid of the saddle, but with men holding on to a rope from either side he gradually quieted down. Taking advantage of the pause the old man crawled on to his back, the blind was removed from his eyes, and we all ran to climb the fence and witness his demise.

For a moment or two Bullet stood still with surprise, and then realizing that something was on his back, he turned himself loose. He pitched as only a Western bronco can pitch, with his head almost between his hind legs and his back arched. He sprang into the air fully five or six feet, reversing his position in the process and keeping it up in quick succession, till it looked as if his rider's head must have been shaken loose from his body. We all looked for both man and horse to come down in a heap, but they maintained their respective positions.

When Bullet found he couldn't unseat him he fairly screamed with rage and went round and round the enclosure, alternately pitching and plunging, for fully ten minutes, when, finding it necessary to slacken his efforts in order to regain breath, he broke into a trot and eventually came to a halt. This gave his rider a chance to settle himself more firmly in his seat and prove to the maddened beast that he was his master.

The old fellow drove the spurs into him, and taking off his old hat, which had been pressed down on his ears, he slapped him with it in the face. This not having the desired effect, he reached down to the ground and seizing a handful of sand rubbed it in his steaming nostrils. Bullet was not prepared to stand much of that kind of work, and after making a futile effort to kick him like a cow, threw down his head and commenced his pitching. He went through the same performance for another ten minutes and with the same result, this time coming to a stand with a regular scream.

At first we had looked on with astonishment and incredulity depicted on our faces, but when we realized that the old fellow really could ride the cheering that we gave him made the whole place ring. When they came to a halt after the second round the old fellow himself was glad to take a breather, but he made no attempt to dismount, merely remarking : ' He sure is a daisy.'

Then it was suggested that he should take him outside, and every one who had a horse saddled there got ready to accompany him, prophesying that by the time they got back Bullet could be thrown into the regular *remouda*. The gates were thrown open, and seeing a chance for liberty he went through them like a shot, proving that he had been correctly named. He was joined on the outside by all the boys who were mounted, and they went off ' hell for leather ', as if the devil was behind them.

I followed on foot, determined to see all I could, but they had not gone more than fifty or sixty yards when Bullet, to show he was still in the ring, threw down his head and renewed his pitching. This time he had the whole world before him and his efforts, if possible, exceeded anything he had done in the corral. The yipping and yelling went on for a minute or two and the old man seemed fairly comfortable, but all of a sudden I saw him sway in his seat and slip round to one side under the animal's feet.

The saddle had turned, and it looked as if the infuriated animal must trample him to death. I ran up as fast as I could and all the boys had pulled up and were forming a circle round him. He was equal to the occasion, however, for on going over he had managed to get hold of the noseband of the hackamore and was holding on for grim death with a hand on each side of the animal's jaws. In this way he managed to keep his head and body off the ground while his feet were still in the stirrups with the spurs hooked into the broad hair cincha and over the animal's back.

The infuriated brute, being unable to bite him, was endeavouring to rake him off with his front feet. How long the struggle might have gone on it was impossible to say, but for the minute or two that it lasted it looked as if it could only have one end, and that we would be compelled after all to consign the old gentleman to a decent grave. He couldn't have held on much longer, when Fred, with great presence of mind, rode up as close as he could to the plunging brute and, seizing a favourable moment, pulled out his gun and shot him through the head just under the ear.

He dropped in a heap like a bundle of clothes, and, to our great relief the old man rolled out from under. He was not in the least flurried. His first care was to shake his foot loose from the cincha, after which he helped himself to a chew of tobacco, got on his feet, and looked at Bullet for some time without comment or remark of any kind. It was apparent he was quite dead, and seeming satisfied he pushed him with his foot, said he was ' a likely kind of a hoss ', and proceeded to undo the cincha.

We all congratulated him on his escape, but he didn't seem to notice it—just said it was a pity to have to kill him —and we all pitched in and rolled him over to free the saddle. That was the end of poor Bullet.

His late rider shouldered the saddle and blankets and we all marched back to the corral. He was offered his choice of the mounts on the ranch, but he said he wasn't interested, and after he had sat long enough on the fence to recover his breath he went back to the house, and that was the last that I saw of him. I never learnt his name, nor where he went, nor where he came from. He was just an incident that came into my life, but made himself sufficiently interesting to be remembered.

We went on with our horse-breaking, and now that my hand was in I forgot for the time all about my letter-writing. Amongst one of the lots that were brought in shortly afterwards was a buckskin mare, my own personal property, and I was interested in her future welfare. She was one of a bunch I had bought from a Mormon who lived on the Gila.

This buckskin had been a foal at foot when I bought her, and gave promise of being something out of the ordinary. As she was now nearly four years old I was resolved to break her. Owing to her connexion with the Church I had christened her Utah, and saw myself in advance the possessor of an exceptional saddle-horse. She seemed to have an excellent disposition and was so gentle from the start that we did not have to throw her.

With very little handling she agreed to lead, and Fred and

I rubbed her all over. We even put a saddle on her but did not attempt to cinch it, for I had determined to break her gently and to practise the old country methods on her. Though recognizing the usual necessity of the rough-and-ready manner of the Western bronco-buster I had never been in love with it.

We rubbed her and petted her and pulled her ears and played with her until we thought we had her as gentle as a kitten, and then while Fred busied himself with some other broncos I said I would take her back into the picket corral and make love to her some more before tying her up. Some of the boys opened one side of the gates for me and I led her through, gentle as a kitten. The gate was closed quickly behind me to prevent the others following, as I distinctly recollect, and I seem to have a faint remembrance of patting her gently on the back, after which all was oblivion.

When I again gained consciousness I was in bed and wondering vaguely what one of the boys, named Perry Tucker, was doing in my room. It seemed to me that, in a hazy sort of way, I had been watching him for a long time. How long I could not form the faintest idea, and I kept watching him now without any immediate object, further than wondering what he was doing there.

Then as my mind became somewhat clearer I noticed that he was looking at me, and I made a move of some kind which caused him to get up and peer into my face. With difficulty I found my voice and asked him if he knew what day it was? He said it was Monday and immediately left the room. All this seemed more or less of a dream, and I felt that I wanted to go to sleep, and took no particular interest as to whether he stayed or not.

Whether I did fall asleep or not is not very clear to me, but the next thing I was aware of was that Fred was standing by the bed and two or three of the other boys were looking in at the door. Fred asked me how I felt, and I said all right, but kept wondering how it could be Monday and asked him what I was doing in bed? He said I had been there since some time the day before, and I presume my mind had been gradually clearing, for I recollected we had been breaking horses on Sunday.

Then he asked me if I recollected having gone to Arizona? This made me think, and I said yes, but that it seemed a long time ago. Then he asked me if I recollected the name of the creek on which we found the stolen horses. This must have been well impressed on my memory, for I said with but slight hesitation, ' Rausensocker!' Then Fred turned to the other boys and said : ' He's all right, fellows ! No one that was dippy could have recollected a name like that.' On which they began to laugh and gave a suppressed cheer.

I had a feeling that I wanted to know what it was all about, but was told I had better stay quiet. I slept for a couple of hours, but the next recollection I have is that I was wide awake and that one of my arms, which was all bandaged up, was hurting me dreadfully. Perry was still in the room and I asked him what had happened ? He said that one of the boys had noticed the mare Utah looking over the bars which served as a gateway to the outer corral with the rope dangling from her neck just as they were about to go to dinner, and they had gone in and found me crumpled up by the fence and had carried me up to bed.

He said I had been unconscious ever since, but that I had been muttering something about my arm as they carried me up, and they had sent for Doc Way, who pronounced it a compound fracture of the left arm. He had put it in splints and bandaged me up. He regretted very much the primitive means at his disposal, and said that if he only had some plaster of Paris he would have put it in a cast and made a real good job of it. I said that something must have happened to it, for it was hurting me like the devil, and I vainly tried to shift into a more comfortable position.

Perry then wanted to know from me what had really happened, but I was unable to enlighten him. I told him that I had a distinct recollection of leading the mare through the gate and of their closing it after me, but after that all the rest was a blank and I have never been able to recollect anything about it. It was evident that Utah must have had a hand in it, but whatever she did she did it so quickly that we were never able to bring it home tó her.

He said the boys intended to take turns sitting up with me during the night. While he was talking, though my arm was hurting me so badly, I noticed I could bend my wrist. This led me to think that my arm could not really be broken, and to satisfy myself I wriggled it around as much as the bandages would let me.

The more I thought of it—and I thought of little else at

the time—the more certain I became that Doc had been mistaken in his diagnosis, and to assure myself I set to work to unloose the bandages. The relief I felt when they came away was beyond expression, and I found that the cause of my trouble was that they had been bound so tight the splints had sunk into my arm.

As I stretched it and rubbed it, enjoying the relief, I had to laugh as I thought that if Doc had only had the means to put it in a plaster cast what an excellent job he would have done. Poor Doc, when he came to see me the next day I felt quite embarrassed at the exposure and wore it in a sling for his special benefit. At the time I told Perry that I was all right, and that there was no necessity for any one to sit up for me. Shortly afterwards I fell asleep and did not awake till the following morning.

I got up and dressed as usual, and beyond a slight dizziness which gave me an inclination to fall over whenever I stooped, could find no ill effects. I was neither stiff nor sore, nor could I find a bruise or a scratch that could have been caused by the mishap. The dizziness lasted for several weeks, and often on horseback made me feel like rolling out of the saddle ; but it passed away after a time and never was so bad that I could not check it by pulling myself together. Just what Utah had done I can't imagine, but she put a slight damper on my career as a bronco-buster. For the time being I had no ambition to shine in that capacity, but it in no way interfered with my letter-writing, and I was enabled to devote the entire day to a much-neglected occupation. I got so busy at it that I entirely forgot everything else, amongst them our expedition to Arizona. It was recalled to my mind, however, that afternoon by the appearance of Cipriano Baca in company with the gentleman we had left to assist him at Clifton, Arizona.

I was still rather hazy in regard to the whole transaction, and I asked them to excuse me a moment till I came to a natural pause in my correspondence. They sat down on a lounge that was in the room, and as they did so it occurred to me that they might have news of Black Jack. I apologized for keeping them waiting and asked if they had seen anything of him.

They smiled at each other, and then Baca drew my attention to a new pair of boots that he was wearing and said they had belonged to Black Jack. At the same time his companion indicated a belt he was wearing which bore an ornamental buckle and said that the gentleman who had accompanied Jack was wearing that the last time he had seen him. It seemed superfluous to make further inquiries. Black Jack's reputation was sufficient guarantee that he had not given up his boots voluntarily, and no doubt the same applied to his companion-in-arms.

They then volunteered the information that the deceased had come to Clifton, and having dolled up in great shape were about to visit some ladies of their acquaintance, and when called upon by Cipriano, in his capacity as a peace-officer, to give themselves up, they had resisted arrest and were promptly put out of existence. Thus ended Black Jack, who was the first of the name that I had happened to come across in that section of country.

In explanation I might remark that the cognomen ' Black Jack ' was a favourite one amongst border outlaws. From the original Black Jack Davy, celebrated in song by every cowboy, and who was no doubt the founder of the dynasty, there have been many Black Jacks. This half-breed Indian, however, was the first to come under my ken, though later on I came in contact with another gentleman bearing the title who was a pure-bred white man named Ketchum, of whom more hereafter.

About this time, in the year 1895, there was really beginning to be some demand for cattle. There were rumours of people being in the country and actually desirous of contracting for their purchase several months in advance of the date of their delivery and paying substantial sums down to bind the contract. All this was very encouraging to the cattle owner, but it also brought about the revival of the rustler. He sprang again into existence with the rise in the price of cattle. The Indian outbreak, which had been the original cause of his disappearance, had been followed by a period of depression which had lasted ten years and rendered his calling unremunerative ; but now he came again like a field of mushrooms after a warm rain. It was an ancient, and at certain periods of history by no means a dishonourable, profession, and from my experience of the New Mexico operators I would judge that the tricks of the trade had been handed down to them in unbroken succession.

Due to the revival of this industry recent legislation had been initiated in the Legislature at Santa Fé which led to the creation of the Cattle Sanitary Board. The registration of brands was now removed from the jurisdiction of the county clerk and placed in the hands of the newly-established board.

Beyond this the law also contained a clause making the acceptance and record of a brand, by the secretary of the board, in itself *prima facie* evidence of ownership in any court of justice. This clause was of great assistance to the legitimate owner, as, naturally, the nefarious gentleman, whose only title was a running iron, was not anxious to expose his delinquency by recording his name and address with the Cattle Sanitary Board. Consequently, when a new brand showed up on the range of which nobody knew the owner an application to the Sanitary Board to record it in your name, if not already recorded, gave you a certain legal right to bar it out and replace it by the brand of the legitimate owner.

The favourite method of those gentlemen of acquiring a herd without the preliminary expense of paying for them was what was known on the range as ' sleepering the calves'. Sleepering was simplicity itself and merely consisted of catching the animal before it left its mother and marking it with the legitimate ear-mark of its owner while neglecting to go through the formality of branding it. It was a simple process and occupied little time, after which one turned it loose and invoked the guardian angel of the rustlers to preserve it from detection until in due time it became old enough to leave the maternal care and become a genuine maverick.

Having reached this stage with the knowledge of its location and general appearance, it was up to the rustler to catch it before any one else detected that it was unbranded ; then he could decorate it with his own brand, or if not already in possession of one, with one invented for the occasion. Then a few dexterous snips with a sharp knife altered the original ear-marks, and there was the foundation of a new herd. That we had to contend to a large extent with this evil may be inferred from the fact that amongst the archives of the W S Ranch are to be found the record of over seventy brands, recorded by me with the Cattle Sanitary Board during a period of some eighteen months, all of which showed up on the range and were intended to cover the W S brand.

In a rough country like ours this sleepering was difficult to detect. It was generally done amongst the outside cattle which clung to the mountains, and after a hard day's ride it was excusable for one not to risk his neck should an ear-marked calf jump up in front of him, even though he actually did not see the brand. Then even in a round-up, which usually contained several thousand cattle, where it was the custom to start by cutting out the cows and calves that needed to be branded, in the dust and confusion a calf that was ear-marked, though unbranded, could easily be overlooked. Also, which was generally the case, the author of the sleepering was pretty sure to be at the round-up, and if he came in contact with his quarry on the drive it was a certainty that it would not reach the round-up ground.

The brands showing up on our range, the majority of which were to be utilized in covering the W S, I naturally recorded as fast as they showed up, and this summary proceeding naturally led to friction with the independent gentlemen who created them. Amongst them was a rather amusing encounter with a gentleman named Holoman.

His given name was Tuk, and I have never been able to ascertain what it stood for. He was one of three brothers who migrated into our country from Texas impelled by the advancing tide of civilization and its accompanying inconveniences.

The oldest brother was Bob, who had in his possession a few head of cattle, some eight or ten, probably strays, as they were profusely ornamented with brands. Bob was a genial soul, in the language of the country 'foot-loose', meaning that he was unmarried and had no encumbrances to hamper his profession. This he openly stated to be that of a rustler or cow-thief, and he didn't give a cuss who knew it. Our personal relations were devoid of malice, and we regarded each other with a mild admiration such as might be exchanged between an inspector of police and a distinguished burglar.

Tuk was the second brother, and a victim of family cares. Though his profession was similar to Bob's, he did not openly assert it. He was a furtive individual and preferred to do his stealing in the dark. He rode wide when he saw you coming, and if compelled to pass closer gave you a furtive look and somewhat hostile greeting, which induced you to look behind and see that he was not taking an unfair advantage of your position. He claimed no cattle on his first arrival, no doubt being too busy with his domestic duties to be of assistance to Bob. The third brother was Pad, presumably an abbreviation for Patrick, who was a youth of about eighteen on his arrival, and gave his services impartially to the general welfare of the clan.

They settled down in Alma, and were not long before making their presence known on the range. It was a disadvantage to Tuk that he owned no cattle, but he apparently had a little money and was able to overcome the difficulty by acquiring the ownership of a few head, the remnant of a brand that had been started by a man named George Roberts. The Roberts boys had purchased a small bunch of cattle from a man named Bob Hanner, who had driven them in from Texas. Bob's real name was Stuart, but as certain authorities in the latter State had been making inquiries about him he preferred to be called Hanner.

We were glad when the Roberts boys purchased his cattle, for Hanner had adopted for his brand a W N with a bar under it, from which he had hoped to derive great profit as it covered the W S. To make this clear I might mention that on the range where the brands were put on with a red-hot iron curves were more in favour than angles. The latter, owing to the proximity of the irons, were difficult to put on with a stamp iron without causing an unsightly blotch and sometimes disfiguring the brand so as to make it impossible to read it.

The W S brand was therefore at this time, and as it had been originally recorded, put on with what was known as a running W—thus ᙍᙍ. Mr. Hanner also adopted this form, only instead of following it with an S, he adopted the letter N, which also, as he said, for fear of disfigurement, he preferred in its running equivalent, and put on thus—ᙍᙍ. Now, it did not require an expert to see that the letter S could easily be converted into an N by the prolongation of either end, and as for the bar underneath it could be produced by means of a running iron or numerous other methods unnecessary to mention.

However, he had only evolved this nice little scheme a short time before the coming of the Roberts boys. I had intended making a protest to the Sanitary Board when the brands were transferred, but when the Roberts boys got hold of it they relieved my anxiety, for the brands having to be newly recorded in order that they should know the ones actually in existence, they agreed to transfer the brand specifically to the right side, which removed it from conflict with the W S, which was always on the left.

The Roberts boys were nice straight boys, and as long as they were in the business our relations were of the best ; but the hard times gave them a distaste for the business and they gradually disposed of most of their herd. They had but few left at the time of the arrival of the Holomans, probably not over twenty or thirty head, and these they got rid of to Tuk Holoman, selling them at range delivery for a nominal sum.

Tuk soon got on to the lay of the land and thought it a pity to waste such a good opportunity. Ignoring such trifles as the records of the brand, he began to brand his increase on the left side. The first of them I saw really belonged to one of his cows, but I remonstrated with him. His excuse was that he was so accustomed to looking on the left side of the animal he paid no attention to what was on the right.

This not sounding convincing and my further protests being unavailing our relations became strained. I wrote to the secretary of the Sanitary Board and asked if it was permissible to record the W N bar brand on the left side, informing him of the circumstances which led to my making the request. His reply was that it was already recorded on the right side, but he didn't see any objection to its being recorded again on the left, and at any rate he would hold it in abeyance till the meeting of the board and would accept no other record in the meantime.

As a matter of fact they did actually record the brand on the left as belonging to the W S, but I did not wait for their certificate, as I considered I had enough to go on. The first calf I met with Tuk's brand on the left side after that I barred out and transferred it to the W S. This led to open warfare, and threats were conveyed to me from several quarters as to what Tuk was going to do with me.

I was not disturbed by Tuk's threats—had it been Bob I would have been more uneasy. But I did have some misgivings as to the legal aspect of the steps I was taking, and I made several efforts in an indirect way to run on to him and see if we couldn't settle the matter amicably, but he always avoided me. One day when I had almost forgotten all about him and his cattle I ran on to him unexpectedly.

I had been out inspecting some corrals that needed repair near the head of the Kellar Canyon and had heard a shot but paid no particular attention to it, thinking one of the boys had seen a deer and shot it. However, as I rode a little farther I met Tuk face to face coming round a corner. I naturally pulled up and so did he, and after eyeing each other for a brief moment he jumped off his horse and pulled his gun out of the scabbard attached to his saddle.

I had no idea that he meant to use it, for I was totally unarmed. The carrying of a long forty-five and a belt full of cartridges had never appealed to me. It was not only cumbersome and interfered with your work, but you were much safer without one. Situated as I was, in constant conflict with a certain element not over-scrupulous in their interpretation of the law, I was much safer to be unarmed. The plea of self-defence might be easily established against an armed foe, but the assassination of an unarmed man was contrary to the ethics of the border and liable to be summarily dealt with. So that, on the whole, I was not greatly disturbed by Tuk's manifestations.

He was in a truculent humour, however, and demanded that I get down and fight him. This appeal to arms seemed rather one-sided, and I pointed out the disparity of our weapons, also demanding to know what he thought we were fighting about. He said I was robbing him of his cattle, and I retaliated that my sole desire was to prevent him robbing us of ours. He had no reply to make to this, but said that he wanted the thing settled once for all and that the present moment seemed to be as propitious an opportunity as he was liable to get.

I agreed with him as to the time and place, saying that if he would put up his gun I had no objection to fighting him with my fists. He sized me up pretty closely before replying, but seeing that I was stripped to my shirt and pants and had no means of carrying a concealed weapon he put his gun back in the scabbard on his saddle. He also took off the pistol-belt and scabbard and hung them on the horn of his saddle. I wasn't much stuck on the encounter, but it seemed a ground-hog case, so before dismounting I suggested that the loser should withdraw all opposition, and that if

he called for time first he should make no further attempt
to brand his cattle on the left side, and I, on my part, would
lay no further claim to any of his calves.

This seemed to suit him, and I got off my horse thinking
I was in for a long and doubtful battle. To my surprise and
relief, however, it only lasted one short round. He came at
me with a rush swinging his arms like an old-fashioned
windmill, made one wild swipe, which I dodged, and
retaliated with a not very vigorous left to the nose as the
force of his swing brought him past me. I had not struck
very hard and must have had my hand rather loose, for it
knocked down one of my knuckles and it has remained down
ever since.

Harmless as I supposed it was, it was enough to finish
the battle. It had drawn first blood, and, much to my
relief, Tuk threw up his hands declaring that he perceived
I was scienced and might as well give in before he got hurt.
He pronounced it ' skienced ', and though I was pleased to
see him surrender it was some time before it dawned on me
what he meant.

As we rode home together he was rather depressed, and as
the trail was rough in places I allowed him to ride a little in
front. As we jogged along I got to thinking over the events
and wondered if my estimate of Tuk had not been doing him
an injustice. I reflected that he might have made use of his
gun, and even if he did not assassinate me might have forced
me under stress to accord him more favourable terms. With
those thoughts in my mind I resolved to let him know before
we parted how much I was indebted for his chivalrous
conduct.

Our way led apart about two miles from the ranch, and
as I rode alongside him I began to express my appreciation
in a somewhat awkward manner. He had eyes like a
ferret and he looked at me piercingly, under the impression,
as he expressed it, that I was 'giving him a game'. Then
seeing that I really meant it he quickly disabused me of
the notion by declaring : ' Why, hell ! I didn't have no
catridge.'

He looked so despondent and his regret at the deficiency
was so sincere that I burst out laughing. He explained in
regretful accents that he had started out with only two or
three cartridges in the magazine of his gun, and these he had
expended in an unsuccessful attempt to shoot a deer, no

doubt the one I had seen cross the canyon. He said he pulled the gun under the impression that he was going to run a bluff and make me withdraw from my position, but I was apparently so unperturbed that he supposed I had caught on and there was no way out of it except to fight.

He was really heart-broken, not so much at losing the fight as that his belt was unfurnished with ammunition. He was also afraid, as he expressed it, that he might have to quit the country. As he explained it, he said that as soon as I had told how he had come to change his brand the boys would never let up on him but would devil him out of the country. His main grievance seemed to being reduced to fighting with his fists instead of his gun, and to relieve my mind I said there was no necessity to say anything about it.

This view of the matter brought him unexpected relief, but he did not seem at all confident that I would adhere to it. I, however, reassured him to the best of my ability, and he left me apparently satisfied. Up to this time I have never mentioned the episode, and he, on his part, though never what might be called a satisfactory neighbour, confined his brand strictly to the right side of his cattle.

CHAPTER XV

TROUBLE AND AMUSEMENT

B UT not all knights of the running-iron were easily disposed of. Our neighbours all over the country were complaining of the inroads made on their cattle. I attended a meeting in Silver City, held by the cattle-owners of Grant and Sierra Counties at the Timmer House Hotel, at which some very drastic remedies were proposed. As these were primitive in method and liable to come in conflict with the law as already established, some of the more timid members of the association withdrew from the assembly. The remedies were never carried out, but they tended to show the pitch of desperation to which the legitimate owners were worked up.

I returned from the meeting in company with Mr. Lyons of the L C Ranch and stayed over with him for several days at the White House. During my stay we rode thoroughly over this range, accompanied by his foreman Johnnie Johnson, also at times by the foreman of the Flying Circle Brand, who rejoiced in the name of Betsy Henderson. They showed us quite a number of cows, apparently the mothers of young calves, which had their heads caved in with a rock and were surreptitiously deprived of their offspring. It was a crude and barbarous method of plunder, but was effective in destroying all traces of evidence, as the bereaved mothers could never hunt up the calves.

Their principal trouble seemed to be with a family named Hall, consisting of four brothers and the old man and his family, who, they said, had come from Texas with an evil reputation. There were others also whom they mentioned as belonging to the same company, notably a man named De Witt. He was usually referred to as ' Skeeter ', due to his temperament and his predilection for working in the dark.

I returned to the ranch and forgot all about them, having sufficient troubles of my own to occupy my attention. However, some weeks later, rumours reached us that open war had broken out between the Hall boys and the L C Ranch. This was followed later by a report that two of the Hall boys had disappeared. Nobody seemed to know definitely what had become of them. They were both stalwart young men, and hints were freely thrown out that they had been caught red-handed stealing cattle and secretly disposed of.

I never found out what really happened, and I don't think their disappearance has ever been accounted for. It led to an open feud, during which the casualties were numerous, mostly on the L C side. Amongst them were two men named Childers, father and son. They were both killed close to the L C Ranch and within a week or two of each other. This guerilla warfare went on for a year or more, till the Halls, whose resources were no doubt exhausted, left the country and took up their residence in the neighbourhood of Deming. There they blossomed into model citizens, and I had frequent interviews with the married son, Tom, when I passed through on my way to and from the ranch. Beyond an intense hatred of Mr. Lyons he bore no ill-will against any one. He was an outspoken, kindly fellow who made no attempt to conceal any of his acts, and I always considered him more sinned against than sinning.

Mr. Lyons himself ended a stormy career in a somewhat dramatic manner six or seven years ago. Whether it had any connexion with his former troubles was never fully established, but he was inveigled into a trip to El Paso on pretence of a cattle deal and while there cruelly murdered. It seemed that he was met at the depot by the prospective buyer, who gave the name of Brown, and having driven off with him and his supposed partner was not seen again till his body was found in the public park about twenty-four hours later. Subsequent disclosures brought out the fact that he had been murdered in a little side street close to the depot. It appeared they drove down it by way of a short-cut, and pretending something had gone wrong with the engine asked Mr. Lyons to hold a flash light for them while they fixed it.

While doing so one of them hit him on the back of the head with a hammer. They then beat him to death with a piece of reinforcing steel they had picked up close by, after which they threw him into the car and drove to the public park, where they disposed of the body in an old wash and where it was found the next day. It was quite a long time before any of these facts came to light, and all they resulted in was that one man got a twenty-five year sentence.

Lyons was an old man at the time, almost seventy years of age, and it seemed that the cowardly thugs who assassinated him were merely hired assassins. The principals to the crime were never found out. I attended his funeral as one of the pall-bearers. He was the author of many acts of which I did not approve, but he was always plucky. That his enemies had to employ professional thugs to get rid of him was proof enough they dared not attack him in the open.

To his credit be it said that he was capable of most generous actions, that he enjoyed the humorous side of life and was an excellent companion. He sang a good song and told many a good story. In camp he was always the life and soul of the party, and was a keen hunter, with real sporting instincts. Peace to his ashes ! With all his faults he was a whole man. I helped to bury both him and his partner, Angus Campbell.

Shortly after the outbreak of cattle-rustling Fred left me. He had got married, and I fixed him up a comfortable house and everything was going smoothly, but we happened to run up against the foreman of the Hampson cattle outfit, which were generally known as the ' Double Circles '. This man, Cole Railston, and Fred had a good deal to say to each other, and it wound up by Cole recognizing him as a gentleman he had previously met in Montana.

The recognition was mutual, only it seemed that Fred at the time was known under another name, which he confessed was Boyd Rochfort. It was a good old French name and there was no reason why he should have been ashamed of it, but it appeared that certain circumstances into which I did not inquire, and which were none of my business, had caused him to change it to the less aristocratic name of Golden.

Whatever it was, it would have made no difference to the W S, and if it was known to Cole Railston I never heard him mention it, although I became well acquainted with him in after years. However, it had marked effect on Fred, for he was never the same afterwards. He became shifty in his manner and evidently dissatisfied with his job. He worked on for nearly a year, during which he made several bluffs at quitting, plainly in the hope that we would fire him, until at length, making up his mind, he told me that he had determined to start a saw-mill at Mogollon.

I gave him all the help I could, and he and his family

moved up there for a time, during which I threw all the trade I could in his favour. He sold out after a few months to our old friend Harry Herman and asked me to assist him in opening a saloon in Alma. I did what I could for him, but the spirit of unrest had got hold of him, and his new profession soon got him into trouble with his family. Before many months there was a separation, and the next thing I heard was that he had pulled up stakes and drifted into Arizona.

From there came reports of him for several years, principally from the neighbourhood of Douglas and Bisbee, where he seemed to be following a somewhat chequered career, and eventually I heard that he had fallen down a well and broken his neck. I was sorry for Fred and would have kept him with me if I could. He had his faults, like all of us, and must have got into serious trouble before coming to New Mexico ; but he did useful work for the W S. He was loyal to them at a time when loyalty to what was known as ' Damned English outfit ' was rare, and the temptation to be otherwise was great.

He was succeeded in his job by Clarence E. Tipton, who had been with us since 1886. The leasing of the land in Colfax County, however, necessitated my being a good deal away from home and making frequent trips to Springer, which at the time was the county seat, and during my absence I usually relied upon Luke, the farm boss, to look after the ranch instead of turning things over to the cattle foreman, as I had been in the habit of doing with Fred.

There was a short interregnum when the post of range boss was occupied by a man named Puckett. This was so brief a period that I had almost forgotten it. But during this time there was an encounter with a bear, which resulted in my becoming the possessor of two baby cubs.

When we first got them, after the death of the mother, they were no bigger than little puppies and were apparently only a few days old, for their eyes were still unopened. Considine had fixed them up a warm nest in an old barrel and was feeding them with warm milk and water with a spoon. The process was not very satisfactory, as they spilled more than half of it, and, not as yet being able to see, poked their noses underneath it in their endeavour to get at it and splashed it up in one's face. We were at a loss how to overcome the difficulty, till some one suggested purchasing a bottle. We had plenty of bottles of sorts at the ranch, both empty and full, but they were not of the orthodox pattern, and our efforts to use them without the aid of a nipple almost resulted in strangulation. Inquiries at the local emporium in Alma led to no result, although they professed to supply everything necessary to human existence from horse-nails to chewing tobacco.

They had heard of such things and babies put in an appearance occasionally in the neighbourhood, but they had other means of subsistence. No ! They were sorry, but they didn't keep them in stock. It necessitated a journey to Silver City, and I undertook to supply the deficiency. It seemed a simple task, and it never occurred to me that it would be in any way embarrassing until I entered the drug-store to make the purchase. There were several people there to whom I was well known, amongst them some of the gentler sex, and as a bachelor approaching middle age my demand for feeding bottles and rubber nipples attracted attention.

Fortunately I was much burned by the sun, but I felt myself growing hot around the ears. I had murderous feelings towards the obliging clerk, who spread his wares out on the counter anxious to explain their merits and varieties. I hastily selected the first that came to hand and with the accompanying box of nipples stuffed them into my pocket. As I left the store I felt that the eyes of the whole town were upon me, and I wasn't really comfortable visiting the place for six months afterwards. Moreover, I missed a lot of useful information that I had hoped to obtain from the druggist. He was a married man and I felt confident would prove a fund of information regarding the infantile amenities of baby bears.

However, having got my bottle I hastily left town and got as far as the Gila that night. I reached the ranch early the following day and was gratified to find my protégés still alive, for I had been fearful they might die of starvation. I was already beginning to feel the anxieties of a parent.

The bottle was just what was needed and at once proved a success. They attacked it with avidity after their long fast, and though we did not allow them to take all they wanted, they became so distended that they looked like two footballs partly blown up. In a few days their eyes were opened and they could see their way about. It was funny to see them shuffle around on voyages of exploration ; they would go along till they met an obstruction, and then stub their noses in the ground, turning a complete somersault, and keep on rolling till they were right side up.

I was for keeping them in the house on account of the warmth, but Considine, who did most of the chores, thought they would do equally well outside ; so he fixed them a nest in an old barrel, which he half filled with hay and laid on its side.   In this they spent the nights, but I think it was really responsible for their early demise, for they only lived about four months.

While they were with us they were the source of constant entertainment, especially at feeding-time, when they fought each other for possession of the bottle.   I had been in too great a hurry to buy one for each of them, and I never could summon up sufficient courage to write for another.   My usual course was to take one on my lap and attend to his wants until he had finished, and then take up the other. As they grew bigger this led to a regular scramble to see who could get there first.

Colonel Morrow, who commanded the post of Fort Bayard, occasionally paid me a visit and called them ' bachelor's babies '.   We christened them Bud and Sis. They appeared to be in good health until one day Bud refused to gambol with Sis and became decidedly sick.   He displayed all the symptoms of acute pneumonia and we applied all the known remedies.   He was brought into the house and kept by the fire, but he lost all interest in his food, and though we administered small doses of good brandy there was only a slight reaction, and after lingering for a few days he quietly expired.

The whole ranch went into mourning over the loss of our first baby and we gave him a first-class funeral, even indulging him with the luxury of a coffin and erecting a headstone over his grave.   The latter consisted of a piece of two-inch pine, neatly dressed and rounded, on which was carved in capitals and with much care, the following inscription :

' HERE LIES OUR FIRST BABY, BUD,
AGED FOUR MONTHS.'

We hoped that Sis might grow to maturity, but she refused to be consoled for the loss of her brother and also refused to leave the house.   She moped and lay all day by the fire in the office and at night followed me to my room and camped in the bed. This continued for over a week, when she began to lose interest in her food and displayed the same symptoms as her brother, and with the same result. Her funeral was an exact replica of Bud's, and we laid them side by side in two little graves, over which we erected mounds.

Their headstones were similar in design and material with the inscription only differing as to the name and the word ' other ' inserted in place of ' first '. We missed them greatly at the time, and for a season or two their graves were carefully attended to. But as other interests intervened they were gradually forgotten, and being close to the ditch, the weeds grew up around them, blotting them from sight as from memory.

Several years later they were unexpectedly brought to mind, after I had quite forgotten them. It was shortly after I got married and my wife and I had returned from our honeymoon to the ranch. I had a good deal of leeway to make up and nothing was further from my thoughts than the romances of my bachelorhood. I was busy writing letters and she was prowling about the place. Suddenly she came in with a very grave face and demanded, ' Who were Bud and Sis ? ' Not divining for the moment what she meant, I asked for an explanation, and then was informed that she had stumbled on to their graves.

The inscriptions had been cut deep and she easily deciphered them. No doubt they looked suspicious, for I had some difficulty in explaining that they were only bears. It was not until I offered to dig them up that she appeared satisfied, and whether she still entertained some hesitant doubts I was never really sure. At any rate, as if by mutual consent, no further allusion was ever made to the matter.

In those days encounters with bears were not infrequent. They really are most interesting animals, and despite what a great many people maintain I never could find that they were destructive to cattle. My personal experience is that they never molest them until they grow old and the procuring of other food becomes difficult, and cattle are not much afraid of them. The same cannot be said about hogs, however, which seem to be the tastiest dish for Bruin, for I have known them break into a pen and push the hogs out in front of them.

We had at this time an interesting family working one of our farms. The head of the house was named De Priest, and he had been married more than once, so that his entourage consisted of the remnants of several families. There were two families of the De Priests ; and his wife, who had been a Mrs. Robinson, had brought a family of her own. I think they migrated from Tennessee, but at any rate they had come from afar, and their possessions being few and scanty they were glad to find some place where they could obtain rest and make a living. This story is entirely devoted to the old man, who had a religious complex.

On week days he was strictly sober, his only weakness being tobacco, a wad of which was always in his jaw and on which I think he mainly depended for sustenance. But on Sundays he held service in Alma and invariably got drunk afterwards. These meetings he had established shortly after his arrival, and they were a great source of amusement to the boys. When convenient they always attended them in a body, and in any case the farm hands patronized them, going each Sunday morning under the guidance of Luke, who pretended to be a devotee and had gained the confidence of Mr. De Priest by drumming up the neighbourhood and bringing them to his meetings.

When he had finished his prayers and delivered his discourse they invariably adjourned to the saloon, where they stood him drinks until overcome ; then they laid him gently in his wagon and he was driven home by one of his boys to sleep off the effects till Monday.

These weekly meetings went on for more than a year, and even blossomed into a sort of Sunday school, as Luke suggested, when they adjourned to the saloon, that the old gentleman should catechize them and see how they were benefiting by his religious instruction. The failure to give a correct answer was to be attended by a forfeit in the shape of a drink to the preacher, and incidentally to the whole congregation. In this way they determined who was to treat and it took the form of a collection.

From the standpoint of the reverend gentleman they were a thorough success and might have gone on indefinitely, had not Luke in his wisdom determined to break them up. He said they were demoralizing his hands, who were not so inured to hardship as Mr. De Priest, and that they all got so drunk on Sundays that they were unfit for work during

the early part of the week. I wanted him to do it without
hurting the old gentleman's feelings, for there was no reason
to believe him insincere, but the spirit of mischief was rife
in Luke, and he went his own way about it.

We had at the time a famous bronco-buster, John
Shannon. He could ride anything that wore hair and
seemed to be solid from the hips up. Otherwise he was a
matter-of-fact individual who never inquired the why or
the wherefore and would have ridden his best bronco over
a bluff if you told him. He and Luke attended one of the
meetings and John was introduced as a new convert and a
fit subject to be catechized after the weekly prayers.

Luke had apprised him beforehand, that if he should fail
to answer and was called on to stand drinks by the preacher
he was to take no notice and pretend not to hear him.   John
took it all in as if it were gospel. He admitted that he was
liable to failure, as a knowledge of the Christian Doctrine
was not within the category of his accomplishments. When
the time came the old gentleman, who was only half shot,
propounded his question, and John, who didn't even know
what he was talking about, not only declined to answer,
but was guilty of the more heinous crime of contumacy,
when a little later he refused to supply the pastor, and
incidentally the congregation, with a drink, in atonement
for his ignorance.

John not only said that the old gentleman had already had
all that was good for him, but on the latter's threat to
excommunicate him, he at Luke's suggestion, took him in
his arms, and having hog-tied him like a calf about to be
branded, placed him in his wagon, covered him carefully
in the folds of a wagon sheet, and directed his boys to take
him home and put him to bed.

The old gentleman protested with all his might against
this ignominious procedure, but the faithful, who considered
it a good joke, only laughed at him. As for his boys, they
were so accustomed to his usual spiritual relapse that when
his cries were smothered in the folds of the wagon-sheet,
they supposed he was in his usual condition and drove him
home without question.   Luke and John got on their horses
and rode back to the ranch.

The first intimation I had of the proceedings was when
Luke came up to where I was writing letters to announce
the result of the meeting and to tell me that he feared the

population of Alma were about to fall away from grace. He was so amused that he was barely intelligible, but when he had disclosed the full account of the transaction I was fearful it might lead to trouble. Neither Luke nor I knew much about the psychology of gentlemen from Tennessee and Kentucky with a religious complex in their make-up, but I had met one or two and had heard more of them.

John was a valuable asset to the W S, and I didn't want him picked off some fine morning with a fractious bronco, so I suggested to Luke that he keep out of the old gentleman's way for a few days till he had time to cool off.

As I anticipated, about an hour later I was called on to meet the crisis. The boy, Willie Robinson, burst in through the door, all breathless and excited. He said his Ma had sent him off in hot haste to say his Pa had gone on the warpath. The boy had run for nearly a mile and I got him a drink of water. It appeared that when they had got the old gentleman home he had fallen asleep and they laid him to rest as usual, but after a time he had got up and vowing vengeance against parties unknown, whom he termed calfropers, had got his gun and sallied forth.

His Ma was greatly frightened and had hurried him off as fast as she could to beg of me to head him off before he got into trouble. He had run with all his might, and the old gentleman was now coming across the field about a quarter of a mile from the house.

Of course I had to appear entirely ignorant of the whole transaction, but I put on my hat and went out. I could see the old gentleman coming along, carrying a gun about six feet long, which he used as a support, stopping every now and then to stamp the butt on the ground as a sort of emphasis. I feigned not to notice him, however, but just strolled along as if with no particular object.

When I got close I expressed surprise at seeing him out on the Sabbath, and asked if he meant to go hunting. My voice was the first intimation of my presence, and he stopped in surprise to stare at me. His eyes were protruding from his head and his chin was festooned with tobacco juice. Having satisfied himself as to my identity, he pounded his weapon on the ground and answered me as follows :

' Hunting ! Hunting nothing ! I'm hunting a damn calf-roper ! I don't know his name, but if ever I get sight of him his calf-roping days are ended ! '

I begged him to tell me the trouble and I would do my best to see him righted. He then unfolded his tale, saying that he had delivered his weekly discourse and was endeavouring to spread the light. The Word was in his mouth—here he endeavoured to get rid of his plug, but failed—when a damned calf-roper named John seized him like he was a damned antelope and hog-tied him. ' Yes, sir ! Tethered me like I was a damned antelope.'

After which he was thrown into a wagon, and, being smothered in a damned wagon-sheet, was driven, he didn't know where. Here his feelings were too much for him, and he would have started in pursuit of the calf-roper had I not restrained him. He said the whole of his congregation were in a beastly state of drunkenness. I assured him that I would do all in my power to see him righted, and that if John was available I would go with him and have him make amends at the time, but I had seen him and Luke ride out about an hour previously and was sure they had gone to camp. After a time I got the old gentleman quieted and took him back to his house, where he put his gun away in a corner, and I turned him over to his wife. There was no reason to think him insincere, but he certainly was an odd combination.

This broke up the prayer meetings at Alma, but the feud with John was carried no further, for when the latter returned to the ranch the old gentleman agreed to bury the hatchet. His religious complex, however, was in no way subdued, for although a competent farmer of a rather benevolent type and ascetic appearance on week-days, it seemed incumbent on him to acquire a certain spiritual comfort on Sundays, so he transferred his activities to Mogollon and Cooney.

At those camps he held forth on alternate Sundays, with entirely satisfactory results, and might have continued doing so to the end of his career had he not been grossly deceived by a pious brother. This gentleman claimed to be an apostle whose vocation was to spread the light. He had attracted general attention on his first arrival, on account of the quaintness of his guise, which consisted of a straw hat and a linen duster, a very unusual garb for that country.

He had taken up his abode with Mr. De Priest and was introduced by the name of Brother Bacon. He was inexpressibly shocked by the general lack of religious feeling in the West, especially on the cow ranges, and seriously remonstrated with me on the wickedness of having the boys work on Sundays. He, however, had no alternative proposition when I offered to turn the round-up loose on Saturday night provided he would have them all together again on Monday morning. He merely sighed and remarked that it was a pagan condition.

He entered heartily into the work of regeneration and attended Mr. De Priest faithfully every Sunday, even to the extent of taking charge of him when it was over and returning him in safety to his family. This continued for several months to the satisfaction of all concerned, for the miners were not only free with their drinks, but also with their money, and they looked on the whole thing as a form of entertainment, so they generally attended in a body.

The only changes that were made were at the behest of Brother Bacon, who was a stickler for decorum in the house of worship. He considered the carrying of arms, which at the time might be said to be universal, a mark of irreverence in what he termed the House of God. Therefore he requested that those attending should either leave them at home or in some other place of safety. The result was that they were generally piled up in the saloon during the ceremony.

One Sunday while taking up the collection he suddenly threw off his disguise, at the same time getting rid of the plate, drew a long forty-five from under his duster, thrust it in the ear of a comparative stranger who was sitting near the door, and bundled him outside before he had a chance to resist. A buggy which had driven up unnoticed was waiting handy, and he and his victim got in and were driven rapidly down the canyon. The immediate impression was that he had gone suddenly mad, for he had thrown away the collection plate, scattering its contents on the floor.

In the wild rush to recover the collection several minutes were allowed to elapse before any one noticed where he was going or the real significance of the event began to dawn upon them. Afterwards all the news that ever returned was that he and his prisoner had reached Silver City and departed on the train for parts unknown. Rumour declared him to be a well-known detective who had long been on the track of a notorious criminal.

The immediate result of the *dénouement* was to destroy religious feeling in both the camps. Though Brother

De Priest was inconsolable and endeavoured to keep them up, he no longer could induce an audience to attend his meetings. The fervour of the neighbourhood and its accompanying moisture had dried up and they perished from sheer inanition.

One of the odd jobs which necessity compelled me to perform about this time was a surgical operation. I was awakened some time about two a.m. by Lem and Tip coming into my room. They had come from camp, about a thirty-mile ride, somewhere near the head of Devil Creek. Tipton's hand was all wrapped up in a handkerchief. They told me that he had got his thumb almost torn off, it being caught in the kink of his rope as he was catching his night horse. It was really in a horrible state, with the flesh torn off and all the sinews and bone exposed.

All I could do was to bathe it with an antiseptic and wrap it with cotton and vaseline. Then when I had bandaged him up and put his arm in a sling I directed him to go the first thing in the morning and seek medical assistance in Mogollon, which was the only place nearer than Silver City that had a resident doctor. However, the next day when they went there they were unable to find him, he having been called away unexpectedly on some urgent case.

Tip's arm was swelling up, and I told him I was sure it was necessary to have an operation, at the same time advising him to hurry off to Silver City. He didn't like the idea of the trip, however, hoping it would get better without it. In this way he kept postponing it for a day or two, until his arm got in such a state that something had to be done to relieve him. He had no faith in the medico at Mogollon and begged of me to undertake the operation.

I didn't much like the idea of tackling it, but he didn't seem to realize his danger, and if he let it go much longer he would certainly lose his arm. Under the circumstances I was bound to do something, so I amputated his thumb with a razor. The operation took place in the bunk-house and Tip sat on the kitchen table. I turned my back to him to keep from being nervous, passed his hand out under my left arm, where I clamped down on it with all my strength, and got through with it as quickly as I could.

I had plenty of bichloride as an antiseptic and the razor was bright and new, but it seemed to me that I took an unconscionable time about it, and when it was over the sweat was dropping from my brow and I felt thoroughly exhausted. As for Tip, he should have been a Christian martyr, for he neither moved nor uttered a sound. When I had him bandaged and bound up he smiled, quite pleased, and picking up the amputated thumb examined it closely and put it in his purse.

What he did with it I could never summon up the cheek to ask him, but I often thought it an odd kind of souvenir to take home to his family. The strange part of it was that he got entirely well ; all traces of inflammation disappeared and except that I had not left sufficient covering for the bone he suffered no great inconvenience. It bothered him somewhat in the cold weather, but a glove and a warm pad almost remedied that. I was filled with pride at the success of the operation, and thought of writing ' Fellow of the Royal College of Surgeons ' after my name.

In 1896 we were faced with a general election, which created a sort of furore in the regions of the West, especially amongst the members of the mining communities. As a rule we didn't take much stock of those matters at the ranch, and I had already gone through several without being unduly excited. On this occasion, however, for the first time in my life, I exercised the privilege of my newly acquired citizenship, by casting my ballot, and, contrary to my expectations, in favour of the Republican candidate. Not that it anyway affected the result, for being a territory we had no voice in the presidential election.

It, however, tended to soothe my wounded feelings, which was in direct opposition to the bulk of the community. To vote at all, being as I considered still a foreigner, was entirely against my principles, and I allowed many years to lapse and the dawn of a new century before again being guilty of such a breach of etiquette. I had no party affiliations and took little or no interest in their policies. In fact, I belonged to that much-despised fraternity known at the time as ' mugwumps ', whose unpardonable crime in the eyes of the politicians was that they allowed the personal character and ability of the candidate to influence their ballot.

Personally I had never intended to forswear allegiance to the British Crown, and the very idea was most distasteful, but Congress in its wisdom had passed an Act—I think bearing date March 1893—in which they made it unlawful for any alien who had not declared his intention, or, as it was more commonly called, ' taken out his first papers ', to acquire real estate in any of the territories. The provisions were in no way retroactive and did not affect the property already purchased. But the exigencies of our position often compelled us to make purchases for self-protection, and it was incumbent on some of us to acquire citizenship.

Mr. Wilson practically lived in England, and often did not come to the country for years, so after considerable hesitation I swallowed the dose, and now I was becoming sensitive over a presidential election. Probably the quality of the candidates also had something to do with it, for this was the advent of Mr. William Jennings Bryan, who had gained the Democratic nomination. He had come to them with a universal panacea for handling the finances of the country, which consisted of what was known as the ' free coinage of silver ', at a ratio of 16 to 1, making them a ridiculous speech about a ' cross of gold ', which really had no bearing on the subject ; he swept the convention off its feet, and they carried him around the hall, and though at the time he was practically unknown to the country, they nominated him without a dissentient voice as the Democratic candidate for president.

Now, the mining sections of the country had gone wild about him and he was universally known as the ' Boy Orator '. Our section had caught the fever along with the rest, and there were meetings in every town and village in the territory, all of them sending their sympathy. Amongst the rest Mogollon and Cooney were no way backward, and there were meetings in both camps, attended *en masse* by the same people. To one of those interesting assemblies we were accidentally invited. We had been riding all day in the mountains and on our way home in the evening found it necessary to pass through the town of Mogollon.

There was an unusual assemblage of people outside what served as the ' Hall of Justice '. It was usually occupied by people playing cards, for it was a sort of annex to the saloon ; but on this occasion it was evidently something important, and we rode up in a hurry to see who had committed murder. We were somewhat disappointed to find it was only a political meeting, but we were cordially received and invited to get down.

All who came from south of the Mason and Dixon Line—in other words, from Texas and Oklahoma—were staunch Democrats, while those who came from Wyoming and Montana were equally rabid Republicans. I didn't relish being thrown into this political turmoil, especially now that I was growing sensitive. They, however, insisted on our taking part in the meeting, and we were shown up to seats of honour alongside the chairman.

When the time came for proposing the first resolution, the procedure of which had already been accorded, I was unexpectedly called upon by the chairman, who was kind enough to allude to me as a worthy representative of a sister industry, to second the resolution. To gain time I asked for permission to read it and was handed a slip of paper. It was the ordinary fulsome resolution, expressing undying support and approbation to the ' free coinage of silver at a ratio of 16 to 1 ' and to our Peerless Leader, the Boy Orator from Nebraska.

As I read it carefully, wondering how I could get out of it, I grew hot under the collar, and requested permission of the chairman to move an amendment, substituting the words ' dried beef or jerky ' for those of ' free silver '. I tried to explain that it would give a much-needed fillip to a vital industry, and the value of each portion could be conferred by attaching to it a tin tag, or label—silver, if they preferred, but I was in favour of the cheaper metal. I had just explained its principal advantage, which was that when the inevitable crash came you at least could eat it, and was on my feet less than half a minute when I was interrupted by a universal cry of indignation.

It was evident that my well-meant remarks were not meeting with favour. There were several suggestions for disposing of my person, amongst which being thrown out on my ear and suspended from the nearest tree or being passed through the crusher of the mill, or dissolved in boiling oil, were amongst the mildest. Perhaps I had not been sufficiently explicit ; but then, it would have been entirely useless trying to explain to an audience the majority of whom entertained a suspicion, almost amounting to a certainty, that the world had not come into existence till late in the eighteenth century—that this question of ' free silver ' and the placing of fictitious values on an unstable coinage had been threshed out centuries before.

Their exhibition of temper was decidedly hostile, but the boys were delighted. They rallied round me as a single unit, gave a whoop—cowboys never cheer—which could be heard over all the racket, and offered to stand by me if I wished to continue. In view of the unfavourable reception, however, we deemed it advisable to withdraw from the meeting. Indeed, had we not been a pretty strong party, nearly all fully armed, we might have been roughly handled. As it was, we withdrew with proper dignity, facing the gentleman who occupied the chair and backing through the door.

Once in the street we heaved a great sigh of relief and adjourned to the saloon for a drink, after which we got our ponies and jogged defiantly down the canyon. On the way I attempted to explain my great admiration for Mr. Cleveland and how it had given me my Democratic bias. And now here was a considerable percentage of a presumably sane electorate clamouring to raise this egregious ass to the presidential chair. Verily, how a great national party could, in four short years, drop from the level of Grover Cleveland to that of William Jennings Bryan was incomprehensible to the budding citizen.

I might have continued in this strain, for I was properly wound up, had I not been interrupted by one of the boys with more material objects in view. He said : ' Hell, fellows, we common cow-waddies ain't got but one vote nohow ! And, hell, we don't need to cast it ! Let us go, fellows, I'm getting hungry,' and he larruped his pony under the flank with his quirt and we all broke into a canter. This ended the free silver discussion as far as the W S Ranch was concerned, and it was no longer considered good taste to introduce it ; for, as I said, politics were pretty well divided on the ranch, but that fall they voted as a unit and they all voted the Republican ticket.

The only one whom I failed to influence was my old friend Pete Branson, the old Confederate soldier, in whose company I had made my first trip over the road, back in 1883. Pete refused to be converted. He didn't give a damn about William Jinkins, as he called him, but he wasn't going to vote no Republican ticket. I even resorted to bribery in this case, for I fixed up a case of beer in Silver City, as if it had come from Chicago, and labelled it, ' To the Old Confederate Stand-by, Pete Branson, as a mark of esteem, from

William McKinley.' This was delivered to him by Jake, who perilled his immortal soul by swearing it was delivered to him off the train ; but Pete wasn't convinced. He examined it doubtfully from all angles, and said he didn't know how McKinley come to hear tell of him. He opened it carefully, and when he found it was beer knocked the neck off one of the bottles, put it on his head and drained it, broken glass and all, wiped his mouth with his sleeve, but said he wasn't going to vote no Republican ticket.

Some years later, at the outbreak of the Spanish War, he was greatly afraid they were going to conscript him. It happened that I sailed from Liverpool the day news arrived of the blowing-up of the *Maine*, and when I arrived in New York everything was in a state of excitement and the outbreak of war seemed imminent. When I got to the White House on my way from Silver City, Pete had heard some talk about it and was in a state of great mental distress.

When he had unhitched our tired horses he led me down to the banks of the stream, about a hundred yards distant, where, seated on the bank and well out of hearing, he put his arm affectionately round my shoulder and unbosomed himself of his grievance. He had got the idea into his head that now the Republicans were in power they would conscript all the old Confederate soldiers to fight their battles.

Now, Pete must have been eighty years of age, or very close to it, but it was useless to point out to him that he had long passed the age of conscription. He said there was no tellin' what them Yankees might be up to, and as he stroked me nervously on the shoulder he said : ' I tell you, Cap, they ain't agoin' to get me. I been there once before and I don't want any more war in mine. What if I am old ? I'm pretty spry and as good a man as most of them Yankees, and I'm goin' to hide till it's over.'

It was in vain that I pointed out to him the personal regard of the President, who had sent him the beer. He said it might be only a trick to incite him. It was only on my promise that if I heard of any movement in Washington towards the expansion of the Regular Army I would immediately come to his rescue and hide him out in the mountains that he agreed to stay where he was, and not put Jake to the necessity of finding a man to replace him.

Poor old Pete, he died some few years later in the hospital in Silver City. He was a staunch old Democrat whose heart was in the right place and who refused to tamper with his colours. Needless to say, he did not have to go to war against Spain or he might have earned a pension.

I ought to mention how we nearly buried alive one of our Scottish friends, Harry Davis. He really wasn't so much a friend of mine, but he worshipped at the shrine of Luke Flanagan, the farm boss, and thought there was nobody like him ; so through my intimate relations with the latter I absorbed some of the reflected admiration. I never was able to fathom the reason for this unusual friendship, beyond personal attraction, for Harry was the descendant of a Covenanter and a worshipper of William of Orange, while Luke was an orthodox Irishman from Connaught and held the memory of the aforesaid William in abomination.

Harry was an independent character with no regular occupation. When he felt like it and wanted to be near Luke he would work for a few days at the ranch and do his best to keep every one idle, for his mind was principally devoted to song and he possessed a musical voice. On the other hand, he wasn't particular about his wages, and if I happened to be absent often went away without them. He usually took up his abode with some sheepmen named McKeefrey, who had come direct from the north of Ireland and had taken up their abode on the Frisco twenty-five miles north of the ranch.

The latter were devout Roman Catholics with all the superstitions and prejudices of their race, but they and Harry were like members of one family, which proved that at least they were liberal-minded. There were originally three brothers, but the youngest had been shot when inadvertently trespassing on some cattlemen before they moved on to the Frisco, so taking the lesson to heart the survivors, Pat and Barney, proved pretty good neighbours.

Harry often disappeared from sight and nobody knew where he was, but whenever he came to the country you were sure to find him at the McKeefrey's. We had a ranch some five miles above them, known as the O-Block Ranch. There was nothing in the space between to attract any settler, for it was all a box-canyon, covered with sand and rocks and subject to overflow whenever there was a rise in the river. Just above the McKeefrey land, however, there was a little nook of unclaimed land, rather less than a rood in extent, which was above high water, and here a derelict family named Graham had taken up their abode.

Nobody knew where they came from or whether they intended to make it their home, and they actually only remained on it some four or five months. There were only the old man and his wife, in the neighbourhood of sixty, and a rather sickly-looking youth, presumably a son, in the early twenties. The old man was apparently a mechanic, for he set up a little shed as a blacksmith shop and did an occasional job, principally shoeing oxen for the Mexicans at the plaza. They were an uncommunicative family who liked to keep to themselves, though rumour, which existed even in that sparsely settled district, claimed they were constantly quarrelling. Anyway, they all disappeared just as mysteriously as they came, and might have been lost in oblivion had not one of the McKeefrey boys happened to pass that way a day or so after their disappearance.

Noticing that the place was deserted he got down and looked into the cabin. He found the old man on the floor with his gun lying beside him. A further examination disclosed that he was dead and had a bullet wound in his body, but a close scrutiny of the gun on the floor revealed that it hadn't been discharged. Further inquiry revealed the fact that the old lady and her son had been seen quite recently on the road to Socorro.

None of these things were troubling Barney or Pat, their only concern was with the old man, to whom they wished to give decent burial. In pursuance thereof they brought him down to their house and set about making him a coffin. This was a matter of some difficulty, for they were not well supplied with lumber. However, with the aid of some empty coffee cases and other scraps of material they eventually constructed a fine roomy casket and lined it with a blanket and shavings.

The only thing remaining was to wake him in true Irish fashion, and this, with the assistance of Harry Davis and all the necessary material, they proceeded to do in a right royal manner. I happened to be going that way the following morning pretty early, as we were building a fence on the O-Block Ranch above them, and I was anxious to see how they were getting on. In passing the McKeefrey place I met Harry Davis on the road.

Harry was extremely happy and was riding up and down

in front of the place, apparently without object, and singing The ' Bonnie Blue Flag '. I gathered between snatches of his song that they had waked Mr. Graham the evening before and intended to bury him that afternoon, and he invited me to the funeral. I told him I would stop on my way back and render what assistance I could and left him oblivious to my answer, for he had recommenced his peregrinations and was alone with his ' Bonnie Blue Flag '.

I went on about my business and spent some two or three hours at the O-Block before I started for home. As I rode down the creek I thought of the funeral and Harry's invitation, so when I got to McKeefrey's in the evening I pulled up and dismounted. Nobody seemed to be around, so I hitched my horse to the fence and proceeded to investigate.

The door was wide open, but there was no one in the house —just the broken meats of the wake and a strong smell of whisky. After some looking around I discovered the two brothers Pat and Barney, in company with a Mexican, fast asleep in the shade, behind the house. Harry was nowhere in sight, but I woke them up and asked about the funeral. They must have overslept themselves, for they woke up with a start and, looking at the sun, surmised it was late. On inquiring about Harry they said he must be somewhere about, and one of them shouted and whistled for him, but met with no response.

On inquiring for the corpse, Pat said he was kind of ' disagrayable ', and they had removed him to the shed before they sat down to eat. This was a little outhouse, nearly all boarded in, built against the fence at the back of the corral, and quite dark. They said they had nothing to do except to coffin him, and the necessary equipment was in the shed along with the corpse. Not having any desire to superintend, I sat down on the steps of the house, while all three of them went over to the shed to perform the last rites for the deceased before we buried him.

They could not have been in there many minutes and I had just heard the sound of the hammer, as they nailed him down, when all three came rushing out again, falling over each other. The Mexican was in the lead and made a bee-line for the mountain, while Pat threw away the hammer which he held in his hand, and Barney was crossing himself and the air all around him.

I rose up to meet them and find out what was the matter.

As soon as one of them could regain his breath he cried out :
' Glory be ! He's come alive, man. He's come alive ! '
While the other said : ' It's his ghost, man ! It's his ghost,
I tell ye ! ' With this Pat ran into the house for his gun,
while Barney went down on his knees and invoked Divine
assistance. As for the Mexican he had entirely disappeared,
and no more was seen of him.

The whole affair was most mysterious. In view of their
previous reports as to the condition of the corpse I could
only put it down to their nerves and the effects of the wake.
I determined to investigate and walked over to the shed.
As I approached it I could hear a racket going on inside, and
it was evident there was something alive, which made it all
the more mysterious. I had hardly reached the door, however, when I met Harry coming out with his mouth full of
shavings. They were also hanging in festoons from his
hair, and as we almost came into collision he shouted :
' Mon ! Mon ! Where are they ? ' And then it dawned
on me that they must have been trying to coffin Harry in
lieu of the deceased.

The whole thing was too funny for words and it was
necessary to calm every one down to get an explanation.
When this came it seemed that when Harry had exhausted
his song he was overcome with sleep. Looking for a place
to lie down the shed seemed nice and shady. He either
ignored or had forgotten about the corpse and threw himself
down on the bench beside it. When the boys went in there
to perform the last rites the place was perfectly dark, the
more so after stepping out of the strong sunlight. Being
in a hurry to get through with an unpleasant task they seized
the first form they laid a hand on. This happened to be
Harry, whose sleep was almost as deep as his neighbour's.

They lost no time in popping him into the box and
immediately began to nail him down. The noise of the
hammering somewhat disturbed him and he moved uneasily
in his sleep, kicking his foot or knee against the lid. This
caused the scare and the scramble and all the subsequent
invocations and trouble. How it might have fared with
Harry is problematical. Fortunately the box was roomy
with plenty of space to turn. He jabbed against a nail,
which woke him up completely ; being unable to get on to
his knees, he pushed the lid up with his back and so escaped
premature interment.

That Harry thought it amusing was manifest, for somewhat later on, when I was in the old country on a visit for Christmas, he put a mock burial in practice on an old man I had sent down from Colfax County to act as gardener at the ranch during my absence.

This old gentleman's name was Charlie Miller and he bore a great reputation around Springer. Every one claimed that he was a first-rate gardener, if he only could be kept sober, but this could only be brought about by keeping him broke.

I resolved to give him a trial and sent him down to the ranch, where he would be farther away though not altogether removed from temptation. At Christmas it was always customary with the boys to have a celebration. It generally lasted two or three days, during which they had a good time and enjoyed themselves. The year I was away proved no exception ; under the presidency of Luke they had a good time and enjoyed themselves. When the time came for them to quit they were all on deck except old Charlie, who, having got the taste of strong drink, refused to quit it.

The result was that he was in a comatose condition when the others were ready to go to work. They were rather at a loss what to do with him, when Harry, who was working there at the time, suggested to Luke that they take him out and bury him. They dug a neat little grave in the garden, not too deep, but sufficient to cover him, leaving his head exposed, after which they carried him out, still insensible, and laid him in it.

Harry was the principal performer and covered him up neatly. About the time he was through Charlie came to himself, and finding he was planted in the ground was scared into sobriety. He begged to be released, assuring them they had mistaken his condition, that he wasn't really dead but had been sleeping. Harry, however, assured him he was mistaken, and as he patted the ground with his spade told him it wasn't seemly in a corpse to be talking.

When they got through they left him to his own devices and the rest went in to supper. Charlie had no difficulty in getting loose, but he was so badly frightened that he immediately left the place and made his way to Alma. From there he managed to get to Silver City, though he didn't travel on the stage, and finally got back to Springer and Colfax County. I found him there on my return, and he told

me a wild tale of how they had nearly murdered him.   He
didn't explain the details, but he told me they forced him to
drink whisky.   Had he not made the latter statement I
would have paid more attention to him.

The last time I saw Harry was at poor Luke's funeral
after he was murdered.

CHAPTER XVI

THE WILD BUNCH. I

THE events related in the last chapter occurred around the years 1896 and 1897, at a time when I was kept very busy going back and forward between Socorro and Colfax Counties. We were shipping cattle regularly from the former place to our newly acquired pasture in the latter, and as every shipment was made I had to go ahead in order to be there to meet them. I had a man named Hughes in charge of the pasture, an excellent fellow, conscientious and obliging, who played a good game of whist and was everything that was desirable in the way of a companion, but unfortunately he wasn't a cowman. It was therefore an agreeable surprise when on one of my trips between Springer and Silver City I met Louie Lloyd or Apjohn at Rincon, and he struck me for a job.

I had heard of Louie occasionally since I had met him years before, but I understood that he had gone into Old Mexico on a mining expedition. On this occasion we had considerable delay at Rincon and we had plenty of time to talk.

We sat down on the end of the station platform and he told me he had just got back from Old Mexico, where he had been with a friend of his named George Lynch. They were in the State of Sonora, where they had had a prospect which gave great promise, but occasionally the bottom blew out of it only to reappear again when they had got farther down. It was luring them on to more strenuous efforts and possible riches when a catastrophe brought them face to face with starvation and compelled them to relinquish their occupation and travel seventy miles on foot in search of food.

Their last shot one fateful evening had disclosed a wealth of some material—I think Louie called it ' galena '. It had a leaden sound and I'm sure it wasn't gold. Perhaps, like the caskets in the ' Merchant of Venice ', the leaden one was the richer. At any rate they stayed awake long into the night discussing their future and what they were going to do with their riches. When morning dawned they snatched a hasty breakfast, took a light lunch along with them, and flew back to the hole they had made in the fissure.

They spent the day drilling fresh holes, stopping every

now and again to admire their property. One of them would
dig out a fresh piece with a pick, admire it, and turn it
over. They would wonder what it really was, but each
time conclude to add a million or so to its value. Then
they would resume work with frantic eagerness, tearing out
great slabs till they had accumulated a great pile.

By evening they were tired and hungry, and taking up
some choice specimens to act as samples they wended their
way back to camp. So engrossed were they with their
future and its prospect of wealth that at first they failed to
notice the condition of the camp. Suddenly one of them
stepped on a piece of bacon which had been trampled into
the ground as if a steam-roller had passed over it. He
slipped and nearly fell down, and with a sudden gasp, as
he looked around, the awful truth was unfolded.

Their camp had been raided as if a cyclone had struck it.
Everything was in confusion. Their blankets were scattered
all over the place with holes trampled in them. Their few
cooking utensils were battered and bruised and all their
provisions were eaten up. What hadn't been eaten was
destroyed, for their only sack of flour wouldn't make a
decent rag and their bacon was chewed and licked and
masticated and then tramped into the ground and rolled on.

At first they were at a loss as to the cause of it, but glancing
around in wonder and amazement they descried a strange
object on the hill-side. What it could be and how it came
there was a mystery ; yet it looked like their one and only
burro. He looked innocent and stupid as usual, but he
had changed his colour. Gradually it dawned on them that
the wretched beast had raided the camp in their absence and
eaten up all their provisions.

Their first thoughts were of murder, and they started out
in search of reprisal. As they climbed the hill, however,
they discovered they were hungry, and they realized the
seriousness of the situation. They had had little refreshment since morning and they were face to face with starvation. It was at least two days' travel to the nearest *hacienda*
and they hadn't a thing to eat.

In crises great men come to the front, and Louie's brain
began to function. The burro looked nice and fleecy ; his
hair was long if ragged, and now was powdered with flour.
Perhaps enough of the precious nutriment could be curried
from him to enable them to reach a settlement.

How gently they spoke as they neared him and how they gasped when he stamped his feet, Louie alone could describe. They led him down the hill-side, Lynch with endearing terms behind him and Louie with his only handkerchief encircled round his neck, and they cursed him behind their beards when he failed to avoid a bramble or insisted on rubbing his side.

They eventually got him on to their tarpaulin and there they proceeded to curry him with the back of their only butcher knife. As they worked they grew rougher and rougher, one of them using a rock. When they finally shook all the dust off him they led him off the tarpaulin, unloosed their curses, and damned him for many generations till he was glad to fly back to his hill-side flourishing his heels in the air. They gathered the spoils in the remains of the flour-sack and added a handful or two that they scraped from the ground. This with a piece of the rind off the bacon, constituted their stock of provisions, which they proceeded to convert into tortias or flapjacks, and hoped to sustain nature with while they travelled the seventy miles.

When the flour was all together, it looked like what a plasterer might have thrown aside as not sufficiently clean for his work. When made into tortias it was uncommonly hard to masticate, much less to swallow or digest. It was lasting, however, for as Louie described it, when you got tired chewing you could fold it and put it away in your pocket for future use, or use it as a napkin while you tried your teeth on another. The burro had shed as much hair as flour.

They packed up their belongings the next morning and after three days' tramping and starvation reached a Mexican settlement where they were able to dispose of the ravisher of their Lares and Penates, which along with their mining tools and other loose objects furnished them enough money to get across the border to reach the nearest railroad. From there, with the connivance of a friendly conductor and some not over-scrupulous brakemen, they managed to ride a freight-train, till eventually they were deposited at, or in the neighbourhood of Batch Station where George Lynch made his home.

Since then he had been assisting Major McClintock, or Old Mac as he called him, to dispense refreshment to the public, and there being as yet no sign of our train, he

suggested that we go up and call on him.   Mac was a famous
Republican war horse.   His place stood about a hundred
yards from the Depot, so we strolled up there.   We found
him in a back room expostulating with some voters.   He
had seven or eight of them in a corner and was laying down
the law to them with a billiard cue.   It seemed that Mr.
Bryan's panacea of Free Silver and the prospect of easy
money had penetrated to the district and some of them had
voted the Democratic ticket.

Mac was in a towering rage over the matter and empha-
sized his remarks by vicious prods of the cue to the delin-
quents while they crowded up in a corner in a vain attempt
to avoid him.   It was evident they were free and independent
voters but they mustn't vote the Democratic ticket.   He
spoke in Spanish and I was unable to understand him, but
there was no mistaking the purport of his remarks.   When
Louie and I had created a diversion, he locked the voters
in the room and joined us outside, but he every now and
again alluded to them in opprobrious terms as rebels and
mutineers.

Before leaving I arranged with Louie to come to the
ranch in Socorro County where I would give him something
to do as a starter.   Fearing I might be absent when he
arrived I gave him a hurried note in pencil to present to
Tipton the Ranch foreman, and he reached there a week
or so after I had seen him.

My experience in life has been that the very worst kind
of an introduction a fellow can bring along with him is one
from the boss, but Louie thought it would help him and I
gave it him.   As I feared, it proved a detriment.   I was
absent when he came and presented it to Tipton.   Tip was
in the habit of hiring his own hands and this was the first
time he had been directed to give any one a job.   Naturally
he resented it.   He and his fellow workers assumed that
Louie, the special friend of the boss, had been put there to
keep track of them, and treated him with latent hostility.

Luke and myself were the only friends he had, for the
short time that he stayed.   I could see how things were
going, but I judged it would only make matters worse to
interfere, and I knew that Louie was a real man and could
take care of himself in an emergency.   This came about
shortly after his arrival.   Charley Schneider, or Dutch
Charley, who had been acting as cook at the ranch for several

years, was really the only bully in the outfit. He had gained a reputation as a killer, as I have related in an early chapter, when he made a widow out of Mrs. Gereen, and he had lived on it ever since.

Louie was naturally quiet and collected, behaving himself like the gentleman he was, and took little or no notice of him, but Charlie having his Dutch courage bucked up, and thinking he had the outfit at his back, decided to make a set at him. He began by being very abusive and Louie considering him drunk, at first took no notice of him. This only made him worse, as he presumed that Louie was afraid of him. After a time he became tiresome and Louie, very quietly, told him to shut up, or if he didn't he would make him.

Charlie was a bigger and heavier man than Louie, but he wasn't built on the right lines. Presuming he had nothing to do but make a demonstration, he jumped to his feet and announced his intention of eating him up. The combat was short and decisive. A right hand from Louie came in contact with Charlie's chin, and it was several minutes after his head struck the floor before he wanted to get up. When he did he made a bluff at drawing his gun, but at this game he was only an amateur compared to Louie. The latter had him covered before he could reach his gun and advised him to be quiet if he didn't want to get hurt, counsel which he decided to follow. Thenceforth Louie had the entire respect of the outfit.

We had a good many cattle in Colfax County at the time, principally culled cows and calves and I was anxious to get rid of them. As soon as I could do so I made a trip to the old country and tried to forget such things as ranches and cows existed. Wilson, who was spending the winter in Egypt, wired me to meet him in Cairo, so after spending a week or ten days at home I went there.

From Cairo we went for a trip to Jerusalem, and arrived there not very long after the visit of the Kaiser.

I left Wilson there and returned home, as it was necessary for me to get back.

When I got to the ranch, I had to face a rather unpleasant situation. A few days before my arrival one of our boys had shot and killed a little boy in Alma. The killing was unintentional, but it occurred under such circumstances as to be almost criminal. Some of the boys were playing poker in a back room of the saloon at Alma, the time was near midnight, long after the usual hours for small boys to retire, but those little boys were playing around the light from the open door of the saloon.

Every now and again one of them would come to the window looking into the back room and make a disturbance, attracting the attention of the players. They would shoo him off and tell him to go home, but he would only run round the corner and come back again as soon as everything was quiet. This went on for quite a time till they began to get tired of it, and one of them undertook to give him a fright the next time he appeared. Unfortunately his hand must have followed his eye, for when he drew his gun at the next appearance intending to shoot out of the window he shot the little boy through the head.

When he realized what he had done he lost all control of himself, and getting on his horse rode off to the hills. He must have wandered about and ridden aimlessly all night, for he returned the next morning and gave himself up. The poor little boy was killed instantly and his parents were distracted. The whole community was very much shocked and the parents in particular regarded it as a wilful murder and by no means an accident. The boy himself took it very much to heart and was desirous of making all the reparation in his power, but all he could do was to give himself up and take his chances before the grand jury in Socorro.

The boy had always been well-behaved and bore a good character and while sympathizing with the bereaved parents I believed him to be entirely innocent of intent. Altogether it was a very unpleasant situation. I did all I could to help him and see that he got a fair trial, for the grand jury found a true bill against him and he was tried at the next sessions of the court. I gave evidence as to his character, and that is all the part I took in the trial.

They found him guilty in the second degree of murder, but he made such a favourable impression on Judge Hamilton, who tried the case, that he only gave him two years. The parents and friends were indignant and inclined to credit the outfit with undue influence. More or less bad blood was engendered, and relations which had never been very cordial were still further strained.

Another event which had occurred during my absence and

which caused me much annoyance was the stealing of my favourite saddle-horse and one of my pet buggy teams by the afterwards notorious outlaws, the brothers Ketchum. At the time they were strangers to the outfit, though we had occasionally heard of them, especially the elder brother Tom, who had inherited the border title of ' Black Jack '. The other was called Sam, but as yet he was unknown to fame.

They came along like the sneak-thieves and murderers they were, claiming hospitality, and repaid it after their kind. My saddle-horse, whom I called Rattler, was a powerful grey and the most wonderful animal for endurance I had ever come across. He had a gait which we called a running walk and which covered some six or seven miles an hour, and I have never seen him tired. Once I rode him from Silver City along with the stage and beat them into Alma. Of course they had to change horses and get the mails, but they used five different teams on the road, while I rode him straight through for the eighty miles.

Him they led out of the stable in the middle of the night, but the buggy team were in the pasture, and though they got the pick of them—a beautiful dark brown I called Major —they failed to capture his mate. The latter was partly a bronco, and evidently ran through the loop when they roped him, for the hair was all pulled off at the root of his tail. Poor Luke was broken-hearted, and I don't think ever got over it. He followed them for days till he found Major, whom they had ridden till he fell down, and he had to be destroyed. But he had no chance against Rattler, whom I afterwards heard they rode into Wyoming and disposed of to some of their friends at the notorious hold-out known as ' The Hole-in-the-Wall '.

I was to become better acquainted with some of those gentlemen in the not very distant future. What was troubling me was the condition of things on the range and the activity of the rustlers. Since the price of cattle had gone up new bands had sprung into existence, and everybody in the whole section seemed to have an interest in the trade. A week or two riding in all directions revealed new brands and devices that were altogether strange to me, and I called Tip to account for it.

A serious talk over the conditions led to his acknowledgment that he was unable to prevent it, and as he was married and his family cares were increasing he said he thought he'd resign. He agreed to hold on, however, until I could get a new man to replace him, and a suggestion from him brought up the name of Perry Tucker, from whom he said he had had a letter quite recently. Perry, it may be remembered, was one of the boys who worked under Fred Golden and who was acting as nurse in my room when I regained consciousness after being knocked out by the mare Utah.

Tip gave his location as being near the line of Old Mexico, but thought a letter sent to Douglas or Deming—I forget which at this time—would most probably find him. It did, eventually, after four or five weeks, and he turned up at the ranch accompanied by two others : the one, a stoutly built man of middle height, was what they called in that country ' fair complected '. He had a habit of grinning and showing a very even row of small teeth when he spoke to you, and he answered to the name of Jim Lowe. The other was several years younger, much taller and darker—in fact, a quite good-looking young man, debonair, with a bit of a swagger. He seemed quite a cut above the ordinary cow hand and undoubtedly had more education. He owned up to the name of ' William McGinnis '.

A short talk with Perry soon settled the business. He agreed to take charge of the outfit and said he would like to have Jim as his assistant and that Mac was a first-rate hand at breaking broncos. This suited me all right, and so they started in to clear up the situation on the W S range. The old saying in regard to a new broom and clean sweeping was acted up to in this case, for Perry soon got rid of all the weak members whom Tip had employed and put new ones in their places.

He seemed to be able to command an unlimited supply, for new hands seemed to show up whenever he wanted them, but as I was very busy building a dam in the river at the time I had no curiosity in regard to their antecedents. They brought about a complete change all over the range, and the stray brands amongst the cattle which had been so frequent before disappeared entirely. Their zeal for everything in connexion with the outfit was beyond all praise. They carried things with a high hand, and if something showed up that was not in accord with the well-known brands of the neighbourhood they assumed without question that it belonged to the W S.

What seemed strange to me at the time was that there

was no particular outcry or protest from the usual quarters, which were well known to us. The rustlers, for the time being, seemed entirely buffaloed. The only times I felt called upon to interfere was to beg of them to exercise sufficient care not to saddle us with a lawsuit. For the rest, I was too busy with the dam to be able to devote much attention to the range.

As soon as we began to move cattle to the road Jim took charge of the trail, while Perry remained on the range and threw the cattle together. It was then that the real genius of the former came under my notice. The way he handled those poor cattle over that long and dusty trail of nearly two hundred miles was a revelation. Frequently they had to go as much as seventy-five miles without water, but he never dropped a hoof, and there was no tail to his herd when he arrived at the road.

Mac usually accompanied him in charge of a bunch of broncos, and when he got through with the trip they were nice and gentle and furnished new mounts for the hands of the range. Truly the way those men handled stock was a marvel.

Another thing about them was that when they got to the road they were most decorous. There was no such thing as drinking or gambling or shooting up the town. Strict discipline was always maintained, and I was frequently congratulated by the merchants of Magdalena on having such a well-behaved outfit. I was very proud of them. The only thing that puzzled me was why they changed hands so often. There was hardly a trip we made to the road that two or three of them didn't want to quit—called away on some unexpected emergency.

They all were good hands and I hated to see them go, but it didn't seem to bother Jim in the least. He seemed always able to replace them by others just as competent. Some of them only worked with us for a single trip. The one I regretted most was a man named Tom Capehart, who had stayed with us for several trips and was Jim's right-hand man as long as he was there. Jim also owned up to being sorry to see him go, but said he was sure to return as soon as he was through with whatever little business he had on hand.

Things were going along very satisfactorily, and as long as Jim and Mac stayed on the job I wasn't greatly worried. One peculiarity that I didn't quite understand was that although the new-comers as they came along acted towards each other as entire strangers I frequently saw them together in the dusk of the evening sitting under a fence in close confab like long-lost brothers.

I called the attention of Luke to this one evening at the ranch, and he said there was something funny going on amongst the outfit, but he had been unable to get at the bottom of it. However, as long as things were going so well it was no affair of ours to inquire into it. They were evidently doing their duty loyally to the outfit, and expressed the greatest contempt for the common cow-thieves, whom they always alluded to as the ' Petty Larceny ' crowd.

It was really the first easy time I had since I took charge years previously, in the sense that I was mentally free from uneasiness. But, alas ! it was too good to last.

When we got to Magdalena with the last herd, which I think was somewhere about the end of September or early in October, Jim told me that Mac wanted to quit. He said there were no more broncos to be broken and that Mac didn't care much for any other class of employment. This was a great blow to me, for I had taken a real liking to Mac. He was always so nice and courteous, with a quiet, gentlemanly manner, that he would have been appreciated in any community.

What he said about the broncos, however, was correct, and I had no objection to offer beyond expressing regret at his leaving. At the same time a man named Bruce Weaver, whom we always called Red, owing to the colour of his hair and his generally ruddy complexion, decided that he would like to accompany him. I had no objection as far as Red was concerned. He claimed to be a rough-rider and a tamer of spoiled horses, but he was a bit of a bluffer.

Jim wasn't particularly keen on his going, and wondered if Mac would take him along with him. I let them settle the whole thing between them. The upshot of it was that Mac came to me as soon as the cattle were loaded and said that if all was agreeable they would like to take charge of the shipment. When I offered to pay him the regular rate I paid all shippers he refused it : said it was a great accommodation to him to be carried so far on his way free of charge, and in any case was glad to get a chance to oblige the outfit. I thought it was very nice of him, especially when he insisted that Red, if he took him along, should give his services on the same terms.

I parted from him with many regrets, and he said he would take good care of the cattle and turn them over to Louie, whom I had already apprised by letter. He thought they might stay a few days with him and get acquainted with the pasture, but intimated that his destination was Colorado just as I said good-bye to him. I went back to the ranch with him and the outfit, intending, as soon as I could arrange it, to pay Louie a visit and make arrangements for the sale of the cattle.

By the time I was ready to leave and to the best of my recollection had got as far as Silver City, I received a letter from Louie saying the cattle had arrived in good shape, and that Mac and Red had gone out to the ranch with him. The former had stayed some three or four days to look over the place and then had gone over to Cimarron, where, as far as he knew, he had taken up his residence for the time being. As for Red, he stayed at the ranch till he developed the smallpox.

He said they had removed him to the pest-house near Springer and were at present engaged in fumigating the ranch with sulphur, which compelled them all to sleep out in the open, but he hoped would be successful in removing infection. The upshot of it was that he wanted me, when I came up, not to come straight to the ranch, but to stay in Springer till he saw me. It was perfectly good advice, which I decided to follow.

When I got to Springer a day or two later Louie had not as yet arrived to meet me, so I resolved to put in the time as best I could till he came. Springer was not a particularly lively place in which to have to spend a whole day without occupation. In pursuance of this resolution I went over to the depot to have a chat with my friend Strong the agent.

He was busy as usual over the telegraph instrument, and held up his hand to indicate silence as I entered the door. I waited patiently till he got through, when he swung round in his chair and began to impart the news. It seemed that there had been a train robbery over on the Colorado Southern at or near a place called Folsom, some seventy miles east of Springer. It had occurred some time in the afternoon of the day before. Nobody had been killed or wounded, but the express car had been detached and the safe blown open, and the robbers, said to be three in number, had escaped with considerable swag.

Particulars did not go much further, beyond the usual intimation that news of the event had been dispatched in all directions on the arrival of the train in Folsom, which had taken place very shortly after the robbery. There had been no attempt to molest the passengers, and the robbers had made no attempt to disguise themselves, but carried out their intentions with celerity and dispatch, had treated the crew courteously when they were not interfered with, and when last seen by these gentlemen were riding full tilt for the mountains in the west.

It was quite an exciting item of news for that neighbourhood, for train robbery was hitherto unknown on that road. It had been considered as a peaceable neighbourhood, at least for a number of years, but I really would not have been much interested had not Strong added that somebody on the train, or amongst the crew, thought that they recognized one of the robbers as having worked for the W S. This was merely a rumour, and I didn't see possibly how it could be true.

That Mac, a paladin amongst cow-punchers, should stoop to train robbery was unthinkable ; and as for Red, he was laid up with the smallpox and an inmate of the pest-house, about a mile out of town. It might have been some of the men who worked for Hughes, but I couldn't think of any of them sufficiently expert for the job. The rest of his news concerned sheriffs and posses which had been organized and gone in pursuit. One of them had come from Trinidad in Colorado to Raton the evening before, under a sheriff named Farr, and immediately gone in pursuit, but it didn't say where. The others had been organized in Folsom, and were confining their activities to that neighbourhood.

I would have thought no more of it had it not been for the mention of the man who worked for the W S. This was bringing it home to me, though I still had no suspicion and would have liked to talk the matter over with Louie. He had warned me, however, to keep away from the ranch on account of infection, and I was settling myself down to await his arrival when I happened to think of Joe Nash at Cimarron. Some talk had passed between us about buying his ranch on the Ponil, and I thought it a good idea to get a team and drive out to see him. He possibly might have some news, and anyway, as I have intimated, Springer was a dull place to wait in.

I at once put the idea in practice, and Bob Cowan, who kept the livery stable and had been in that business since the days of the Overland Route and the Santa Fé trail soon had me rigged out.

Nothing more exciting than the fighting of mosquitoes occurred during the trip till I had gone rather more than half-way to Cimarron. Then my attention was attracted by a man coming along the prairie parallel to the road and in my direction. He wore no hat and was gesticulating wildly, and evidently anxious for me to wait for him. He was a small man, of what might be termed insignificant stature, with very fair hair and light eyebrows, and his eyes were bloodshot and red.

He had evidently undergone a severe shock to his system, and he begged me for God's sake to take him in to Springer. I told him I had just come from there a couple of hours previously and was on my way to Cimarron. I offered to take him there, but he said it was an absolute necessity for him to get to the railroad and in touch with the telegraph.

Eventually I told him to climb into the buggy. As he got in he showed me his coat-tail, which was torn, and said it had been done by a bullet. It was only on this statement that the train robbery occurred to me, and I asked him what he had been doing.

He then told me that he was a special officer of the Colorado Southern Road and that he had accompanied the sheriff's posse in pursuit of the robbers. He told me all about the train being held up near Folsom, which I already knew, and went on to relate how they had at once started out from Trinidad in company with Sheriff Farr and a strong posse, acting on information received saying the bandits were headed for Cimarron.

They had come by rail to Raton, where, having procured horses, they set out the same evening for Cimarron. They then got information that the supposed robbers had already gone through and up the Cimarron Canyon, so as soon as they had rested and got some further help they proceeded to follow them. They were successful in locating their camp and had been able to creep up on them. There were only three of them there when they first saw them, and one of them they had shot down as he was going to the creek for some water with a canteen in his hand.

He believed that some of the posse recognized him as a

man named McGinnis, and he was sure that he had been killed, for they saw him roll into the *aroya*. There must have been a number of others in hiding, however, for they had hardly bowled over McGinnis when they were met by a regular fusilade. Then commenced the most dreadful battle between the sheriff's posse and the bandits. The fighting was fast and furious, and he thought the sheriff had been shot down, but the horse which he had been riding, and which was strange to him, had taken fright at the noise and bolted while his gun was still in the saddle.

He pursued him to recover the weapon, as he was anxious not only to capture the robbers but also to avenge the sheriff, but the beast was evidently unbroken and he never was able to come up with him. A most plausible tale for the newspapers, but I thought it rather fishy. The beast had led him a merry chase, and he must have spent the whole night in pursuit of him.

When I asked how it came he had given up the pursuit he said that the beast had got away in the dark and he found himself lost in the mountains. He was very proud of the hole in his coat as a proof that he had been in action, but when I congratulated him on his narrow escape and said it was fortunate that the damaged garment had not been in touch with his person at the moment of impact, he didn't take it quite kindly.

When I took him back to Springer, as soon as he reached the telegraph he imparted his news to the Press. For a week or more the leading journals of both Pueblo and Denver devoted large capitals and long columns to his prowess.

When the result of the action came to be summed up a day or two later, it appeared that the bandits, who were only three in number, despite their two casualties had had all the best of it. The sheriff's posse consisted of some eight or ten men, and with all the advantage of surprise and the wounding of two of their opponents at the first volley, the third member of the party, who was known to the authorities by the name of Franks, or something similar, had not only whipped the posse off, but had killed three of them and wounded a fourth, while his victory had been so complete that he had been enabled to carry his wounded companions and all their impedimenta away with him.

True, one of these companions, Sam Ketchum, had only

been able to ride twenty miles or so till he gave out, the result of a broken arm, but then he did not have the right stuff in him. I was glad when I heard of his capture, as he was one of the brothers Ketchum who previously had abused our hospitality and stolen my pet saddle-horse from the ranch in Socorro County. On the other hand, I must confess to a certain amount of gratification that my friend Mac had escaped and was not killed by the first volley as reported by the agent, for he and his companion had got out of the country, leaving no trace.

The exploits and the picture of the special officer were kept before the public for a considerable time afterwards. He had evidently got hold of some credulous reporter and was using him to the best advantage. There was only casual mention of poor Sheriff Farr and the others who had sacrificed their lives in pursuit of their duty. The whole credit for dispersing the bandits, who had left of their own accord, and the capture of Ketchum, when he wasn't present, was given to the ' Special Agent '. No mention was made of the horse that had led him astray so opportunely from the scene of battle, nor the particular portion of his garment that came in contact with the bullet. The horse had been found the next day quite close to the scene of action. It was quietly grazing and undisturbed, but some one had evidently removed the gun from the saddle. The place where I met the gentleman was at least fifteen miles from the scene of action, and the time was the following day. Of such stuff are our border heroes made : all it needs is a press agent to manufacture them.

Louie and I stayed in Cimarron for several days to see if there was any further news, and a fresh posse was sent out after the bandits. They took Ketchum into custody and sent him *via* Taos to Santa Fé. As for Mac and his companion, they could get no trace of them. They had disappeared into space and apparently that was the end of them. I returned to the ranch in Socorro County, where the news of the hold-up of the train and the subsequent battle in the Cimarron Canyon had preceded me. Every one was on the tiptoe of excitement to know if Mac and his companion had been captured. I was able to assure them that up to the time I had left Cimarron no news had been heard of them.

CHAPTER XVII

IT was more than a month later that Jim Lowe brought me the news of Mac being taken. Jim had been out in camp in our horse pasture, nearly twenty miles from the ranch, and I wondered how he could have heard it. He told me Tom Capehart had brought him the news, having just ridden over from Lincoln County, fully three hundred miles or more from the scene of action in the Cimarron Canyon in Colfax County. It seemed he had got to the ranch sometime after midnight the night before. His horse and himself were in the last stages of exhaustion, but he had borrowed a fresh mount from Luke and gone straight to the camp in the horse pasture in search of Jim, and now they had come to consult me as to the probability of getting Mac out on bail and to know if I was willing to act as security.

I wondered how many members of what was usually alluded to as the 'Wild Bunch' I had in my employ, but as I had made some effort previously to get some information on this point from Perry, without result, I did not again refer to it. I told them I would be willing to go on his bond should I get the opportunity, but I didn't believe the offence was bailable. The penalty for train robbery in New Mexico was death, and I feared that the best I could do was to certify to his good behaviour and use what influence I could amongst friends to obtain a mitigation of his sentence should he be found guilty.

I then asked Tom, whom it was evident must be the man the authorities called Franks, how Mac had been taken. The following is the account he gave me. That he did not intend to commit himself was evident from the start, for he made no direct allusion to the cause of Mac's trouble, merely saying that he had been wounded, shot twice through the body. Owing to the long rides he had been compelled to make in his wounded condition in order to get away from his pursuers, and being unable to give proper attention to his wounds, he was in a pretty weak condition when they got down into Lincoln County, where they intended to seek employment.

This made it necessary for Mac to lie out in the hills, while Tom looked around for a job and made occasional trips to the nearest settlement in search of provisions and other necessaries. He didn't think it was well for Mac and himself to be seen much together, for Mac's description was in all the papers, also a pretty good likeness of him, while so far no mention had been made of him nor any attempt to publish his picture.

There was merely a vague description of a man they called Franks, which stated his height and possible complexion, and which might have been him, and then again might not. Anyway, there was a little isolated cabin not far from Mac's retreat the owner of which had taken up a claim on which there was a good spring, where they were in the habit of getting water. He (the owner) lived all alone there, and they were on friendly terms with him and accustomed to turn in there, whenever they passed by, to get a drink or some article of food, with which he occasionally supplied them.

When Mac's wounds were nearly better, or at least had stopped running and ceased to hurt him, they decided they would go back to Socorro County and the W S, as Tom did not succeed in getting a job where he was, and Mac was not disposed to look for one in that place owing to the unpleasant publicity given him by the newspapers, and their numerous placards posted all over the country offering a reward for his capture, copies of which had been mailed to all the peace-officers in New Mexico.

They consequently decided to make for the W S as the only haven of refuge. They agreed to meet at the little cabin on the following day, and Tom went off to procure provisions and ammunition and other such necessaries as they might need on the journey. They figured it would take them at least a week or ten days, as it was practically the whole width of New Mexico—about four hundred miles—and it was necessary to carry their food along with them, as they proposed to avoid as far as possible visiting any of the towns.

All would have gone well had it not been for the cruelty of fate. It seemed that some horses had been stolen quite recently from a ranch in that neighbourhood, and the sheriff was out with a party looking for the thieves. The isolated cabin and its owner were under grave suspicion of being a hold-out and an aider and abetter of the horse-thieves.

The result was the sheriff and his party made a raid and took possession of the place before sunup on the very same morning that Mac and Tom had arranged to make use of it. Their idea was that the horse-thieves were in the habit of using it as a rendezvous, and they practically held the owner as a prisoner and made him conceal them in the cabin till such time as the thieves would turn up.

The first to arrive, according to arrangement, was Mac. He had no ammunition for his gun, so he left it in his saddle when he hitched his horse up, and there were only two cartridges in the pistol in his belt when he walked in amongst them. They had seen him coming and were laying for him, thinking him to be one of the horse-thieves for whom they were looking, and the owner had been unable to give him warning as he was practically held a prisoner. The result was that Mac walked in amongst them quite innocently, and was astonished when he found himself covered and was told to throw his hands up. Mac's idea was that he was wanted on account of the train robbery. He was determined not to give in voluntarily. He jerked his gun and shot one of them through the wrist, then having no more cartridges went at them with his fists. They were compelled to beat him into insensibility before they could subdue him.

It was only after they had him secured and saw his wounds, which were not as yet healed, that they became aware of his identity. The sheriff, it seemed, had a description of him in his pocket with the offer of the reward, which I believe was five thousand dollars, in large letters. When they found who their captive was and the importance of the arrest they gave up all idea of the horse-thieves and took Mac, as soon as he was able to move, to the nearest town and the railway.

All these facts Tom had learned from the owner when he arrived an hour or two later. There was nothing he could do single-handed, so he came straight to the ranch with the news and to see if Jim could help him. This all occurred just three days previously, and how he managed to cover the distance in that time was marvellous. He never explained how he did it, but he must have supplied himself with fresh horses to accomplish it. The horse he rode into the ranch the night before never recovered.

He had certainly done all he could for poor Mac, who

must have had the deuce of a time making that ride from Colfax County with four bullet-holes in his anatomy. Truly Mac was out of luck, and it occurred to me that it might be advisable to change his trade if he ever got out of this scrape without having his neck elongated. They were most anxious I should go on his bail, and assured me that I need not be uneasy about the money as they would willingly furnish it. I told them about the Special Agent, and how he already suspected me, and that I thought it would be more advisable to testify to his previous good behaviour.

They had to be satisfied, for this was all I could do in the matter, and Tom said if it made no difference to the outfit he would like to stay out in the horse-camp with Jim. I told him that as far as I was concerned I had no objection, but thought it advisable that he should avoid putting himself in evidence as far as possible.

The situation was becoming complicated. I was genuinely sorry for Mac, and wished that he had been able to get out of the country, but I didn't want to get the outfit mixed up in the business. As yet I had no direct evidence that any of the others belonged to the 'Wild Bunch'. It was a few days later when we got the papers detailing the capture. It said he had put up a desperate resistance, and that they only had identified him when they saw the shirt which he was wearing was all covered with blood. They then made an examination and found the partly healed wounds. He apparently was still wearing the same shirt he had been shot in.

I couldn't help contrasting his stamina and nerve with that of Sam Ketchum. The latter had only a broken arm —there was no intimation even that it had been badly shattered—yet he threw up the sponge before he had gone thirty miles and had so little recuperation that he died of it afterwards in prison. Mac had ridden over three hundred miles with four bullet-holes in his body, had been unable to change his bloody shirt for over a month, and still put up a very respectable fight at the end of it. Tom was inclined to blame himself very much as the cause of it, as he maintained that if he had only got to him in time with the ammunition he would have cleaned up the whole outfit when he walked in among them.

As for Mac, they took him to Raton and placed him in prison, where he was duly indicted by the grand jury for train robbery.   He was tried at the following term of court there, which took place in a comparatively short time after his capture.   He made a most favourable impression during his trial on both judge and jury.   The latter found him guilty, but with a strong recommendation to mercy.   They sentenced him to life imprisonment, and he was taken to Santa Fé, and for a year or two we heard no more about him.

I made several inquiries about him during that time, but was never able to see him.   Mr. Bursum, of Socorro, was warden of the penitentiary at the time, and Mr. Gilian Otero was governor.   Mac's good behaviour must have impressed them most favourably, for at the end of that time he was pardoned out.   He paid me a visit on his release and thanked me for what he said I had done for him.   I really had only certified to his good behaviour while in the employ of the W S, but he said it was more or less due to it that he had procured his release—a statement which I take the liberty of doubting.

Meantime things went on more or less as usual.   At the ranch every one was pleased that Mac had not been hanged, but I was sorely perplexed as to the status of the outfit.   They were the most loyal and satisfactory outfit that I had ever had in my employ, but I couldn't help thinking that the whole thing might blow up, although I still had no direct evidence that I was harbouring any more outlaws.

However, a few months after Mac was convicted, one morning, while I was busy with letters, a middle-aged stranger slipped into the office, and came so quietly that I hardly noticed his presence till he bade me ' Good morning.' I then asked him what I could do for him, on which he gave me his card.   On it was printed ' Pinkerton Detective Agency '.   His own name was in the corner in smaller capitals, and to the best of my recollection it was Byrne or Burns.   I kept the card for a long time as a souvenir, but like a good many of my bachelor relics it got lost in the shuffle after I was married.

My first impression was that he had come in connexion with the late train robbery near Folsom, and probably wanted information about Tom.   But to my relief he quickly disabused my mind by telling me that the affair he had come to see me about was a train robbery that had taken place a year previously at a place they called Green Mountain in Wyoming or Montana.

It seemed that the train had been held up there, probably by some of the same band who were now at the W S. The express car was detached and the safe blown upon. A great quantity of swag had been secured by the robbers : amongst others, a large packet of National Bank bills consigned to some bank in the State of Washington or Oregon. These bills were quite new and were still to be signed by the bank president. A number of them had been traced after they were put into circulation. Some had come to the bank in Silver City and were traced back to the store in Alma.

He had come to investigate the matter. Another peculiarity in connexion with the bills, which he had neglected to mention in the first place, was that when the outlaws blew off the door of the safe they had also blown off the corner of the packet in which the bills were contained, so that all the bills were bereft of a corner and easy of identification, and he pulled one out of his pocket to show me. The store in Alma had informed him that they got the bills from a man named Johnny Ward, who was in our employ, and he wanted to know if he could interview him.

Now there were two boys with the name of Johnny Ward in our employ, and they were distinguished by the soubriquets of ' Big ' and ' Little '. The latter had been with us for several years and had been in our employ when Tipton was foreman. He was well known in the country, and there was no reason to suspect him of having any collusion with the train robbers, other than that Perry had kept him on when he got rid of most of the others. Big Johnny Ward, however, was a new-comer, and was undoubtedly one of the ' Wild Bunch.' By what name he was known to the authorities I never heard, but I often wondered how he escaped detection, for he carried about with him a most peculiar mark, which he was unable to get rid of. This was a spot on one of his eyeballs resembling a second pupil. There was no mark or scar nor any indication that it was the result of an accident, and in all probability it was congenital, but there seemed to be no possible means of disguising it. He always wore his hat well tilted over so as to keep it in the shade, but it was impossible to come close to him without observing it. The very fact that he always wore his hat at that angle would of itself be an object of suspicion and a clue to his identity.

I naturally supposed that it was this latter gentleman he was after, but Little Johnny Ward happened to be somewhere on the premises, and I volunteered to go and get him. When I did so, to my astonishment he owned up without demur to having had the bills in his possession, and produced some more of them from his pocket. He said he had undoubtedly paid some of them to the store in Alma in exchange for tobacco and ammunition. He accounted for them saying he had received them from a man named McGonigal, one of the transients who had worked with Jim on the trail for a couple of weeks or ten days. He had come there along with another man who claimed to be his brother, though he in no way resembled him, and all I can recollect about them is that one of them always wore a red handkerchief round his neck and answered to the name of Neale.

Johnny had sold him a horse when he was leaving, or two, if I rightly remember, for he had a considerable amount of the stolen bills. The detective made no attempt to recover any of them, merely asking leave to copy the numbers, and he seemed entirely satisfied with Johnny's statement. When the latter had gone I had quite a conversation with the detective. He seemed to have all the train robberies and other crimes on the tips of his fingers, as well as an accurate description of their perpetrators, although he made no mention whatever of Mac's recent escapade on the Colorado Southern—probably thought it might be too personal.

During the interview he drew a photograph out of his pocket and handed it to me to look at. It was somewhat faded, and he must have been carrying it round with him for a considerable time, so I took it over to the window to examine it. There were three or four men represented on it, the majority standing up, but one of them sitting down and all dressed in the usual cowboy outfit. He asked me if I recognized any of them. As I handed it back to him I told him that I certainly recognized the man sitting down, and possibly one of the others.

He then asked me if I knew the name of the man sitting down, and I told him that the only name I had ever heard for him was Jim Lowe. That it was Jim there could be no possible doubt, for he had the identical grin that he always wore when he spoke to you. The other one might possibly have been Capehart, but I couldn't be sure of it. The photograph had been taken some years before, and Tom was many years younger than Jim.

The Pinkerton man wanted to know if I had ever heard any other name for him, and when I told him ' No ', he said that it was Butch Cassidy, or at least that was the name he was known by to the authorities. I told him that all I knew about him was that he was the best trail boss I had ever seen and one of the best men that the W S had in their employ since I had known them. I also said that he had great influence with his men, and that none of them ever got drunk or shot up the town or were guilty of any other foolishness while he was over them.

He said that despite the good character which I gave him there was hardly a State or a territory south of the Canadian line that wasn't anxious to get hold of him, and that there was a large reward offered for his capture. He was well known as the brains and leader of the best-organized gang of outlaws that had appeared in the country for more than a lifetime, and that he thought his own outfit would be willing to pay something like twenty thousand dollars for him. I forget the exact amount he mentioned, but know it was quite a large sum.

He also informed me that it was the custom of those gentlemen when they had committed some especially daring outrage in one section of the country, for the parties who were actually engaged in it to seek temporary employment at as great a distance from the scene as possible, where they remained under an assumed name and in seclusion till the excitement and the public interest in the matter had quieted down. The next job they undertook was always entrusted to a different gang and in an entirely new section of the country. But it was all carried out by a thoroughly organized gang and Jim—or Butch, as he called him—was undoubtedly the head of it.

He said that their information in regard to express shipments was uncanny, and that they must undoubtedly have some means of gaining inside information which was causing the authorities no end of worry. He said that he had no idea where Jim had disappeared to after his last exploit,

which occurred some years previously, till he saw him in
Alma that morning as he was coming to the ranch.

It seemed to me that I stood a good chance of losing the
outfit I was so proud of.

I asked him if he had any intention of trying to arrest
Jim, or what he was going to do about it, but he assured me
that his only business was in connexion with the bills which
had been traced as part of the plunder taken from the
train at Green Mountain. Moreover, he said : ' I'm not
such a fool as to attempt it in this neighbourhood. If I
wanted Jim here I'd need a regiment of cavalry at my back.'

He left me shortly afterwards, saying that all he had to
do now was to find McGonigal. He probably might be able
to locate him from the description I had given him, but he
was very unlikely to be travelling under that name, and
that was the last I ever saw or heard of him. When Jim
came to the ranch I thought it only right to give him all the
information I had received from the detective, and to my
surprise found that he already knew all about it.

He only grinned when I told him the name he had given
him, and said that he and Tom had already spotted him.
In fact, they had stood him a drink when he returned to
Alma. As he put it, they suspicioned who he was, and they
invited him to drink to make sure. He supposed that he'd
have to pull out before very long as it was more than likely
they might send after him ; but, as it was, he liked the
country very much and had no immediate intention of
leaving it.

We were still shipping cattle and I had no intention of
firing him. He did, however, go rather sooner than I
expected, and just before we took the last herd to the road.
It was Perry who took the initiative. He told me just
before going to the road that after we had got rid of that
shipment he thought he would like to quit, as he had other
interests in Arizona that he would like to attend to. I
asked him just to hold on for a little time till I could find
some one to replace him, and he then suggested that I put
Jim in charge of the outfit.

Under the circumstances as disclosed by the Pinkerton
agent I didn't see my way to doing this, and we called Jim
into consultation to ask him what he thought about it.
I asked him if he was in my place and knew all the circumstances connected with his career whether he would feel

justified in offering him the job, and without the least hesitation he said he wouldn't. I told him that I would like to be able to keep him for a permanency, especially on the trail, but as it was he had too many strings to him.

I would have had no objection to his staying on till we got through shipping cattle, but with Jim it was *Aut Caesar, aut nullus.* If I didn't want to give him the outfit he didn't want to stay on, and so it was arranged that Perry should take that last herd of cattle to the road and Jim would make his preparations for leaving. He said that Tom would stay on with Perry till we got the cattle off our hands.

Tom did stay on for a considerable time afterwards, principally out at the horse-camp, only paying occasional visits to the ranch or Alma. Just when he left the ranch I am not quite sure, for I happened to be away from there at the time ; but it must have been at least four or five weeks after Jim had taken his departure.

In regard to the latter, I said good-bye to him when we started for Magdalena. Despite the bad character given him by the Pinkerton agent I was sorry to lose him. The only thing he asked me for on receipt of his wages was to let him have an old pair of raw hide kyacks that were lying around the stable. For the benefit of the uninitiated I might mention that a kyack is a contraption for use on a pack-saddle. Our range being so very rough and mountainous as to make the use of any kind of a wheeled vehicle an impossibility, we were compelled to do all our work with a pack-outfit.

Our kyacks were rather different from those generally in use. The usual ones, of Spanish or Mexican origin, were simply deep pockets hung on each side of the saddle ; but ours were made of an oblong frame ten to twelve inches wide and twenty to twenty-four inches long, and about twelve to fifteen inches deep, covered with raw hide, with the hide on the outside.

We nearly always used cedar or juniper boughs in constructing them, as they proved to be stouter and more lasting than ordinary lumber, and we bound the corners with thong instead of nailing them. The raw hide was put on wet, and when it contracted it made a handy receptacle, which was very light and strong and proof against all kinds of rough usage. They carried pots and pans or dutch-ovens or rock-salt or anything you put in them without galling the horses' sides or in any way interfering with blankets or other stuff that was put over them.

They were also very convenient for carrying flour, as a fifty-pound sack just fitted into them. I never saw them in use elsewhere, and we were inclined to look on them as our own speciality.

I gladly let Jim have a pair and said good-bye to him. He told me that he was taking Red Weaver along with him. The latter had come back to Alma after he got cured of the smallpox, but we didn't employ him at the ranch ; in fact, I objected to him as being entirely too rough with his horses.

I supposed that I had seen the last of them, but not more than ten days or two weeks after I had said good-bye, while I was in Magdalena, I got a telegram from the sheriff of Graham or Apache County in Arizona. It was sent from St. Johns, and merely asked if I knew two men, giving the names of Jim Lowe and Bruce Weaver. It contained no further information, and after thinking the matter over I sent him a reply saying I did.

It was not until I returned to the ranch a bit later that I was able to discover the reason of it. I then found out that Jim and Red had made a raid before leaving. It was in no way connected with the W S, and I think was meant to do them a favour. There was a man on the range, one of our neighbours, who owned a few hundred head of cattle. They were bought somewhat later by the W S, who took the whole brand, —02. At this time he was classed with some others as being a member of the 'petty larceny' crowd. He was particularly obnoxious to the outfit, as he always made a great show of being virtuous. They had much more respect for Bob Holoman and his crowd.

It seemed that Jim and Red before they left were determined to get even, for they took every saddle-horse he possessed, not leaving him even one, and he had to walk several miles to his nearest neighbour to borrow one. They certainly made a clean sweep of his horses, and I think that it largely induced him to sell out at a reasonable figure. Whether word had been sent to the sheriff in Arizona I never found out, but he must have had some sort of suspicion, for he detained them at St. Johns, where they purchased provisions.

He held them until he could communicate with me at

Magdalena. His telegram merely asked if I knew them, and I replied that I did, but it must have been entirely satisfactory, for he allowed Jim to go his way with the horses, but he detained Red—whom, it seemed, Jim claimed, was a stranger he had picked up on the road—on the ground of his suspicious appearance and his not being able to give a more definite account of himself.

He was, however, unable to establish any definite charge, and after some further inquiry turned him loose, and he came back to Alma. I afterwards heard that Jim was anxious to get rid of him as he regarded him as merely a bluffer with no definite claim to be classed as a member of the ' Wild Bunch '. Where Jim went to at the time I don't know, but I heard of him about a year later as being in the mountains in Colfax County ; at least I heard of a couple of mysterious strangers who had visited the camp of the survey party who were surveying the tract sold by the Maxwell Grant Co. to Mr. Bartlett of Chicago, and afterwards known as the Bartlett Ranch, on the Vermejo.

The description of the men was not very definite, but I at once recognized the raw hide kyacks which they had with them, and which were so unusual as to attract the attention of the surveyors. From it I surmised that Mac and his party must have concealed whatever loot they had taken off the train somewhere in those mountains, and that Jim, and probably Tom Capehart, had gone there to recover it. That Jim had not much faith in Red he had told me before when I commented on the fact that the smallpox had kept him from being along with Mac at the train robbery. Jim said that Mac was better without him. He claimed that he lacked the necessary courage or sand when it came to a show down. He was anxious to be wild and woolly and considered in the confidence of the ' Wild Bunch ', but he was really only used as a messenger, and that they always paid him well for his services with instructions to keep his mouth shut if he didn't want to hear from them unpleasantly.

Anyway, Jim disappeared for the time being, taking all of Ashby's horses along with him, and Red returned to Alma as soon as he was turned loose by the sheriff at St. Johns. How Jim had managed to arrange it was a masterpiece of diplomacy. Red also had some consolation, for was he not actually arrested as an outlaw and could swagger

around with his head in the air as became a border hero ?
He also must have gained some more substantial reward,
for he was enabled to live in that neighbourhood without
working for six months, when he was killed in a duel with
Pad Holoman.

In 1899 Wilson and I purchased a tract of land on the
Ponil. I determined to put as much as possible of it under
cultivation and raise alfalfa for hay for the cattle. To do
this it was necessary to have an experienced man to look
after it, and much as I hated losing Luke at the Ranch in
Socorro County, I determined to send him up there. I
didn't say much to him about it at first, for I knew he was
unwilling to be separated from me personally, and he had
always acted more or less as my guardian angel since he had
followed me from the old country.

Luke was outspoken and absolutely incorruptible, and
though he had many good friends his faithfulness to the
W S had made him some bitter enemies. I was always
fearful that some of them would take advantage of him some
day when he had a little more than was good for him.
There was not much danger for him as long as he was sober,
for he was fearless and generally well armed, but he occasionally went on a ' tear ', and at those times I was always a
bit nervous. Anyway, I thought if I got him up to Colfax
County he would be more independent, have plenty do to,
and get away from such a mean crowd.

When I got ready to make the change I decided that
I would take my buggy and team up there also, as it would
be much more useful to me there where I could drive all
over the country than in Socorro County, where I was
practically limited to one or two roads. I made all the
necessary arrangements for Luke to drive them up there.
It would probably take him ten days or two weeks, according
as things went smoothly or otherwise, but it would give him
an opportunity to see the country, and I would go ahead of
him by train and see that everything was in order for him
to take hold when he got there.

I always blame myself that I didn't see him started on
the road before I left the ranch. As arranged, he was to
leave the next day after I did. I went to Silver City on the
stage and took the train from there, expecting that Luke
would start early the next morning, and I thought no more
about it.

When I got to Springer the following afternoon I made arrangements to go to Cimarron with Louie and look over the situation—had actually hired a team and was all ready to start when some one came rushing to me with a telegram that had just arrived from Silver City. I thought that it must be some communication from Luke in regard to something I had forgotten, till I opened it, when I found that it was from a gentleman named Porterfield, who kept a drug-store in Silver City.

He said he had just arrived from Mogollon and had been requested to wire me the news that Luke had been murdered there on the afternoon of the day I had left the ranch, which was the 9th of November, 1899. There were no further particulars except a request to return at once.

Fortunately the train going south had not yet gone through Springer, and I just had time to run over to the depot and get a ticket, so I went straight back to Silver City.

All the way there I was harassed with doubts and speculations as to how it could have occurred and what had brought him to Mogollon just before leaving. It was the greatest shock I had received so far in my experience. I didn't know at the time just who had killed him, but I naturally supposed that it was one of the gang or some of their agents. I had been fighting them for years now, and they had dealt a mortal blow when I thought I had the best of them. It was a good deal like being stabbed in the back when you weren't looking.

When I got to Silver City I learned that the crime had been committed by a man named Saunders, a cowardly loafer. It was only a short time before that I had seen a man with one arm in a sling threaten to pick up a stone and run him out of the camp. It seemed that some new-comers who had recently got hold of the Last Chance Mine had been shocked at the Western habit of going about armed and the reckless manner in which they loosed off their guns on slight provocation.

They had requested the authorities in Socorro to appoint a town marshal, and Saunders had been appointed. Vested with a little authority he used to swagger round the camp with a gun on him, talking big to complete strangers and demanding drink for his forbearance.

I find it difficult to write calmly about the matter after

the lapse of a quarter of a century. Nobody who knew him paid the least attention to him, and it was in a feeble attempt to assert his authority that I had seen the one-armed man run him out of camp. He merely threatened to pick up a rock and take his gun away from him, but that was enough for Saunders to make himself scarce when he wasn't bucked up with a drink.

Luke had gone to Mogollon the day I left the ranch to say good-bye to some of his friends who lived there, as he expected to be on the road the following morning. Like all men in that country he wore a gun till he got there. As was customary on his arrival he took it off and placed it in charge of a man behind the bar at the hotel. A man named Johnson was the proprietor. After that he spent a couple of hours going around with his various friends and having an occasional drink. When the time came to leave he got his gun and mounting his horse started out of camp for the W S.

As he passed the hotel coming from the livery stable another man named Johnson, who partly to distinguish him from the hotel proprietor was known by the name of ' Big Dog ', came out on the street and stopped him.

Big Dog insisted that he get down and take a farewell drink with him, and naturally Luke complied. They went into the bar in the hotel, where there were several others, and they were all asked to join, including the proprietor, who was behind the counter and serving them. While they were about to drink Luke's health and wish him good luck, after they were served, it appeared that Saunders, who had been sneaking round the corner as usual, came into the hotel bar.

Nobody paid any attention to him, and none of them except the proprietor, who, from behind the counter and facing the door, knew he was there. According to his own story, he claimed that he called upon Luke to take off his gun, but if he did it is equally certain that nobody heard him. The first intimation Luke had of his presence was when he put his left arm round his neck from behind and made pretence of taking his gun away from him. That he was completely taken by surprise was evident, for he still had his glass in his hand untasted. He even didn't know till he looked round, when he said : ' Damn it, man ! Let me go ! What's the matter ? ' These were the last words uttered,